The Transition
of China's Urban
Development

The Transition of China's Urban Development

FROM PLAN-CONTROLLED TO MARKET-LED

Jieming Zhu

Foreword by Urlan Wannop

PRAEGER

Westport, Connecticut
London

Library of Congress Cataloging-in-Publication Data

Zhu, Jieming, 1957–
    The transition of China's urban development : from plan-controlled
to market-led / Jieming Zhu ; foreword by Urlan Wannop.
      p. cm.
    Includes bibliographical references.
    ISBN 0–275–96427–2 (alk. paper)
    1. Urban policy—China. 2. Urbanization—China. 3. Land use,
Urban—China. 4. Free enterprise—China. I. Title.
HT384.C6Z48 1999
307.76'0951—dc21   99–18720

British Library Cataloguing in Publication Data is available.

Library of Congress Catalog Card Number: 99–18720
ISBN: 0–275–96427–2

First published in 1999

Praeger Publishers, 88 Post Road West, Westport, CT 06881
An imprint of Greenwood Publishing Group, Inc.
www.praeger.com

Printed in the United States of America

The paper used in this book complies with the
Permanent Paper Standard issued by the National
Information Standards Organization (Z39.48–1984).

10 9 8 7 6 5 4 3 2 1

To My Family

Contents

Figures and Tables

Foreword

China's accelerated urbanization in the two closing decades of the twentieth century has been larger than experienced at a comparable stage of industrialization in any Western country. It has occurred in circumstances of a headlong transition from state control of a non-market in urban land to relaxed acceptance of market competition urban property development.

The economic surge of this remarkable period in China's history has transformed old cities and created new metropolises. The urban impacts of political and economic transitions have been particularly visible to Western visitors, who inevitably spend much of their time in city centers where their hotels lie. Visitors are variously awestruck by the scale of construction, excited by the pace of building, and sometimes apprehensive about potential future environmental and social problems when residents of the districts of high-rise blocks running to the urban horizon gain higher incomes and expect commensurately higher living standards.

Few visitors understand the processes by which so much of the face of urban China has been so rapidly transformed since the death of Mao Zedong. For almost 30 years after 1949, prime urban sites in Chinese cities were effectively "free goods." The subsequent onslaught of demand by both private and quasi-public investors put heavy stress on public policy and on official practice in managing urban development. Chinese officials had to learn rapidly, and their management of new processes was inevitably sometimes tenuous. New rules had to be devised to respond to unfamiliar conditions. New means of property development emerged.

Jicming Zhu's authoritative and detailed account of property development in Shenzhen arises from his research there. He sets his analysis in the context of experience of urbanization and property development policy in China as a whole. The special economic zone of Shenzhen grew over what as recently as 1980 was a landscape predominantly of rice paddy fields farmed from traditional villages. The Hong Kong to Guangzhou railway track snaked across the green landscape. But in only 10 years between 1985 and 1995 the single new metropolis of Shenzhen grew by a population of more than 2.5 million. By comparison, it took 50 years for the population of 32 new towns in the United Kingdom to be developed by 1.4 million.

Shenzhen is an extreme case in China because of its exceptionally high speed of growth and because it had a unique regional relationship with Hong Kong in the late years of Britain's lease prior to its termination in 1997. But Shenzhen is widely significant because it has magnified many of the features of China's modern experience of urban change and of reform in property development. The account of Shenzhen's experience is important because not only China but many other newly industrializing and commercializing countries face a long further history of urbanization.

Urlan Wannop
Helensburgh, Scotland

Acknowledgments

This book would not have been possible if it were not for those individuals and institutions that I feel helped one way or another. I should mention two of my alma maters, Tongji University and the University of Strathclyde, which have molded me under two distinctively different cultures, yet with the same goal of exploring the unknown with rigor. I owe my intellectual debt to Professor Le Dehua of Tongji and Professor Urban Wannop at Strathclyde.

This book is derived from my Ph.D. dissertation, written in Glasgow between 1990 and 1993. In this connection, I would like to express my gratitude to Professor Urban Wannop, whose kindness, guidance, and tolerance as a supervisor with my deviation away from the path of traditional planning research were particularly encouraging to the gestation of this project. I benefited tremendously from my fellow researchers, who collectively created a warm "team" atmosphere that was sharply in contrast with the cold, drizzling Scottish weather most of the time. Also, I wish to acknowledge the financial support to this research by the Committee of Vice-Chancellors and Principals of the Universities of the United Kingdom and the University of Strathclyde.

I am indebted to all of the developers, real estate agents, planners, and government officials of Shenzhen who participated in my interviews, particularly to Wang Fuhai and Chen Hongjun of Shenzhen Institute of Urban Planning and Design for their valuable assistance during my fieldwork in 1993 and 1997.

Last, but not least, this book was greatly facilitated by my research project (RP960039) funded by the National University of Singapore.

Abbreviations

CCI	Capital Construction Investment
CCP	Chinese Communist Party
FFYP	First Five-Year Plan
GTJ	*Guojia Tongji Ju* (State Statistical Bureau)
GTJCSJDZ	*Guojia Tongji Ju Chengshi Shehui Jingji Diaocha Zhongdui* (Urban Social and Economic Survey Organization)
GZJG	*Guoyou Zhichan Jingyin Gongsi* (State Assets Management Corporation)
IFTE/CASS	Institute of Finance and Trade Economics, Chinese Academy of Social Sciences
IPA	Institute of Public Administration
SEZ	Special Economic Zone
SFNB	*Shenzhen Fangdichan Nianjian Bianjibu* (Editorial Committee of Shenzhen Real Estate Yearbook)
SFYP	Second Five-Year Plan
SGGJ	*Shenzhenshi Guihua Guotu Ju* (Shenzhen Planning and Land Bureau)
SGGJNF	*Shenzhenshi Guihua Guotu Ju Nanshan Fenju* (Nanshan Planning and Land Bureau, Shenzhen)
SOE	State-Owned Enterprise

SQZGLXB	*Shenzhenshi Qiye Zhidu Gaige Lingdao Xiaozu Bangongshi* (Shenzhen Enterprise Reforms Committee)
SSBJJKZJK	*Shanghai Shi Banian Jiejue Juzhu Kunnanhu Zhufang de Janjiu Ketizhu* (Shanghai Housing Situations Research Team)
SSEZ	Shenzhen Special Economic Zone
SSTJ	*Shanghai Shi Tongji Ju* (Shanghai Statistical Bureau)
STFG	*Shenzhen Jingji Tequ Fazhan Gongsi* (Shenzhen Special Economic Zone Development Corporation)
SZTJ	*Shenzhen Tongji Ju* (Shenzhen Statistical Bureau)
TVE	Township-Village Enterprise
ZSKRY	*Zhongguo Shehui Kexueyuan Renkou Yianjushou* (Population Research Institute, Chinese Academy of Social Sciences)

Chapter 1

Introduction

Although the city as a form of civilization has been in existence for more than 5,000 years, and nearly half of the world population live in cities, understanding of the production of this entity is far from thorough. Urban governments try to manage a balanced urban development with dimensions of social and environmental considerations but have been frequently frustrated by the unsuccessful implementation of plans thoughtfully prepared to guide urban growth. Development of the urban built environment is one of the most important sectors of the urban economy and one of the most conspicuous aspects of urban growth. Understanding the city as a human settlement will be enriched, and the management of urban development will be enlightened, by the knowledge of the process through which the built environment is produced and consumed.

The incorporation of market forces into the economy and the revival of market-oriented land and property development in cities have led to a tremendous change in the Chinese coastal cities since 1980. The economy in transition from plan to market provides a great opportunity to understand the formation of Chinese urban built environment in the background of institutional change. A fundamental change that has occurred in Chinese urban construction is that land and property, which used to be passive factors of the planned economy and pure accommodation for production and consumption, have become investment mediums, besides their utilitarian function. Both practitioners and academe are intrigued by how institutional change interacts with the behavior of market players during the process of real estate development, and it is intellectually fascinating to explore how land and property as a production factor without prices are transformed to an asset priced in a nebulous market. This book reveals how the Chinese urban built environment is shaped by the characteristics associated with an emerging property market and a unique property development industry.

ECONOMIC REFORMS: INTRODUCTION OF THE MARKET FORCES

Significant changes with a single goal of developing the national economy have been initiated since 1978, symbolized by formal integration of the Four Modernizations (agriculture, industry, science, and defense) into the new Constitution of the People's Republic of China. Endorsed by the Fifth National People's Congress in March 1978 and then by the Third Plenum of the Eleventh Central Committee of the Chinese Communist Party in December 1978, a social transformation spearheaded by the economic reforms was launched aiming at a grand dream of national advancement. The rigid, centrally controlled system was to be revised in order to build vigor into enterprises that were mostly state-owned. Market approaches were suggested to make urban enterprises efficient in their production. The reforms were expected to stimulate the inactive urban economy, which had been, as believed, stifled by central planning. The new policies called for a shift of strategy from overemphasized self-reliance to a participation in the world market and from inward-looking, self-sufficient production to outward-looking trading in the context of globalization.

Decentralization of the economic management was to be carried out, and coexistence of a variety of economic entities was to be tested. The central government was determined to carry out a systematic change to enhance the performance of the national economy. However, as an unprecedented institutional transition in China's history in terms of the scale of the economy and the magnitude of the populace involved, this strategic reform lacked operational targets and well-prepared plans. The initial measures adopted were meant only to introduce market mechanisms to the planning system and thus to raise economic productivity. Since then, China has been transforming toward a decentralized economy with a mixture of market forces and planning controls.

Although impressive social and economic progress had been made under the leadership of the Communist Party-led government (Putterman & Rueschemeyer, 1992), the administratively planned system and its supportive political structure were held responsible for many political upheavals and economic problems during the period 1949–1979. After the disastrous Cultural Revolution, instigated by the same party, when the economy was virtually reduced to a standstill for a decade, the people's discontent with the poor economic performance became widespread and prevalent. A wave of cries for changes reverberated around the country.

Following the death of Mao Zedong in 1976, a group of reformers, led by Deng Xiaoping, managed to return to the political platform and started what were later called economic reforms. In retrospect, it was an absolute necessity for the Communist Party and the government to change their stance from emphasizing the ideology of "class struggle" to pursuing economic growth, as the legitimacy of the Chinese government was in jeopardy after 30 years of rule without success in raising the life quality of its people to a level on a par with that of other developing nations.

Two characteristics of the economic reforms stand out. First, the reforms started in a top-down manner aiming to validate the existing political regime. Second, the reforms were meant only to improve productivity and enhance economic efficiency. It was never in the central planners' minds to replace the centrally planned system with a capitalist market economy but rather to make the planning system more flexible and decentralized. The economic reforms were used as an instrument to legitimate, rather than to undermine, the existing political structure. The only change was that socialist pragmatism substituted for socialist idealism. Through advocacy of four cardinal principles (i.e., the socialist road of development; the dictatorship of the proletariat; the leadership of the Communist Party; and Marxism-Leninism-Mao Zedong thought) socialism and associated state ownership are still the cornerstones of the political system.

Constrained by the constitutional and ideological barriers, the Chinese economic reforms have declared explicitly that socialism is the foundation, and public economy remains a leading sector of the country. The president and party secretary, Jiang Zemin, asserted that "without a state-owned industrial sector, there can be no socialism" (CND, 1998). It is understood that old institutions, which used to play a principal role in the old planning system, still determine the reforms (Chen, 1992). Old politicoeconomic forces are still at work. The reform process turns out to be a result of ideological battles rather than a matter of economic rationality. In this context, it is understandable that there has been no blueprint to guide the unprecedented transformation. The liberal try to push the reforms forward, while the conservative intend to hold the existing system. Nevertheless, a desire to build a strong economy has given liberals a powerful mandate and forced politicians on the two extremes of the political spectrum to unite. Pragmatism has prevailed as a result. Pragmatism and political rhetoric determine an approach of trial and error for the implementation. "Groping for stones to cross the river" is a succinct adage revealing the underlying philosophy. The piecemeal, step-by-step trial determines that any useful instrument and policy may be adopted if they deliver the goods. The salient characteristics of pragmatism implanted in the process of reforms imply that eventual consequences may betray the original rhetoric. In spite of the party's assertion to keep state-owned-enterprises alive, sales of loss-making small- and medium-sized firms are quietly carried out in some provinces (CND, 1998). Local economic experimentation is often given a free rein, and legislative or even constitutional constraints can be ignored (Hamer, 1996).

The Chinese economic reforms are aiming to change to an economy where most transactions are conducted at market prices. A market economy is composed of independent individual producers and consumers, and their relationships are determined in the market and by the market mechanisms. Government is an actor to regulate production and consumption, not superior to others with regard to the role it plays and the power it has (Howe, 1978). Having been under the central planning system for 30 years, China will find the route to market long and rough, as transition will entail drastic changes to the economy and thus to the society.

Following the dogma of Marx and Engels, China set up a socialist, centrally controlled economic system with predominant state ownership of production means, soon after the People's Republic came into existence. Under the system, utilization and allocation of resources, including land, were determined by the central plans. Many urban facilities were used free of charge. If there were prices for some items, the prices were neither derived from interactions between demand and supply nor used to guide allocation. Urban reforms, in which urban land management is an important component, are propelled by the success achieved in the rural reforms that have improved farmers' welfare significantly. Like the rural reforms intended to raise agricultural productivity, urban reforms are meant to introduce market forces to the process of urban development. Prices are recommended in urban infrastructure. In 1984, about 30 cities started to impose fees for wastewater drainage. The measure was said to have reduced unnecessary discharge of effluent and created a designated fund for the maintenance of drainage systems by the fees collected. With roads and bridges in very poor condition, some cities in Guangdong experimented with toll collection in order to set up a financial resource for their improvement (Cao & Chu, 1990).

The urban land and property sector has to change in order to coordinate the changing economic system. It is recognized that land and properties should not be provided as free goods. As an economic asset, properties have to be commercialized and priced by the market. The process of real estate commodification and marketization was initiated immediately after many Chinese coastal cities were opened to foreign investment. Market orientation opens the gate to the participation of market forces in the urban economy, as well as in land and property development. Attempting to speed up urban development and to facilitate direct investment in manufacturing and services, new approaches are intended to establish a market for land development and building construction. "*Yinniao zucao*" (to attract birds by building nests) and "*zucao yinniao*" (to attract birds to build nests) were two initial methods of marketization for property development in the early 1980s, when shortages of premises impeded inward investment from materialization, and the state's fiscal capacity was clearly not adequate in coping with the situation in the booming coastal cities. Since then, a functioning property market has emerged and has been seemingly responsive to market demand. Property prices and rentals, established as a result of commodification, have been adjusting according to the equilibrium of market demand and supply.

DIVERSE URBANIZATION IN REGIONS

China is a vast country with 31 provinces, autonomous regions, and municipalities directly under the central state (excluding Taiwan). There are great variations in terms of the stage of the local economy, natural setting, and local culture. Regarding the level of urbanization, for example, 51.7 percent of the population lived in areas defined as cities and administered by urban governments in 1989; the figures were 59.3 percent in the Eastern Region, 40.1 percent in the Central Region, and 28.3 percent in the Western Region (see Figure 1.1). Industries are much more developed in the Eastern Region than in the Central and Western Regions. The latter two achieved only 48.8 percent and 34.2 percent (1989), respectively, of the Eastern level with respect to the gross output value of industry per capita (Hsueh, Li, & Liu, 1993). In terms of attracting foreign investment, the differences between the regions are even greater than in manufacturing production: the Central Region's and Western Region's shares accounted for only 9.3 and 3.9 percent, respectively, of the total foreign investment in China in 1995 (see Table 1.1).

Bearing this broad picture in mind, the author feels that it is impossible to have a discourse on China's urban transformation both comprehensive in nature and representative of the whole country. There is not a single typical Chinese city representative of this vast country. Instead, the case study approach is employed in order to achieve an in-depth understanding. Shenzhen is chosen as a case to examine the process of market-led urban growth. It is deemed appropriate and sensible to situate Shenzhen in the context of the Eastern Region, which is in the front line leading the nation toward modernization. The Eastern Region includes 14 open coastal cities and several loosely defined economic development areas, such as the Yangtze Delta, Pearl River Delta, and Liaodong Peninsula. What has been experienced in the Eastern Region will sooner or later be experienced by the Central and then the Western Regions, if the economic reforms proceed as expected. In this connection, Shenzhen and the Eastern Region represent the future of Chinese urbanization.

Figure 1.1
Map of China

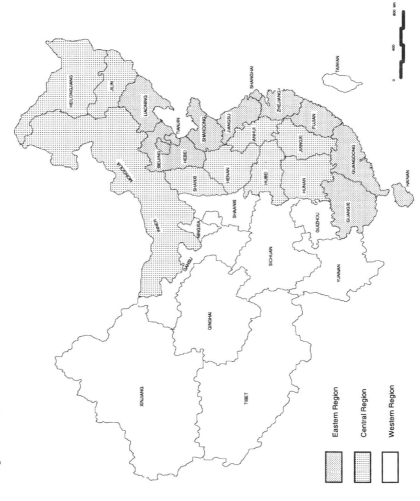

Eastern Region

Central Region

Western Region

Source: Courtesy of S.S. Han.

Table 1.1
Chinese Cities in Three Regions (1995)

Region	Urban Built-up Area as % of Total	GDP as % of Total	TIFA[6] as % of Total	Foreign Investment as % of Total
Eastern Region[1] Cities	51.8	65.0	65.2	86.8
Central Region[2] Cities	34.3	23.9	23.4	9.3
Western Region[3] Cities	13.9	11.1	11.4	3.9
Coastal Cities[4]	9.2	14.5	21.9	20.4
SEZ Cities[5]	1.6	3.2	4.6	12.7

Notes: (1) The Eastern Region comprises Beijing, Tianjin, Hebei, Liaoning, Shanghai, Jiangsu, Zhejiang, Fujian, Shandong, Guangdong, Guangxi, and Hainan, with a land area of 1.3 million square kilometers. (2) With an area of 2.8 million square kilometers, the Central Region consists of Shanxi, Inner Mongolia, Jilin, Heilongjiang, Anhui, Jiangxi, Henan, Hubei, and Hunan. (3) The Western Region includes Sichuan, Chongqing, Guizhou, Yunnan, Tibet, Shanxi, Gansu, Qinghai, Ningxia, and Xingjiang, with an area of 5.5 million square kilometers. (4) All coastal cities are located in the Eastern Region. (5) There is a total of five special economic zones (SEZs). Shenzhen, Zhuhai, and Shantou are in Guangdong Province; Xiamen is in Fujian Province; and Hainan Island is a provincial SEZ. (6) TIFA stands for total investment in fixed assets.
Source: GTJCSJDZ, 1996.

THE CASE OF SHENZHEN

The special economic zones (SEZs) are the first comprehensive experiment for the feasibility of economic liberalization, without running the risk of opening the whole country to deregulation. In August 1979, the first two SEZs (Shenzhen and Zhuhai) were set up in Guangdong Province. Two months later, two other SEZs (Shantou and Xiamen) were established in Guangdong and Fujian Provinces, respectively. The zones are designated as a vehicle to establish an economy alternative to the extant planned system. Foreign inward investment is looked upon to bring much needed capital and production expertise in order to make good use of local resources and the labor force. The central government would not play a key role as it had usually done under the old regime in the establishment of SEZs' economy and finance of their land and property construction. During the process, an economy with market orientation is expected to be accomplished and to demonstrate the workings of a market to the whole country.

Nevertheless, the zones are meant to be only economically special, politically remaining the status quo. The SEZs serve as controlled laboratories for experimenting with the capitalist management of economic operations, before working out suitable models for the rest of the country. Free-market models need to be tested and tried in the Chinese socialist context before they can be adopted. New technologies and modern management related to market economy are expected to come with inward investment, which are critical to national modernization. Liang Xiang, the first mayor of Shenzhen, clearly stated that the objectives of the SEZs were to draw investment from overseas (*Beijing Review*, 23 January 1984):

1) Through preferential policies these zones could use large amounts of foreign investment in a better way, import advanced technology, and acquire scientific techniques and management—all of which would enable the country as a whole to develop economically at a quicker pace. 2) By dealing regularly with the foreign capital, we can further observe and understand the development of and exchanges in the modern capitalist world, and keep abreast of changes on the international markets and in science and technology. 3) Through co-operation, we can learn modern construction and management methods and train professionals.

Situated on the east coast of southern Guangdong, the Shenzhen special economic zone (SSEZ) is part of the Shenzhen municipality (see Figure 1.2). Prior to 1979, Shenzhen was a small market town for Bao'an County, which was an agricultural jurisdiction within the Chinese administrative hierarchy. The SSEZ has a territory of 327.5 square kilometer, or about 16 percent of the Shenzhen municipality. Overlooking Dapeng Bay in the east and the Pearl River Estuary in the west and separated from new territories of Hong Kong by only a stream in the south, Shenzhen is one of the major channels for inland China's trade and contacts with the world market via Hong Kong. In 1979, there was a population of 71,400 living in the SSEZ. It had increased to 1.6 million by 1996.

Since 1980, Shenzhen has achieved astonishing success in its economy and urban growth (see Table 1.2). In terms of ownership structure, Shenzhen's economy was mainly driven by the state-owned sector in the beginning, when there were no private enterprises at all. The share of state-owned manufacturing enterprises in the total gross output value of industry declined to 26.7 percent in 1990 (SZTJ, 1991). It further went down to a mere 9.0 percent in 1996, whereas the domestic private sector and foreign sole-proprietary firms produced 19.0 percent, and other non-state sectors (such as collective ownership, joint-venture, public-listed firms) produced 72.0 percent (SZTJ, 1997).

Shenzhen is an exception in the way that it has been built, the speed of the economic growth it has achieved, and the geographical location it has enjoyed. However, Shenzhen is becoming less exceptional. Shenzhen is meant to be an exemplar for other Chinese cities to follow if its development can live up to reformers' expectations. It could be an exception if it failed, or if its experience were unique. Hong Kong used to take a lion's share from the total inward investment into China. Due to the geographical, cultural, and linguistic proximity to Hong Kong, Guangdong absorbed a great amount of foreign capital, 41.9 percent in 1990, for example (GTJ, 1991). Shenzhen has benefited greatly from foreign investment not only

Figure 1.2
Map of Shenzhen

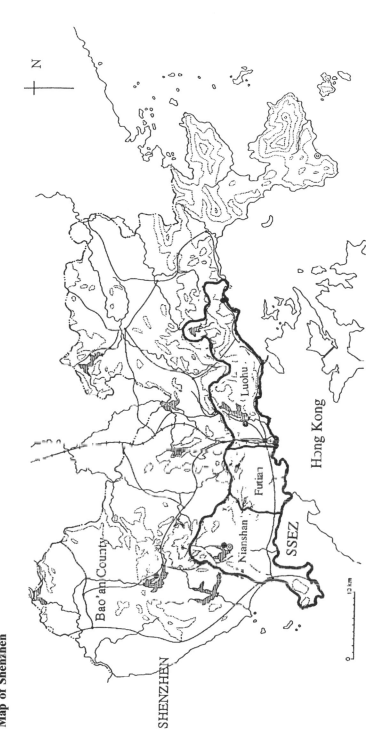

Table 1.2
Economic Performance and Urban Development of Shenzhen

	1980	1981	1982	1983	1984	1985	1986	1987
GDP (Million ¥)	270	496	826	1312	2342	3902	4165	5590
Percentage of GDP Contributed by Construction Industry	12.2	15.5	26.5	25.5	23.4	15.7	13.6	10.0
Investment in Built Environment/GDP (%)	46.2	54.5	76.6	67.5	66.4	70.8	46.0	38.6
	1988	1989	1990	1991	1992	1993	1994	1995
GDP (Million ¥)	8698	11566	17167	23666	31732	44929	61519	79569
Percentage of GDP Contributed by Construction Industry	9.7	9.1	7.2	8.4	10.9	13.8	11.6	11.4
Investment in Built Environment/GDP (%)	39.9	37.6	34.3	32.6	37.1	41.6	34.0	36.1

Source: SZTJ, 1996.

because of being close to Hong Kong but also because of the preferential policies (exclusive in the 1980s) it offered. In 1986, Shenzhen took 16.7 percent of the total foreign direct investment committed in the country (GTJ, 1987). However, a noteworthy phenomenon is that foreign investment, which used to concentrate in a few localities, has diversified to more regions since 1990. The portion of total foreign investment taken by Shenzhen declined to 9.4 percent in 1990, 2.9 percent in 1992, and further to 2.4 percent in 1993 (SZTJ, 1994; GTJ, 1994). Other cities are following suit by opening up their economies with the blessing of the central government. Shenzhen is becoming less exceptional in the role that foreign capital has played in economic expansion.

Overseas capital has been critical in turning Shenzhen from a tiny market town to a modern metropolis. Nevertheless, Shenzhen is not principally built by foreign capital, as is perceived. Shenzhen, due to its exclusive preferential policies in the 1980s, was attractive as well to domestic enterprises. More domestic enterprises came to register in Shenzhen than did foreign ones. Local enterprises' investment in urban physical construction accounted for 35 percent, while that of foreign firms accounted for only 18 percent in the period 1979–1996 (SZTJ, 1997). On the other hand, foreign participation in urban physical development has not been exclusively in Shenzhen since 1990. For example, Guangzhou saw 23.4 percent of the investment in real estate made by investors from overseas, Beijing saw 16.0 percent, and Wuxi saw 12.5 percent in 1994 (*Guangzhou Tongji Ju*, 1995; *Beijing Tongji Ju*, 1995; *Wuxi Tongji Ju*, 1995).

Shenzhen's achievements have led the central government to allow more cities to open up to economic liberalization. Another aspect of the successful Shenzhen story is often overlooked but equally significant in the contribution to the city's spectacular accomplishments: inward domestic capital. Domestic enterprises venturing into Shenzhen attracted by the economic freedom have achieved great success in raising productivity and profitability. Shenzhen has demonstrated that home enterprises can achieve what foreign ones can achieve under market conditions. Therefore, the expected exemplary role of Shenzhen to Chinese urbanization cannot be dismissed because of its unique background and exceptional growth since its inception.

STRUCTURE OF THE BOOK

From 1949, when the People's Republic of China was founded, up to 1998, China experienced dramatic changes over a wide spectrum. The 50-year history can be roughly divided into two periods: an era of central planning (1949–1978) and an age of economic reforms (1979–present). Chapter 2 briefly examines the characteristics of urban development of the two periods, and key events are highlighted to reveal their significance to the path of China's urbanization. After this broad background, Chapter 3 focuses on the case of Shenzhen to investigate an emerging property market in the transitional economy. Against a conceptual elaboration of real estate in a market system, the performance and behavior of the Shenzhen property market are analyzed against the backdrop of real estate commodification and marketization. Two modes of land provision in parallel, a salient and crucial feature of the Chinese gradualist urban reforms, are identified in Chapter 4 as a main contributor to Shenzhen's unique urban development process, which is echoed in other Chinese cities. The gradual and incremental urban land reforms are then elaborated within a broad framework of institutional change. Gradualism is used by the local government as the means and tool for local growth. The local property development industry, itself a product of the economic transition, is a key player in property development. Chapter 5 is thus devoted to unveiling the route the Shenzhen local developers have been taking toward attaining recognition of real independent enterprises. However, the remaining planning elements due to gradualism compromise the property market as well as the property development industry. Chapter 6 lists the implications of gradualist land reforms before drawing a conclusion about the role that should be taken by Chinese city governments under institutional change.

Chapter 2

Chinese Urban Development: From Socialist Central Planning to Socialist Market Orientation

The founding of the People's Republic ushered in a new era of a centrally controlled system. Centralization is a recurring phenomenon following divisive civil wars for the local interests in the long Chinese history. Planned economy, nevertheless, was imported from Russia because of the Communist ideology and thus was new to Chinese society. Under this framework, industrialization was pursued fervently to strengthen the country in the interest of nationalism, whereas urbanization, a concurrent event with industrialization, was suppressed by the Chinese planning ideology. Centrally controlled urbanization was carried out without a land market, which subsequently gave rise to a "socialist" urban structure. The grand economic reforms since 1979 have led China to a new stage. Market-led urbanization has introduced two significant phenomena: rural industrialization and commodification of urban housing. Market forces are introduced to play a role in urban development. Dynamic urbanization ensues from the re-emergence of land markets that had disappeared with the arrival of central planning. Urban restructuring is gaining momentum in changing socialist Chinese cities to resemble capitalist ones.

SOCIALIST URBANISM: INDUSTRIALIZATION WITHOUT URBANIZATION

When the Chinese Communist Party (CCP) defeated the Guomingdang Nationalist government and commenced its governance over the country in 1949, the paramount task on the new government's agenda was to develop a new socialist China. A planned economy of central control was adopted following the Soviet model because of the common ideology of perous new people's city" (cited by Murphey, 1953:27). The first Shanghai mayor of the new government, General Chen Yi, made it clear that the new government was to "change industrial policy from that of dependence on imperialism to that of serving the Chinese people" (cited by Murphey, 1953:27). Thereafter, the new production system under central planning did not seem to give a free hand to the urban private sector, which still contributed more than 63 percent to Shanghai's output in 1953 (Howe, 1981). Before the private sector was to be nationalized and put under the reign of planning in the near future, the existing industrial cities' role was restricted to maintaining the status quo. The fate of the coastal industrial cities was further compounded by the international situation at that time. The international embargo and hostile confrontation in the early 1950s made coastal regions vulnerable to possible attack. It was planned to evacuate Shanghai residents and to transfer factories to the interior regions. Between 1950 and 1957, 425,000 personnel, including professionals and ordinary workers, were relocated from Shanghai to key cities (*zhongdian chengshi*) with given industrial significance, which were planned as important producer cities, to help urban construction and industrial production (Shi & Gao et al., 1989). The Ministry of Construction Engineering was set up in 1952 and took charge of building new cities. It was understood that old industrial cities would not be relied upon for national industrialization.

Construction of new cities by new regimes is not unique from the perspective of the long Chinese history. It had been a tradition in China that every new dynasty made great efforts to build a new capital city as a symbol of the arrival of a new era. During the process, old structures would have to make way for new buildings, if the old buildings were in the way of new construction. The Communist government regarded itself as a pioneer to lead China into a brand-new era. New socialist cities could best serve as a manifesto of socialism in physical form. The drafted plan for Beijing city firmly believed that the capital of socialist China should be not only the political and cultural center but a great industrial city. It went to the extreme by declaring Beijing to be restructured into a heavy industrial city from a traditional cultural and administrative center. Ten grand "socialist" buildings were planned for the new capital immediately after the new government came into power and were completed by 1959, the tenth anniversary of the founding of the People's Republic. For the party leaders, Beijing was no longer the imperial capital for emperors and scholar-official elite but the new center for socialist China and its proletarian and Communist Party elite. The imperial north-south axis was soon shifted to a socialist east-west axis in Beijing's urban structure. The antiquities of city walls and many buildings were relentlessly torn down to make way for new thoroughfares. "*Pojiu lixin*" (to eliminate the old in order to build the new) is a revealing slogan that explains succinctly what has happened since 1949 in the Chinese cities. "As much as one-fifth of the existing buildings and dwellings in Taiyuan and Lanchow were taken down to make way for new construction, although these buildings were still in good condition" (Fung, 1981:275). It was estimated that the demolished buildings in 175 cities in 1956 amounted to 2.48 million square miles (Fung, 1981). "*Pojiu lixin*" did not cease and was forcefully continued in the 1960s–1970s "Cultural Revolution," when thousands of historical relics and artifacts were destroyed.

Plan-Controlled Urbanization

Because of continuous upheavals caused by World War II and the following civil war, the proportion of urban population to the whole declined from 27.2 percent in 1943 to 10.6 percent in 1949, when the war ended (Sit, 1985:6). The ensuing rehabilitation (1949–1952) and the subsequent First Five-Year Plan (FFYP) (1952–1957) saw the country rebuilt upon the rubble and debris. Urban population increased steadily to 15.4 percent in 1957. However, the migration of the population to cities was much controlled by the government. Free movement of population was curbed to the minimum by the introduction of the household registration system (*hukou zhidu*) in 1954, which effectively fixed residents in localities where they had resided, as all sorts of civil rights were associated with the household registration certificate. Spontaneous migration from rural areas to cities was virtually non-existent. During the FFYP, 6 new cities were built, and 20 cities expanded substantially (Cao & Chu, 1990). The new urban construction was apparently led by 156 Soviet-assisted manufacturing projects. Before the execution of the FFYP, the central government had categorized all existing cities into four groups with priorities according to the degree of heavy-industry components and the number of industrial projects to be constructed (see Table 2.2); 694 large plants were then assigned to, and planned for, the 39 cities in categories I, II, and III.

Because of the emphasis placed upon construction of producer cities and investment in productive components, attention was paid to the erection of plants, while infrastructure and urban services were ignored. Ironically, urban planning as a tool of effective management of urban development was not highly regarded under the central planning system. It could be attributed to the characters of the party leaders, who hailed from the countryside without credentials for handling modern industrial cities. Large-scale industrial development without coordination of urban planning gave rise to chaos, poor performance of investment, and thus waste of scarce resources. The national leaders, with revolutionary zeal but without urban management experience, tasted the complexity of urban industrialization and had to learn to be rational and reasonable. For the sake of improving performance of industrial investment, given limited fi-

Table 2.2
Categorization of Cities, 1952

Category I (to be developed as heavy industrial bases)	Category II (to be developed as major industrial cities)	Category III (to be developed as industrial cities)	Category IV (to remain as what they were)
Beijing	Jilin	Tianjin	all other cities
Baotou	Anshan	Tangshan	
Xi'an	Fushun	Dalian	
Datong	Benxi	Changchun	
Qiqihar	Shenyang	Jiamusi	
Daye	Harbin	Shanghai	
Lanzhou	Taiyuan	Qingdao	
Chengdu	Wuhan	Nanjing	
	Shijiazhuang	Hangzhou	
	Handan	Jinan	
	Zhengzhou	Zhongqing	
	Luoyang	Kunming	
	Kanjiang	Neijiang	
	Wulumuqi	Guiyang	
		Guangzhou	
		Xiangtan	
		Xiangfan	

Source: Cao & Chu, 1990: 37.

nancial resources, allocation of industrial projects might have to consider how to make use of urban facilities in the old existing cities. Therefore, all cities were re-categorized in 1954 according to the revised national development strategies (see Table 2.3). Taiyuan, Wuhan, and Luoyang were upgraded from the second league to the first league, which clearly indicated the focus of urban development in the Central Region. The significant shift in the priority of locational selection for major industrial cities occurred in old metropolises Shanghai, Tianjin, Dalian, Qingdao, Zhongqing and Guangzhou, upgraded from category III to category II. The central planners realized that the old industrial cities, especially coastal metropolises, might as well be used for the efficiency of new industrial investment. The enthusiasm for building brand-new socialist cities without association with decadent semicolonial and semifeudal old cities was obviously dampened by limited resources. Beijing's removal from category I in 1952, not appearing in any category at all in 1954, showed an emergence of a sense of rationalization and discretion. The development of Beijing would have to carefully consider its history and the role it would play.

The leaning toward building new socialist industrial sites in the interior region was not without problems. Inadequate resources scattered among numerous construction sites gave rise to a serious problem of investment inefficiency. In his speech "On the Ten Great Relationships" to the Central Committee of the CCP, Mao Zedong stated that industrial develop-

Table 2.3
Categorization of Cities, 1954

Category I (to be developed as heavy industrial bases)	Category II (to be developed as major industrial cities)	Category III (to be developed as industrial cities)	Category IV (to remain as what they were)
Taiyuan	Jilin	Tangshan	all other cities
Baotou	Anshan	Nanjing	(small and
Lanzhou	Fushun	Hangzhou	medium sized)
Xi'an	Benxi	Jinan	
Datong	Shenyang	Kunming	
Wuhan	Harbin	Guiyang	
Luoyang	Tianjin	Baoji	
Chengdu	Dalian	Changsha	
	Changchun	Nanchang	
	Jiamusi	Nanning	
	Shanghai	Huhehaote	
	Qingdao	Zhangjiakou	
	Zhongqing	Xining	
	Guangzhou	Yingchuan	
	Shijiazhuang		
	Handan		
	Zhengzhou		
	Fularji		
	Zhuzhou		
	Hegang		
	Kanjiang		

Source: Cao & Chu, 1990: 43–44.

ment in the interior regions should rely on the support of more efficient production in the coastal cities. The issue of relationship between "bone" (plants) and "fresh" (infrastructure and services) was also raised, as a disproportionate amount of investment was made in plants, while little was made in residential and service sectors. However, economic rationality never triumphs over political fanaticism in an ideological regime. In 1957, Mao Zedong confided his ambition by declaring overtly that China should aim to catch up with Britain in 15 years on major industrial productions (Ma et al., 1991). Socialism could be justified as superior to capitalism only by economic strength. In contrast to the First Five-Year Plan period, when industrialization was mainly driven by the top-down, state-sponsored, and Soviet-assisted industrial projects, the Second Five-Year Plan (SFYP) period (1958–1962) was characterized by the politically motivated mass industrialization movement at grassroots levels. The developmental focus shifted from the key cities, to almost every urban and rural locality and from the dependency on the Soviet Union's technologies and assistance, to the reliance on the indigenous efforts and passion. In 1960, 100,000 plants were under construction nationwide in order to increase the contribution of industrial products to GDP so that the share of manufacturing would surpass that of agriculture in the national economy (Cao & Chu, 1990:72). This movement, coined as the Great Leap Forward, initiated in 1958 and ending in 1960 as a total failure, was also the beginning of indigenous rural industrialization. Mass movement resulted in mass urbanization. Urban population rose to 19.7 percent in 1960, an increase of 5.1 percentage points within four years (GTJ, 1990).

Meanwhile, self-contained, manufacturing-led satellite towns were planned and built around metropolises, aiming at containing further expansion of cities that were already considered too big to manage. The socialist ideology deemed urban problems such as shortage of housing for low-income residents, social segregation, traffic congestion, and environmental pollution as evils related to the uncontrolled growth of capitalist cities. Thereby, socialist cities should adopt a new urban form to avoid these urban problems. Urban problems, nevertheless, occurred in Chinese cities. The size of cities was reckoned the chief culprit for the urban predicaments. The ultimate solution was logically for the national urbanization policy to emphasize the development of small cities and containment of large cities, in spite of the fact that larger Chinese cities were actually associated with greater efficiency of their industrial enterprises because of the economy of scale and benefits of agglomeration (Pannell, 1992).

City size had to be restricted, and urban sprawl had to be prevented. Some factories and their workers in metropolises had to be relocated from the central city to the manufacturing-dominated satellite towns. Eight satellite towns were constructed in Beijing, six in Nanjing, and five in Tianjin. Shanghai had planned and built seven satellite towns since 1958 (see Figure 2.1). Development of Wujing, Minhang, Jiading, Anting, and Songjiang had commenced since the late 1950s, while Baoshan (with the construction of Baoshan Steel Mill) and Jinshanwei (with the establishment of Jinshan Petrochemical Plant) since the 1970s (see Table 2.4). Each of these satellite towns specialized in certain sectors of manufacturing. In 1982, the population of satellite towns in Shanghai accounted for about 7 percent of the total municipal urban population, producing industrial products representing 13 percent of the municipal total in value (Zheng, Zon, & Song, 1984).

Merits of metropolises were thus overlooked and probably overshadowed by urban problems. Not intrinsically belonging to large cities, urban problems arose from inadequate investment in urban infrastructure and incompetent management by the inexperienced city governments. Planned decentralization is not necessarily an appealing measure to be accepted by the concerned factories and workers. Given choices, Shanghai industrial enterprises would rather remain in the central city. Only 11.9 percent of the total number of enterprises operational in seven satellite towns migrated from the central city. Workers whose "work units" had moved to satellite towns "voted with their feet": only 28.1 percent of them

Figure 2.1
Map of Shanghai Municipality

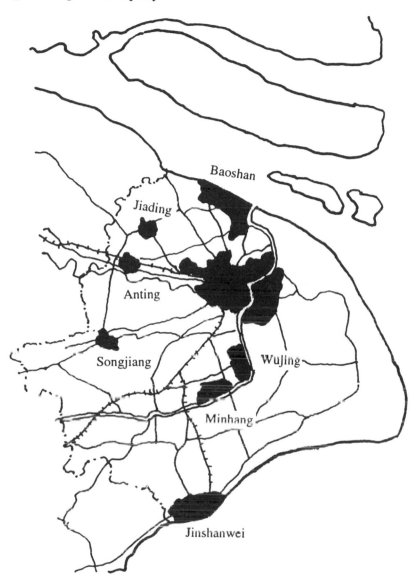

actually settled where they worked, and the rest commuted between their workplaces and residence in the central city (Zheng, Zon, & Song, 1984).

Since 1966, when the infamous Cultural Revolution started, urban development had virtually been at a standstill. The "Third Front" program between 1964 and 1971, the creation of an industrial base in remote inland

Table 2.4
Satellite Towns of Shanghai

Satellite Town	Distance from Central City's CBD (KM)	Number of Residents (thousands)	Size (ha)	Main Industry	Total Number of Enterprises	Number of Enterprises Migrated from Central City
Baoshan	18	165	2,400	metallurgic	114	0
Wujing	25	13	376	chemical	21	2
Minhang	31	67	794	machinery and electrical	59	15
Jiading	33	56	693	instruments and researches	65	7
Anting	33	10	230	automobile and machinery	26	10
Songjiang	40	69	632	machinery and light industry	74	10
Jinshanwei	72	45	1,000	petrochemical	12	0

Note: CBD = central business district; ha = hectares.
Source: Zheng, Zon & Song, 1984: 15.

provinces to prepare for the envisaged war, drained finances for the development of other cities (Naughton, 1988). Urban youths were sent to
the countryside in the "up to mountains and down to villages" movement
(*shangshan xiaxiang*), which ostensibly advocated the necessity of re-
education of urban high school graduates by peasants, according to Mao's
revolutionary tenets. Between 1962 and 1979, 17.8 million urban youths
either voluntarily or obligatorily migrated to the countryside. One-third
of them, or 5.8 million, were sent during the heat of the Cultural Revolution (1967–1970). Most urban youths came from large cities such as
Shanghai, where 1.25 million young residents had to abandon their much
liked urban life (Gu, 1997). The food shortages and famines that ensued
from the Great Leap Forward also forced city governments to re-rusticate
urban residents. Urban population decreased to 12.2 percent in 1965. It
further dropped to 11.2 percent in 1970 before reviving to 12.1 percent in
1978. Cities in the Eastern Region experienced negative population
growth of 0.79 percent in the period 1965–1970 (GTJCSJDZ, 1990).

Urban Land Management System Prior to 1979

Before the 1949 revolution, private land-ownership was the norm in
China. In the countryside, most agricultural land was owned by landlords
who either hired peasants to do farming or leased it to tenant farmers.
Urban land, like rural land, was owned by private individuals as well as
the government. The conversion of rural land-ownership from landlords
to peasants through the Land Reforms, which confiscated land of landlords
and redistributed it to peasants, commenced soon after 1949. Meanwhile,

urban land-ownership remained largely unchanged, except that the land owned by foreigners and the Kuomintang government was confiscated and converted to state ownership. In 1953, the cooperative movement in the countryside abolished private ownership of farming land and replaced it with collective ownership. Change of urban land-ownership started with the socialist reform of private industries in 1956. Private properties and land were gradually converted to be state-owned, and by 1958 the conversion had been almost completed in all cities. After the people's commune movement in the countryside and ownership transformation in cities, private land-ownership virtually ceased to exist, though the nationalization of urban land was not officially finalized until the 1982 Constitution (IFTE/CASS & IPA, 1991).

Universally recognized as one of the most important production factors, land had been excluded from economic transactions by the socialist principle of state land-ownership that considered any kind of land transaction unconstitutional and unlawful. Clause 4, Article 10 of the 1982 Constitution stipulates: "Urban land belongs to the state. Land in the countryside and in suburban areas belongs to collective ownership unless the law stipulates that the land is state-owned. Residential land and family plots also belong to the collective ownership. No organization or individual may appropriate, buy, sell, or lease land, or unlawfully transfer it in any way."

Due to the nature of the overall state economy and the centrally controlled economic system, the government did not see it necessary to subject land users, most of them being state-owned enterprises, to a system of land utilization with compensation. It was reckoned that planning control was supposedly more efficient than the market system, and thus planned land allocation would meet users' demand without implications of affordability and market bias. In 1954, a government decree removed the nominal utilization fees and rentals for using urban land by state-owned enterprises, government offices, and civic institutions (Fung, 1981). According to central planning, urban land was allocated to users through administration channels that spared land users payment of any fee or price, and urban land users had no rights to transfer the land they occupied. From 1954 to 1984, urban land in China was virtually free goods and was not regarded as an economic asset. Land was assigned according to land users' investment plans, and site selection was negotiated and determined between users and urban planners based on the city land use master plan (see Figure 2.2).

Urban development was a result of top-down plans, instead of an outcome of bottom-up initiatives and interactions between private and public interests. Marxist doctrines consider that land does not have value, though it is a necessary factor for production, and thus income from any property should be abolished. Landowners as a class were eliminated with the nationalization of land. There was no profession of real estate developers

Figure 2.2
Land Allocation Process Prior to 1979

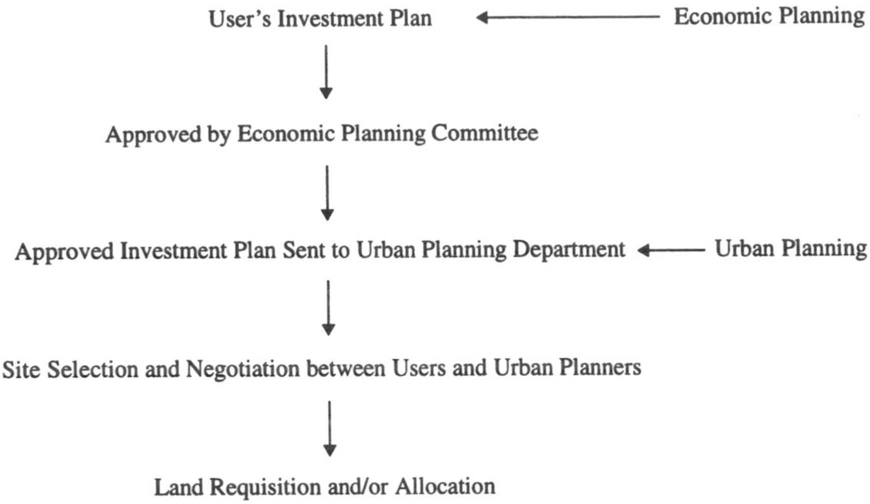

User's Investment Plan ◄————————— Economic Planning

↓

Approved by Economic Planning Committee

↓

Approved Investment Plan Sent to Urban Planning Department ◄——— Urban Planning

↓

Site Selection and Negotiation between Users and Urban Planners

↓

Land Requisition and/or Allocation

because all premises were constructed by state-owned construction companies at the command of governments, and therefore there were no property markets. Under the predominant state ownership and administrative command system, individual initiatives were largely suppressed, and market demand was ignored by the rigid top-down controls. The absolute state ownership of urban land under the centrally controlled socialist system has led to a dramatically different structure of socialist cities (French & Hamilton, 1979). The absence of land markets was blamed for having profoundly impaired the internal efficiency and productivity of the former Soviet cities (Bertaud & Renaud, 1994).

FORMATION OF URBAN STRUCTURE WITHOUT A LAND MARKET

The system of free and administrative allocation of urban land appears economically irrational and thus tends to be inefficient. Nevertheless, it is an integral part of the overall economic strategy for the purpose of expeditious industrialization. Given the hostile international embargo, it seemed that China had few options but to be self-reliant. After a brief rehabilitation after the civil war, a strategy of state-led, rapid industrialization was adopted to emphasize development of heavy industries to build a framework for the economy under construction. This military-styled development demanded all necessary resources under state control. Urban land being one of the indispensable resources for industrialization, its nationalization was an essential thrust to make the urban land-ownership system compatible with the economic system and the policy of rapid industrialization. Although the Marxist ideology contributed to the formulation of free land use policy, as Marx believed that land was not a commodity and thus should be owned by the state and allocated to users according to their needs instead of their economic power, the socioeconomic situation was principally responsible for the adoption of this policy. In China, the socialist ideology was adopted and shaped in the socioeconomic context. Sociohistorical necessity determined state policies, which were later coated with Marxist-Leninist-Mao Zedong ideology (Tang, 1994).

All evidence suggested that in order to speed up industrialization to catch up with capitalist countries, the government had to mobilize all resources. Prices of agricultural produce were held artificially low in order to subsidize urban workers. Prices of natural resources were controlled by plans to ensure low costs for production. Housing for urban workers by the name of "workers' apartments" was provided with heavy state subsidies. State-developed residential communities were located near factories to enable workers to commute short distances and thus to devote more energy to production. Many in-kind benefits were given only to workers of manufacturing industries, such as benefits covering childbirth, retirement, sickness, death, injury, and disability. Free land allocation was deemed fundamental in this context. Sustainability of economic growth and proper maintenance of facilities were forsaken by the government, which knew little of economics but was keen on large-scale industrial production. The categorization of "consumer" and "producer" cities revealed the government's obsession with narrowly defined production. "Consumer cities" were often referred to as parasitic and unproductive. Therefore, it was logical that priority should be granted to the productive enterprises in order to fulfill the goal of rapid industrialization, whereas services were not considered productive undertakings.

In order to ensure that factories could obtain desired land plots, price mechanisms in the land management system were probably deliberately ruled out, so that market forces would not undermine the plan-controlled land allocation. The determination of land use by the ability to pay would, in those revolutionary leaders' minds, jeopardize the urgent need of industrialization and assist only cities with "unproductive" services of consumption. Land was meant to be allocated according to needs, of which industrialization was paramount. Manufacturing was thus privileged in land allocation, and, as a result, the proportion of industrial land use in Chinese cities was much higher than that in capitalist cities, where land was allocated by the market (see Table 2.5). Industrialists' demand usually overtook others' in land allocation. Investment in urban housing and services was compromised because of shortages of funds. In spite of the ex-

Table 2.5
Urban Land Use Structure: Comparison between Japanese and Chinese Cities
(percent of total land use)

	Japan (average)	Nanjing	Ningbo	Shanghai	Jinan
industrial	13.0	34.2	30.5	24.4	37.5
residential	76.0	29.1	28.3	32.5	28.4
others	11.0	36.7	41.2	43.1	34.1

Source: Zhongguo Shehui Kexueyuan, 1992.

istence of long-term urban land use plans that tried to guide cities toward a rational land use structure, it was not uncommon to see factories located in a city's central business district. Quite a number of manufacturing factories occupied central locations in downtown Shanghai even in the 1980s.

An urban economy was thus structured without participation of the land market. During the period 1949–1979, when Chinese urban construction was completely controlled by government plans, the absence of a formal land market to coordinate land allocation among competing users resulted in an inefficient structure of land use and inequality among land users (IFTE/CASS, 1992). Land use changes were extremely difficult due to occupiers being protected by most de facto rights over their premises, which was an obstacle for potentially more efficient land users to have access to the land occupied, if not impossible to acquire land in the right location and at the right time. Without mechanisms to receive market feedback, the plan-guided investment in the urban built environment often led to mismatches between what was demanded by marketplaces and what was supplied by plans. Underinvestment and overinvestment occurred in the Chinese cities in the process of urbanization.

Free resources encourage users to overconsume, let alone to consider affordability. Waste and excessive claims arose as land applicants often demanded more than needed by their investment schemes. Land squandering was prevalent (Fung, 1981), evident by rapid expansion of some industrial cities (see Table 2.6). Many cities uneconomically adopted great squares in their city plans. "[T]he area of the municipal central squares in the urban plans of Lanchow, Loyang and Harbin exceeded the 9 hectare Tiananmen Square in Beijing" (Fung, 1982:275). The excessive land supply in so-called new industrial cities contrasted sharply with the extremely parsimonious land use plans applied to "old industrial cities," which were the traditional manufacturing bases of the country (Zhu, 1996). Government policies favored the former by directing almost all resources to construct new industrial bases, and thus the latter were neglected because of financial constraints. The old industrial cities suffered from underinvestment in urban infrastructure. Lack of funds to maintain the existing building stock caused urban degradation. A too-high population density in the

Table 2.6
Change in the Size of Built-up Areas of Selected Chinese Cities (square kilometers, 1949–1957)

	1949	1957	% Growth
Beijing	109	221	103
Xi'an	13	65	400
Zhengzhou	5	52	940
Hefei	5	57	1040
Jinan	23	37	61
Tianjing	61	97	59

Source: World Bank, 1993: 43.

Table 2.7
Population Density in Selected Chinese Cities (thousands per square kilometer, 1983)

	Shanghai	Guangzhou	Beijing	Xi'an	Hefei	Lanzhou
urban population density	40.6	32.0	11.6	10.9	8.9	5.6

Source: Zhu, 1986b: 15.

old industrial cities resulted from insufficient development of new housing estates and related urban facilities, while the generous land development in the new industrial cities gave rise to a too-low population density to sustain urban public services (see Table 2.7). One neighborhood in Shanghai had a residential population density of 293.5 thousand per square kilometers—one of the highest in the world (Zhu, 1986a). As the largest city in China, Shanghai built only 22.8 million square meters of housing from 1950 to 1980, its monetary investment accounting for merely 0.49 percent of city GDP. Over 30 years, housing stock increased only 58 percent, despite expansion of city GDP 6.7 times and of urban population from 4.2 million to 5.8 million (SSTJ, 1981). Housing shortages were pervasive. In the period 1953–1978, 8.83 percent of Shanghai GDP was invested in fixed assets, 1.82 percent in infrastructure, and 0.54 percent in utilities (SSTJ, 1981). As a result, the contribution made by the construction industry to city GDP was as insignificant as 1.1 percent (see Table 2.8), in sharp contrast with that in cities of similar size under the market economy, where the construction industry should be a pillar of the urban economy. Without mediation of land and property markets, top-down plans tended to misallocate resources in urban construction (see Tables 2.9 and 2.10). Underinvestment strained urban functions to the limit, whereas overinvestment unnecessarily wasted valuable resources.

Because of the socialist principles and pervasive state ownership, urban housing was regarded as welfare distributed to workers according to their

Table 2.8
Investment in the Built Environment of Shanghai (1953–1980)

Period	% of GDP Contributed by Property Industry	Investment in Fixed Assets as % of GDP	Investment in Housing as % of GDP	Housing Construction (Million sq m)
1953-57	2.3	6.6	0.6	2.94
1958-62	1.3	9.8	0.3	3.75
1963-65	1.1	6.7	0.3	1.37
1966-70	0.6	5.3	0.1	2.07
1971-75	0.9	10.4	0.3	3.46
1976-80	1.4	11.6	0.9	9.18
1953-78	1.1	8.6	0.4	17.56

Source: SSTJ, 1996.

Table 2.9
Investment in Utilities of Shanghai

Year	1957	1962	1965	1970	1975	1978
Investment in Utilities as % of GDP	0.36	0.17	0.41	0.18	0.67	0.99

Source: SSTJ, 1980.

Table 2.10
Urban Investment as Percentage of GDP

	Shanghai (1950-80)	Japan (1960-80)	USA (1975-83)	Germany (1976-80)	UN Recommended Standard
Investment in Fixed Assets/GDP	8.83	32.40	18.11	22.09	33.0
Investment in Infrastructure/GDP	1.82				
Investment in Utilities/GDP	0.54	3.12	1.46	1.8	4.0
Investment in Housing/GDP	0.49				

Sources: SSTJ, 1990; *Chengshi Jingji Yanjiu*, 1993, No. 1: 15.

needs. The low rental for housing was consequently determined by the then low wage system. On the one hand, the low rental remained unchanged until the early 1980s, when it became a nominal charge in comparison with greatly increased wages over the years. On the other hand, due to a misconception of housing as a consumption good rather than a basic need of urban residents, only a disproportionate amount of funds was channeled into urban housing investment, whereas a lion's share of capital investment was put into industrial projects. Housing development was consistently kept very low in proportion to the total capital investment over three decades. National housing investment as a proportion of GDP averaged only 1.5 percent from 1949 to 1978. Urban housing problems then emerged, were exacerbated by continuous negligence, and became a crisis in some places where underinvestment led to a severe housing shortage. Insufficient rental income resulted in poor maintenance of the existing housing stock. Inadequate housing investment coupled with rapid growth of the urban population in the late 1970s because of the return of many rusticated urban youths in the Cultural Revolution gave rise to widespread deterioration of housing conditions in many Chinese cities; 192 cities witnessed a reduction in housing area per capita from 4.5 square meters in 1952 to 3.6 square meters in 1978. One-third of urban households were officially categorized as in overcrowded conditions (Wu, 1988). Shanghai became a victim of the central planning as it ignored adequate investment in urban physical and social infrastructure for sustainable urban growth (Zhu, 1996). According to a population census conducted in 1982, 47.6 percent of urban households in Shanghai had housing problems to various degrees: poor housing qualities such as dilapidated structures and lack of amenities, overcrowding, and homelessness. Average housing floor area per capita was merely 4.7 square meters, and 25.1 percent of households were virtually homeless as they temporally lived with their parents or relatives while waiting for government assignment. About half of the total housing floor areas were substandard without necessary facilities (SSBJJKZJK, 1983).

INITIATIVES FOR URBAN REFORMS

The economic reforms proceeded from rural areas to urban districts and from manufacturing industries to financial establishments. The great success of agricultural reform, indicated by a substantial increase in agricultural output, has changed the organization of farming from collective communes to a household responsibility system since 1978. It then led reforms to the urban domain, where the industrial sector involved many tough problems such as distorted commodity prices and deep-rooted socialist welfare. The urban reforms tried to replace comprehensive and direct state involvement in the enterprise decision-making process with interventions in production via indirect levers such as taxes, subsidies, and macroeconomic policy tools. A market dimension was purposefully added to economic operations where state-owned enterprise rights to make decisions were confirmed (Gray, 1982). Industrial decision making was to be guided by economic indicators rather than dictated by administrative cadres. According to a series of surveys carried out by the China Economic System Reform Research Institute, by 1984, 51 percent of randomly sampled enterprises had gained autonomy to a certain extent, and 77 percent of them found it necessary to bear market situations in mind in their production (Zhang & Zhang, 1987).

Urban reform is a general umbrella under which comprehensive—nevertheless, gradual—changes are initiated to install market mechanisms in the process of urbanization. One of the goals for the urban reform is to abandon the rural-urban dichotomy and to re-establish cities as the centers of economic organization from a wider perspective. The Chinese economy used to be separated into two entities: urban industries and rural agriculture. The two spheres did not necessarily intersect. The heavy industries, which were the emphasis on the state agenda in order to build up military strength for national defense, might not benefit the rural economy directly. Instead, resources were mobilized to build industries at the expense of peasants. Agriculture was made to contribute to the process of industrialization. The benefits of industrialization and urbanization hardly trickled down to farmers working in the fields. The town–country division was strikingly reflected in the three systems of household registration, social security, and land (Zhou, 1997a).

Under provincial governments, which were the first-layer local governments under the central government, there were two parallel administrations of governance: prefectures, which governed counties (the agricultural units in the Chinese administrative hierarchy) and cities, which were directly responsible to the provincial governments. Therefore, there were no direct linkages between rural and urban economies in governance, which was extremely important in the central planning system. The economic integration of towns and the countryside started with the abolition of prefectures and transfer of their subordinate counties to the leadership of cities. This structural change in administration is called *shidaixian*, literally meaning "cities-leading-counties." The leading role of the city has thus been explicitly established to usher in an epoch of city-led regional development for the first time in Chinese history.

The market-oriented urban reforms demand decentralization to give city governments autonomy in the management of urban economy, and urban economic units are to be transformed from so-called *danwei*[1] to real and independent enterprises. During the urban reforms, a diverse range of issues has been touched upon, such as commodity prices, labor wages, taxation, labor market, social security, education, medical care, and housing. The relationships between the central state and local governments and between governments and enterprises have also been dealt with. The urban economic transformation is therefore comprehensive and far-reaching to the extent of changing everyone's economic welfare, social status, and even cultural values.

The changes in the governmental role from a production organizer to an economic regulator and from direct administrative controls through directives to indirect managerial guides with monetary and fiscal policies have indicated a replacement of administrative means with economic levers. Financial accountability is instilled in the urban governmental management. Fiscal expenditure for investment in infrastructure and urban maintenance is gradually institutionalized by designating a proportion of enterprise revenues, instead of previous ad hoc grants, which were subject to changes of the central policy and to personal negotiations. Fiscal decentralization was first attempted in the wake of the catastrophic failure of the top-down Great Leap Forward in the 1950s, when the central government was forced to delegate power to local governments in their conducting management of urban development in the ensuing economic recovery. Shenyang was the first city granted autonomy to withdraw 5 percent from enterprise profits and to use it as a special fund for urban construction. Later in 1962, this policy was applied to 64 cities, including Beijing, Shanghai, Tianjin, the capital cities of 26 provinces, and 35 other cities (Cao & Chu, 1990). However, the following anarchical Cultural Revolution canceled this local autonomy.

Before the fiscal reform in 1984, which changed the fiscal system from profit remittance to taxation levy, 5 percent of remitted industrial and commercial profits had been collected as Urban Maintenance Fee since 1978. Urban Construction Maintenance Tax has been introduced to replace the Urban Maintenance Fee since 1985. Urban construction has thereby been linked with the performance of the local economy. The cost factor in utilizing urban facilities is concurrently built into the framework of urban management. Since 1984, about 30 cities have implemented this practice by charging, for instance, for drainage in order to set up a fund for the maintenance of a drainage system. In 1985, 113 cities collected fees from enterprises for using infrastructure. This initiation of commodification of urban services has a profound impact on urban development.

To open up local economies became a paramount task for the governments at various levels, which saw a lackluster performance of self-sufficient production. Chinese cities were searching for appropriate strategies to embark on economic liberalization. In 1981, Shashi and Changzhou, two medium-sized cities, were designated for a pilot study of urban reforms that would change comprehensively the urban system molded under central planning to one with market orientation. Since 1983, the five large cities of Chongqing, Wuhan, Shenyang, Dalian, and Nanjing were added to the list for urban reforms. Later in 1984, 14 coastal cities (Dalian, Qinhuangdao, Tianjin, Yantai, Qingdao, Lianyuangang, Nantong, Shanghai, Ningbo, Wenzhou, Fuzhou, Guangzhou, Zhanjiang, and Beihai) were designated as "open cities" for foreign inward investment where special zones could be set up coined as "Economic and Technological Development Zones" to entice technologically advanced foreign investment.

The economic reforms so far have been acclaimed a great success regarding welfare for citizens. The quality of life for the Chinese populace has greatly improved. Moreover, the most remarkable change in Chinese society is that market mechanisms have begun to play an important role in the operation of economy and society. The economic reforms have led to considerable increases in production and consumption. National income per capita rose by 8.3 percent a year between 1978 and 1995, compared with an increase of 3.9 percent in the period from 1953 to 1978 (GTJ, 1997). *The Economist* (28 November 1992) commended: "China's economic performance in the fourteen years since then (1979) has brought about one of the biggest improvements in human welfare anywhere at any time."

Urbanization in the Countryside—Rural Industrialization

One of the effects of the Great Leap Forward (1958–1960) was the initiation of rural industrialization where "commune and brigade enterprises" using local materials and rural labor were developed to support agricultural production (Byrd & Lin, 1990). "Walking on two legs" (*liangtiaotui zoulu*) was the policy advocating parallel development of big, modern manufacturing in cities and small, primitive industrial production in the countryside. Following Marxist ideology, it was believed that rural industrialization could lead to the erasure of three differences: between the city and the countryside, between industrial and agricultural production, and between manual and mental labors.

The new economic policy broke the ideological taboo to which Chinese peasants had been subjected for three decades by dismantling communes and restoring households as basic farm units, that is, the regime of household responsibility. Market-driven initiatives implanted a powerful engine in the rural economy and thereafter saw significant progress in farming productivity (Putterman, 1993). Peasants were exhilarated by the betterment in their living conditions. For instance, the gross agricultural output value increased by 108.4 percent during the period 1980–1985 in Jiangsu Province (United Nations, 1991). However, the problem of labor surplus soon arose due to improvement in farming efficiency. A considerable number of potential emigrants would flood the cities as had been happening in many developing countries where urbanization meant people leaving the countryside for urban life. The urbanization of population had been kept artificially low (19.4 percent in 1980) because of the control of free migration by the state since 1954.

Having realized it would incur huge social and financial costs to accommodate rural–urban population transfer, the Chinese government adopted a policy that allowed little growth of large metropolitan areas but encouraged development of rural townships. In this context, a new form of urbanization took place, "to leave farming but not to leave the countryside (*litu bu lixiang*)." This policy was to alleviate the migration pressure in existing urban areas, as most cities had problems of housing shortages and infrastructure inadequacy because of underinvestment in the past, as well as underemployment due to an ill-structured economy shaped by the planning system. Many cities were not ready to absorb inflows from their rural hinterland. Thus, the township-village enterprises (TVEs) came into being. These were small and medium-sized enterprises in rural regions to make use of local materials and to provide non-agricultural employment to those made redundant by the primary farming, known in China as *xiangzhen qiye*. Most TVEs were owned by township (*xiangzhen*) governments or village communities. Although the history of TVEs can be traced back to the 1950s, when millions of farmers were mobilized to establish small labor-intensive village factories to produce goods for local consumption, TVEs flourished only in the 1980s.

In retrospect, rural enterprises have had a great economic and social impact on Chinese urbanization. In 1978, only 9.5 percent of the total rural labor force was employed in TVEs, accounting for 7.0 percent of the national labor force. The ratio of TVE workers to the total rural labor force jumped to 27.9 percent in 1993, translating to 20.5 percent of the national labor force (Wong & Yang, 1995). In 1976, there were 1.1 million rural enterprises employing 17.9 million workers and producing a total gross income of ¥27 billion (Chang & Kwok, 1990). In 1993, 24.5 million TVEs were in operation and employed 123.5 million people with a production of ¥3,154.1 billion, which represented about 40 percent of the nation's total industrial product (Wong & Yang, 1995; Chang & Wang, 1994), while it was only 9 percent in 1978. Rural industries have become one of the major forces in changing farmers' lifestyle, reinforcing agricultural infrastructure, and building up a local social service system. There is a general trend in the relatively developed regions that rural manufacturing has become a pillar of the rural economy with respect to output, employment, and its significance in production.

Looking into varieties of the township industry, two salient models emerge. The first model is those TVEs under private ownership. These TVEs are usually far from large cities, and thus urban industrial assistance is hard to obtain. Enterprises are usually small and simple and do not require much technology and capital investment. An average private enterprise in Wenzhou, for instance, consisted of only three workers in 1985 (Dong, 1992). The second model is the southern Jiangsu model, where TVEs are mostly owned by township and village governments. They are located in areas close to large cities, where support by large, state-owned industries from cities is available in the forms of technical support and subcontracting. Those TVEs are usually ancillary workshops to manufacture parts and accessories for the city partners. A coalition between rural indigenous industrialization and spillover of upgrading urban industries is formed, by which TVEs can receive technological assistance and market access. The phenomenon of more developed TVEs being closer to the central city of Shanghai suggests that there should be a strong linkage between TVEs and city industries (Hou & Zhao, 1995). Those TVEs are most likely the spillover of manufacturing from Shanghai central city, where an upgrading in economic and land use structure has been under way. TVEs in southern Jiangsu and northern Zhejiang benefit greatly from the retired workers from Shanghai factories returning to their hometowns. Shanghai engineers and technicians are invited to be their part-time staff, providing assistance at weekends because of the adjacency of those TVEs to Shanghai. The complementary relationship between rural industries and urban enterprises will promote a new division of labor and a coordinated development between the rural and urban economies. In 1988, peasants in Jiangsu, Zhejiang, and Shandong Provinces, which are of the second model, accounted for 17 percent of China's rural population, but they represented 43 percent of the total rural industries and produced 50 percent of the total TVE output (Naughton, 1995).

Nevertheless, TVE-led urbanization does not look completely sanguine. Urban industries tend to contract out undesirable production, usually with pollution, to TVEs, which are not in a favorable position to bargain. Dispersion of industries across the countryside creates problems of environmental degradation and low efficiency in production as local supporting infrastructure is not good. The planning control for TVEs may be lax, suggested by a low degree of intensity in land use in Shanghai suburbs where land is scarce (Hou & Zhao, 1995). Four adverse issues are identified in the urbanization process of the region Changjiang Delta, one of the most developed regions in China: inadequate infrastructure, agricultural degradation, destruction of natural resources, and environmental pollution (Wang & Zhang, 1995). Urban industrial development has invaded the rural agricultural base aggressively in the form of joint ventures with TVEs. This urban sprawl has given rise to a conflict between industrial development and agricultural production. It is reported that more and more TVEs in the southern coastal regions have been shaping joint ventures with overseas capital since 1992, intending to absorb advanced technology and to open up foreign markets (Wong & Yang, 1995). Technological and managerial upgrading is probably key to the further success of TVEs in future. However, the future development of TVEs needs to be scrutinized and assessed in order to find the right direction for this alternative route of urbanization.

Urban Housing Reforms

After the Chinese Communist Party came into power in 1949, private housing was gradually phased out by the government policy of conversion to state ownership, according to the prevailing ideology. Property right conversion reached its climax in the Cultural Revolution, when almost all urban housing was under public ownership. Although there were still some properties held by private owners in the 1950s and the early 1960s, private property investment and development had virtually vanished. In the production of urban housing, government was the sole supplier, while other kinds of housing developers and investors were effectively excluded and eliminated. Under the general planning framework, which was pro-manufacturing-related investments, investment in housing was given a low priority. Inadequate finances for housing development inevitably resulted in housing shortages. Housing floor area per capita, a widely used indicator in China to measure housing provision, declined to a very low level in the 1970s. Acute housing inadequacy was basically, on the one hand, caused by underinvestment in housing for a long time. The fact that the state was the sole supplier of urban housing explained that housing provision was at the mercy of state plans, and housing conditions would not be improved as long as housing investment remained a low priority on the government agenda. On the other hand, an absence of housing markets and thus prices led to inequality in distribution, because housing welfarism delinked housing demand from affordability and excluded pecuniary contribution from residents. As a result, urban slums re-appeared as the unfortunate urban residents who were not properly accommodated by public housing built temporary and informal shelters to cope with basic housing needs. Patches and pockets of dilapidated housing re-emerged as an embarrassing part of the supposedly socialist cityscape of many Chinese cities after the 1950s slum clearance movement.

In this context, housing reforms were tried to put an end to the welfare provision of urban housing. Urban workers used to be assigned flats, upon availability, and then paid nominal rentals, reportedly accounting for only 1 percent of the household income. It became necessary to mobilize more funds into housing investment and to promote various modes of housing development. Decentralization of housing provision and commodification or privatization of housing were consequently the two thrusts for the initial housing reforms in the early 1980s. As opposed to housing provision being solely dependent on the state prior to 1978, *danwei* and private capital were urged to participate in the construction of housing. While housing commodification, facilitated by private capital, would be a long and slow process due to demand constraints, directing more investment from *danwei* into housing for employees seemed without much resistance.

With the gradual progress of the state-owned enterprise reforms, enterprises were allowed to retain profits after contracted submission to the supervisory authorities and given autonomy to decide how the retained profit should be invested. Housing, as a benefit in kind, had always been in the compensation package for urban workers. Although under transformation, the ownership of enterprises remained unchanged, and state

Table 2.11
Growth of Extrabudgetary Funds (1952–1991)

Period	Extrabudgetary Funds as % of Total Funds*	Annual Budgetary Funds in Average (Billion ¥)	Annual Extrabudgetary Funds in Average (Billion ¥)	% of Extrabudgetary Funds Controlled by Enterprises
1952-59	9.7	29.6	3.2	67.4
1960-69	15.0	43.2	7.6	83.6
1970-79	22.2	84.2	24.0	89.3
1980-89	46.2	168.1	144.3	96.8
1990-91	49.4	304.3	297.6	97.8

Note: *Total funds is the sum of budgetary funds and extrabudgetary funds.
Source: Caizheng Bu, 1992.

property ownership and state management of its enterprises did not give enterprise managers incentives to look forward to the long-term prospects. Instead, the partial reforms had induced short-term behavior among state-owned enterprise managers and workers. Housing provision remained under social welfare. The only difference was that enterprises replaced the state as the major providers.

With strengthening of profit-making state-owned enterprises' financial capacity, housing provision in the 1980s increased substantially compared to the decades in the past. The extrabudgetary funds (Wang, 1995), the finances outside the planning control and mainly administered by enterprises, had been growing at rates much faster than the expansion of budgetary funds since commencement of the economic reforms (see Table 2.11). Over 90 percent of total housing investment was financed by the state budget in the form of capital construction investment in 1979. By 1988, the state was responsible for only 22 percent of the investment in housing, and enterprises' financing of housing increased to 58 percent (World Bank, 1992). As a result, the benefits in-kind to workers, of which housing was the biggest component, increased dramatically in the total compensation package.

Housing commodification was carried out initially by raising housing rentals to the degree of full cost recovery for the existing housing stock, on the one hand, and commercializing housing development for new supply, on the other. It was recommended that the housing market be regulated by market affordability. A commercially viable housing lease market should be created to sustain a sizable housing stock for leasing. The first commodity housing sales were tested in some cities in two provinces of Shanxi and Guangxi, where prices of housing units were set to cover the basic construction cost. Later, hundreds of cities participated in the experiment of sales of housing stock to tenants at market prices. In spite of the fact that housing prices did not include profits, which were the norm for any commercial development of properties, the relatively high prices, along with prevailing low wages, deterred a sizable demand for this scheme. The housing cost was about 10–20 years' income for an ordinary household at the time (Wang & Murie, 1996). The experiment had to be abandoned due to demand constraints.

Having realized low purchasing power in the urban housing market, the government was prompted to try a scheme of subsidized sale of housing. In 1982, pilot housing commodification was tried in the four cities of Changzhou, Zhenzhou, Shashi, and Shiping. Individuals paid one-third, and the rest were paid one-third each by the state and the enterprise to which the prospective buyer was attached. By the end of 1983, 1,619 housing units had been sold in these four cities (Cao & Chu, 1990). Then, the experiment was extended to more than 120 cities and 240 towns nationwide by 1984. The buyers obtained the "partial property rights," as they paid only one-third of the market prices.

The 1988 *State Council Plan for Housing Reform in Urban Areas* sets the guidelines for the rent reform and homeownership promotion. Determined by the characteristic of gradualism in China's reforms, a prudent, step-by-step approach was adopted in transforming the urban system in order to avoid the grievous disruptions inflicted by the "shock therapy" used in the former Eastern European socialist countries. Housing reform was complicated by its existence in a web of overall urban reforms where different sectors did not proceed at the same pace. Rental increments and housing commodification were closely related to tenants' ability to pay, which was further affected by the wage system reform. Under the existing framework, workers' remuneration was made up of a low cash salary and provision of payment in-kind in the form of heavily subsidized housing, health care, education, and other benefits. Thus, raising housing rents had to be in tandem with wage adjustment by cashing out in-kind housing benefits. Nevertheless, the slow pace of wage reform constrained the momentum of housing rental increases. The procedure of raising housing rentals was consequently designed to increase rents to cover maintenance cost as a first step and then eventually to raise rents to cover the full economic cost of housing development as a commercial undertaking.

Low rents not only undermine good maintenance of housing stock but also are a main culprit causing inflation, which became phenomenal in the 1980s, given the fact that urban households spent only about 1 percent of their cash income on housing and thus had a relatively high purchasing power for durable commodities. Low expenditure for housing also led to unreasonably high demand for housing and thus to difficulties in fair housing distribution. The voucher model was first implemented in Yantai, Shandong. The vouchers, used only for paying for housing rents or purchases, were deemed cashing out of in-kind benefits incorporated into the total compensation. The use of vouchers was to control the money supply so as not to fuel inflation, which was menacing enough at the time to cause social unrest. The issuing of housing vouchers was connected with gradual rental increases. The fashion of gradualism determined that the raised rentals were still far from the market rate. However, inequity in public housing distribution was redressed by the introduction of rental surcharges on households holding "excessive" housing space.

Simultaneously, a drive for privatization was initiated to sell housing to those who could afford it. The so-called commodity housing was to be delivered by the property developers rather than by the government or *danwei*. It was based on the premise that housing rentals would be increased gradually, eventually to the point that buying housing units became a more sensible decision than renting. Because many urban tenants were still not required to pay rentals at a market rate, renting public housing was substantially more economical than buying private housing. Constrained by a weak demand because of low wages and purchased only by those who could afford it and were in a long queue in the process of applying for public housing, commodity housing amounted to only 1.7 percent of total housing provision in Shanghai in the period 1981–1985. It then rose to 11.7 percent in 1986–1990, when the wages of workers were raised considerably due to the progress in economic performance (SSTJ, 1997). Private housing was still not the norm in urban China. However, the significance of housing privatization is that private finance is mobilized, and housing development is partially commercialized. The old Chinese public housing system neither sustains maintenance of existing stock nor encourages production of new supply. The old housing delivery system impeded the free flow of urban laborers as they were bound by housing units which were largely assigned through *danwei* where they were employed. Delinking housing supply from *danwei* enables reforms in the labor market by enhancing labor mobility, a very important aspect of the urban reforms.

Decentralization of housing financing stimulated housing investment by the common interests between enterprise managers and employees. The participation of *danwei* in housing production has considerably alleviated housing shortages and improved the livelihood of urban residents. Nevertheless, the housing allocation, maintained as a part of compensation to workers, is *danwei*-linked. Inequality in housing benefits between employees who have been given them and those who have not remains as it was before. Inequality in housing benefits among interenterprise employees arises as state-owned enterprises do not fare equally in the market competition. An unconstrained demand because of pecuniary affordability pushes for more supply of housing from well-performing enterprises, while workers in loss-making enterprises are not able to have the benefits to which other fellow citizens are entitled. Social welfare administered by the state is redistributed by enterprises, resulting in unequal redistribution of social welfare among urban citizens.

The scheme of rental increases with housing vouchers was still confined to the experimental cities, partly due to resistance from the social groups with vested interests that were most likely in the powerful position to influence policy making and partly because of the abrupt interruption of the Tiananmen political upheaval in 1989. The extent and the scale of rental increases in other cities were not up to the level that could make maintenance of housing stock commercially viable and purchasing of housing units economically sensible. As for housing commodification, housing freely available at market prices in the newly founded, though fledgling, market remained a privilege for a small minority who became richer during the economic reforms. In Beijing, for instance, only 3.7 percent of commodity apartments were bought by private individuals in 1988 (X. Wang, 1995). Lack of housing finances was a major issue constraining demand; also continuous provision of welfare housing by *danwei* dampened the private demand for commercial housing. In order to meet housing needs of their employees, some *danwei* even bought units from the commodity housing market and then sold them to applicants at a large discount. The proportion of commodity housing purchased by *danwei* was 47.5 percent during 1979–1987 and went up to 79.8 percent in the period 1988–1991 in Shanghai (SSTJ, 1997). Housing applicants had no incentives to purchase housing from the market directly. The formation of a housing market was sabotaged by an ever-growing social group, because of the success of *danwei* in the investment in housing, that had vested interests in maintaining the status quo in order to keep their already materialized gains. The housing provision by *danwei* did not weaken, but enhanced, housing welfarism and did not encourage private investment in housing.

Although the state-owned enterprise reforms were intended to change *danwei* into real enterprises and to delink social responsibilities from enterprise operations, the gradualist reforms required *danwei* to be partially responsible for housing supply. Partial commodity housing, because of embedded subsidies by the state and/or *danwei*, created ambiguity in property rights. Nominal owners had only use rights, a component of property rights, as they paid just partial prices for the housing. Having seen the long-term nature of the urban enterprise reforms, the central government issued the third State Council guideline for housing reform in 1994 to confirm "a system of reasonable cost-sharing among the state, *danwei* and individuals." Full privatization of urban housing will hinge on the wage reform to exclude enterprises from housing provision and on the financial reform to create a financial market where potential buyers can procure mortgages to finance housing purchases.

Thereafter, the second-round housing reform plan since 1991 has aimed at mobilizing sufficient funds to finance housing development and investment and raising the share contributed by residents from their living expenses in owning or renting a flat. As a test, Shanghai implemented a provident fund scheme, contributed to by both employers and employees each at 5 percent of wages initially, to appropriate and designate finances only for housing investment. Low-yield housing bonds became a mandatory investment for residents assigned welfare housing, and the fund was designated for housing development. Together with the cashing out of housing benefits, housing rental increased by 3.7 times during 1991–1997, and it is expected to rise to the level of 15–20 percent of household income eventually. Since 1994, Shanghai has had a scheme of sales of public housing to sitting tenants. Flats are sold at a discount that takes into consideration factors such as tenants' number of years serving in *danwei* and entitlement to benefits based on seniority, deemed as cashing out of housing benefits that the tenants deserve over the years of low-waged employment. Up to the end of 1996, 51 percent of salable public housing was sold to 659,000 households, representing 20 percent of total urban households (Zhang, 1998).

Progress in housing privatization and commercialization would not be achieved if there were no economic advancement. Economic growth has raised people's income substantially and greatly improved the quality of life and living standard of Chinese urban residents. Average income for an employed adult in Shanghai increased by 2.3 times over the five years from 1990 to 1995. Housing costs as part of household expenses increased from 4.6 percent (1990) to 6.2 percent (1995) (SSTJ, 1996). The percentage of commodity housing sold to private individuals was 20.2 percent for 1988–1991 and then rose to 35.6 percent for 1992–1996. Provision of commodity housing in the total housing supply rose from 11.3 percent (1986–1990) to 41.4 percent (1991–1996). Per capita housing space rosed from 4.5 square meters in 1978 to 8.7 square meters in 1996 (SSTJ, 1997).

Urban housing reforms are a multipronged scheme. Together with changes in housing finance, housing delivery, and housing market, housing as a social security is equally emphasized to integrate with the new housing system. The new concept of "basic housing project" (*anjiu gongcheng*) is introduced to cater to low-income urban families experiencing housing hardship, with selling prices covering just basic construction cost. Three urban housing forms—commodity, partial-welfare (sustained by *danwei*), and social security housing—coexist to constitute a transitional housing system for Chinese urban residents. Housing commodification has also stimulated market orientation in housing design and neighborhood planning. "Comfortable housing project" (*xiaokang zhuzhai gongcheng*) is advocated by the government in anticipation of the future forms of housing estates (Wang & Cheng, 1995). It sets out guidelines for the standards of housing designs, housing facilities, and neighborhood layout. Niches are left to the private sector, which is encouraged to use new building materials and stress local characteristics in design and planning.

Due to the complexity of the urban reforms and gradualism in the social transition, it remains a long journey for China to develop a housing in-

Table 2.12
Increase of Urban Population (1978–1996)

Year	1978	1983	1988	1993	1996
Non-Agricultural Population as % of Total Population	12.9	17.9	20.7	23.5	24.6

Source: ZSKRY, 1997: 204.

dustry and housing stock operating in the property market that is supported by property financial institutions, real estate consultant services, and property management firms. Many challenging issues unique to the country need constant examination and evaluation. The success of the urban housing reforms will depend on the systematic installation of market mechanisms in the economy and coordination with reforms in other sectors. One critical issue remains outstanding: how to phase in market mechanisms and phase out socialist welfarism in a gradualist fashion while efficiency and equity are equally taken into consideration.

Urbanization—Impact of Market Reforms

Under the previous centrally planned economy, urbanization was slow. In 1949, 10.6 percent of the population lived in cities; this figure increased to only 12.9 percent in 1978. With the economic reforms to liberalize the economy, to set people free from rigid economic controls, and to release abundant initiatives from the ideological cage, a variety of economic entities was emerging to break the dominance of the state economy. Rapid urban growth took place. By the end of 1996, urban population reached the level of 24.6 percent of the total national population. Within a span of 18 years (1978–1996), the urban population doubled, while there had been an increment of only 22 percent in the period 1949–1978 (see Table 2.12).

This accelerated development is largely attributed to the participation of new non-state sectors, such as private and collective companies, joint ventures, and foreign investors. The phenomenon is manifested in the rural areas by the flourishing rural townships built up by small private and collectively owned manufacturing and services. On the one hand, the urbanization of the country is, to a large extent, driven by the rural townships as waves of modernization have effectively radiated into the rural hinterland in material provision and technology transfer. In 1982, 31.3 percent of the total urban population lived in small towns. This figure rose to 42.3 percent and 47.7 percent in 1984 and 1986, respectively (Goldstein & Goldstein, 1990). By 1986, rural enterprises absorbed 76 million rural laborers, rising from 33 million at the end of 1984 (Shen, 1990). On the

Table 2.13
Floating Population in Selected Chinese Cities

Year	1984	1985	1986	1987	1988
Guangzhou	0.50	-	0.80	1.15	1.17
Shanghai	1.02	-	1.83	-	2.09
Beijing	0.30	0.60	0.90	1.15	1.31
Taiyuan	-	0.24	-	0.26	0.30
Wuhan	0.35	0.50	0.81	-	0.75*

Note: * = figure of 1990.
Source: Li & Hu, 1991.

other hand, economic prosperity brought about by the economic reforms and opening up of the urban economy due to market orientation was creating jobs in cities. The urban tertiary services permitted free entry of self-employed individuals to provide services as tailors, barbers, peddlers, salesmen, real estate agents, and so on. According to a survey of 74 cities and towns, approximately 28 percent of peasants migrating to cities since 1949 did so in the period 1977–1982 (Taylor, 1988:759). About 16 percent of workers recruited for urban jobs during 1978–1990 were peasant migrants (Chan, 1994:111).

In spite of rural industrialization, which tries to anchor farmers to the land where they have been living for generations, and expansion of the urban economy, which offers non-agricultural jobs, the capacity of absorption is limited, given the fact that rural underemployment has been a perennial problem in China (Buck, 1930; Taylor, 1988). It is exacerbated by the large-scale release of rural labor surplus because of the recent rapid rise in agricultural productivity spurred by the economic reforms. Thus, spontaneous, rural-to-urban migration occurs without official sanction, which was essentially required in the central planning era. It starts with the journey to a city to explore prospects of finding a job. About 60 percent of the so-called floating population (persons traveling to cities for various purposes) are peasants from the nearby countryside (Zhou, 1997b). With increasing exposure to market mechanisms, Chinese cities are witnessing a rapid increase in the number of the "floating population" (see Table 2.13). In 1988, 69 percent of the floating population were temporary migrants, accounting for 9 percent of permanent residents in Beijing. The magnitude of potential emigrants rose with the further opening up of cities. The "floating population" represented 33 percent of the total urban residents in the more market-oriented city of Guangzhou in 1988, rising from 10 percent in 1980. Shanghai accommodated temporary migrants to the degree that they accounted for 11 percent of the urban labor force (1988) (Li & Hu, 1991). In 1993, 1.39 million temporary emigrants (49 percent of the total) stayed more than six months, and 0.81 million (29 percent) stayed more than one year in Shanghai (Zhao & Zhu, 1998).

Table 2.14
Distribution of Number of Cities in Regions (percent)

Region	1949	1965	1976	1988	1994
Eastern	50.0	39.6	35.6	37.3	44.7
Central	40.4	42.6	44.2	41.7	37.1
Western	9.6	17.8	20.2	21.0	18.2

Sources: Xia, 1992; Liu, 1996.

Most of the temporary emigrants were engaged in low-pay, dirty, and dangerous jobs that were not permanent.

Cities have to re-draw the map of social-geographical delineation shaped in the socialist regime with the ostensible concern of equality. "Zhejiang Village" in Beijing has been developing since 1985 with about 1,000 "floating population" coming from Zhejiang Province. The number reached 70,000 in the early 1990s. From a social concentration of temporary migrants of the same origin and with the same dialect, it has developed into a self-regulated community with self-provided social facilities such as schools, clinics, and child care, which are usually provided by the urban government (Wang, 1995).

Cities have been urged to lead national development since 1983, when the new economic strategy was ushered in. It is explicitly stated that the city should lead the countryside and that the city government should coordinate the municipal economy where agriculture is a component. Reorganization of governmental structure is attempted to abolish the dichotomy of rural and urban governance. Urban jurisdiction is extended to encompass suburbs and county towns in order to provide urban governments with opportunities for comprehensive urban development. With an emphasis placed upon the role of cities, many market towns that were previously not deemed as urban places and their residents not as urban population have been upgraded to the status of urban places. There were 3,052 officially designated urban places in 1983. Due to the reclassification, the number of cities and towns jumped to 6,506 in 1984 and further to 11,523 in 1995 (GTJ, 1997). Because of the re-definition of urban population and extension of urban boundaries, the number of the populace who reside within the urban administrative jurisdiction increases significantly, though those people have not changed their residence and occupation. The proportion of urban residents to the total national population was 23.4 percent in 1983, and it rose to 31.6 percent in 1984 and drastically increased to 70.4 percent in 1996 (GTJ, 1997).[2] As for the geographical location of market-oriented urbanization since 1978, it has inclined to the Eastern Region and changed the direction of plan-guided urbanization. The distribution of the number of cities in regions has shifted to favor the regions near the east coast (see Table 2.14).

Table 2.15
Investment in the Built Environment of Shanghai (1981–1995)

Period	% of GDP Contributed by Property Industry	Investment in Fixed Assets as % of GDP	Investment in Housing as % of GDP	Housing Construction (Million sq m)
1981-85	2.9	22.1	2.1	20.25
1986-90	5.3	32.5	3.6	24.48
1991-95	6.4	50.2	10.6	37.80
1979-95	5.4	40.6	7.4	85.88

Source: SSTJ, 1996.

URBAN RESTRUCTURING WITH A LAND MARKET

Under market orientation, urban capital investment has shifted its preference from manufacturing to services. In Shanghai from 1950 to 1985, 67.3 percent of total investment in capital construction was made in the manufacturing sector, while only 30.0 percent was in the service sector. In the period 1991–1995, capital investment in manufacturing declined to 42.2 percent of the total, and in the tertiary industry it jumped to 56.6 percent. City GDP contributed by services increased from 21.6 percent (1953–1980) to 35.8 percent (1981–1996) (SSTJ, 1997). With the nationalization of ownership, urban land became a state asset. It ceased to be a commodity that could be transacted in the market. Since the commencement of the economic reforms, land has been re-considered as a commodity. Although its ownership remains unchanged as a state monopoly, its use rights are detached from ownership. Land use rights can be purchased and held for a period at a premium. Moreover, so-called land use rights can be transferred, assigned, bequeathed, or mortgaged at the lessee's will within the validated term. Since then, the real estate sector has become an important component of the urban economy. Property development as an economic activity contributes substantially to the general national product and employment. In Shenzhen, the value of construction output accounted for 21.2 percent of the city's total product, and the industry employed 22.2 percent of the total workforce in 1989 (SZTJ, 1989). Similarly, land and property built on it regain the characteristics of an economic asset with market values.

Market forces apparently influence the allocation of economic resources to the urban built environment, as central plans are, to a certain extent, replaced by market mechanisms. The emerging market is more responsive than plans in meeting market demand. It constitutes a sharp contrast to urban construction under the previous regime, where investment in the urban built environment was neglected (see Tables 2.8 and 2.15). Properties as economic assets are sold and bought at prices determined in the market. Property prices have been changing and adjusting according to

45

Table 2.16
Property Development in Manufacturing and Service Sectors, Shanghai (millions of square meters)

	Factory	Office	Shop	Hotel
1949	10.30	2.30	3.25	0.23
1980	26.46	3.37	2.43	0.54
Average Yearly Increase Rate, % (1949 - 80)	3.10	1.24	-0.93	2.79
1985	34.85	4.25	2.98	0.73
1996	55.13	11.27	6.56	2.28
Average Yearly Increase Rate, % (1980 - 96)	4.69	7.84	6.40	9.42

Sources: SSTJ, 1986, 1997.

market situations, and price benchmarks were set up and broken by new records until 1994, when property oversupply descended upon some booming Chinese cities for the first time since 1949. Shanghai witnessed an explosive growth in building construction over the last decade, and the quantity of property completed was many times the amount built over the 30 years before 1980 (see Table 2.16). It was reported that "a fifth of the world's cranes straddle 20,000 building sites, making Shanghai the world's biggest construction site," with 5,000 construction firms employing 1.4 million construction workers (*Business Times*, 4 December 1995). More funds have been committed to the urban infrastructure since 1980. Investment in Shanghai infrastructure as a percentage of its GDP was 2.97 percent in 1981–1985 and then rose to 5.67 percent (1986–1990) and 10.38 percent (1991–1995). It increased to 13.10 percent in 1996 (SSTJ, 1997).

The value of location begins to be reflected in the property market. Price signals are sent to property developers about which location is highly valued, and this is where new projects should be built. The land value gradient exhibited by cities under the market system appears in Shenzhen, to which the central place theory seems to apply. The central area of Luohu has the highest degree of accessibility, and thus properties there fetch the highest value. Property values diminish outward from the center because of the reduction in accessibility. The dynamism of locational change is apparently built in the land market, where the land value gradient changes as infrastructure development over time has altered the relative accessibility of locations. Due to the changing value of locations over time, the interrelations of property values between Luohu, Futian, and Nanshan (the three districts in the Shenzhen special economic zone) are changing accordingly. The locational differentiation is also highlighted by property vacancy rates: Nanshan as the poorest location has the highest vacancy rates, whereas Luohu as the best location has the lowest vacancy rates.

In contrast with the past under central planning, when the central busi-

Figure 2.3
Map of Shanghai Central City

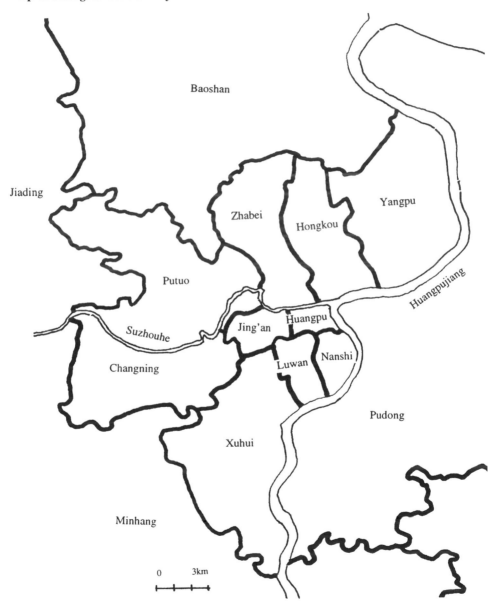

Table 2.17
Investment in the Built Environment by District, Shanghai, 1996

District	Area (sq km)	TIFA (million¥/sq km)	Investment in Commodity Properties (million¥/sq km)
Huangpu	4.54	2638.3	1575.3
Jing'an	7.62	1067.5	702.0
Luwan	8.05	708.7	520.9
Nanshi	7.87	611.3	407.6
Xuhui	54.76	260.5	134.5
Changning	38.30	225.0	132.5
Hongkou	23.48	225.7	118.0
Putuo	54.83	130.1	45.8
Zhabei	28.50	113.1	43.8
Yangpu	52.13	106.3	30.9
Pudong	522.75	71.3	19.3
Baoshan	424.63	49.7	4.0
Minhang	370.75	17.5	3.7
Jiading	458.80	6.9	2.5

Note: TIFA stands for total investment in fixed assets, of which investment in commodity
properties is a component.
Source: SSTJ, 1997.

ness districts were abandoned, and investments were mainly made to the peripheral areas and satellite towns, the central area of Shanghai has received more investments than other districts since 1980. Huangpu, Jing'an, Luwan, Nanshi, and Xuhui are the central urban districts, and their locations have been rediscovered (see Figure 2.3). Investment in the built environment appears to comply with the land rent gradient. Between 1985 and 1991, when the land market was not fully open to market competition, new urban construction mainly took the form of new investment on vacant sites. Nevertheless, good locations were identified by the market forces. Factories and housing were largely built on the outskirts, whereas offices were constructed on vacant land in the intermediate areas between the city center and outskirts, as the central area was fully utilized. Urban redevelopment has, however, taken place due to the participation of the land factor in urban construction since 1991. Demolition occurs in downtown, where the market land value pushes the low-end users out by the high-end users (see Table 2.17). Shanghai is witnessing a market-led urban restructuring. Industrial spaces are moving out of Huangpu, Jing'an, and Putuo districts and transferring to suburban Baoshan and Jiading. To some extent, residential spaces are replaced by offices in Huangpu, Luwan, Jing'an, and Nanshi districts, while new housing estates are built farther away from the city center to cater to the displaced residents.

Economic restructuring toward services is echoed by the development of high-rise buildings demanded by offices and required by inevitable intensifying use of land. Between 1980 and 1995, 1,411 tall buildings were erected in Shanghai, of which the tallest was the 420-meters Jinmao, de-

Table 2.18
Structural Change of Shanghai Land Uses (1952–1994)

Land Use	1952		1989		1994		Average Yearly Increase Rate	
	Area	%	Area	%	Area	%	1959-89	1989-94
Total	4,886	100	16,652	100	22,094	100	3.4	5.8
Manufacturing	1,064	21.8	4,774	28.7	5,573	25.2	4.1	3.1
Housing	2,489	50.9	8,535	51.3	11,907	53.9	3.4	6.9
Services	688	14.1	1,355	8.7	2,098	9.5	1.8	9.1

Source: Hou, 1996.

signed by the architectural firm of Skidmore, Owings and Merrill in 1998, whereas only 82 high-rise buildings were built during 1912–1979 (Xu & Xu, 1997). Urban land use structure has been transformed by market-oriented urban investment (see Table 2.18). Shanghai is convincingly moving from an industrial city toward a service center. During the process, the re-emerging land market has facilitated the formation of a new urban profile of a revived cosmopolitan city.

NOTES

1. *Danwei* refers to a variety of state-owned enterprises and institutions where most urban residents were employed in the Chinese centralized economic system. A *danwei* is a work unit having such attributes as personnel power, communal facilities, independent accounts and budgets, urban or nonagricultural purview, and public sector (Lü & Perry, 1997:5–6).

2. The degree of urbanization, represented by the ratio of the number of urban residents to the total population, was suddenly inflated by many counties being classified as cities. Therefore, the data should be handled with caution, as much of urban population growth between 1983 and 1990 was due to changes in official classification of urban settlements. Many counties are upgraded to the status of cities, while populations within the boundaries are actually still engaged in rural farming.

Chapter 3

An Emerging Property Market
in the Transitional Economy

The economic reforms, initiated for the rural agricultural sector, have marched into the urban domain and brought much change to the urban economy. Because there was a lack of mechanisms to receive feedback from the marketplace in the centrally-controlled system, investment into the urban built environment was inadequate due to its low priority in the government investment agenda. Urban reforms are intended to redress the problem of urban underdevelopment. One of the most significant changes has been that land is no longer a means of production given free to users. Urban land has become a commodity with a price. Consequently, development of buildings has become an entrepreneurial undertaking. The property market, an important component of the market system, arises from the horizon of forerunner cities and shapes itself in the process of urban changes. Many Chinese cities, especially those coastal cities experiencing dynamic economic growth, are undergoing a tremendous transformation in their profiles. However, property market being an imperfect market and compounded by the gradualist economic reforms, a unique property market in Chinese cities has emerged. A challenge facing China's urban governments is to understand property as an economic asset, the characteristics of property development, the nature of property investment, and the meaning of property in a wider context. Government development controls have to learn to blend market forces with extant planning elements.

REAL ESTATE IN A MARKET SYSTEM

The urban built environment under the market system is shaped by numerous individual players and primarily determined by private developers and the state. The government is mainly responsible for the provision of urban infrastructure and public projects such as social housing and civic structures, while the private property development industry decides what buildings should be developed at what locations within a statutory framework. The private real estate industry is "the main progenitor" of changes in urban physical form (Fainstein, 1994; Reckinger et al., 1991). The state comes to intervene in the private interest-dominated property market by taking on roles such as subsidizer or investor only when there are perceived market failures (Healey, 1991; Pagano & Bowman, 1995; Lassar, 1990; Imbroscio, 1997).

Real Estate as Economic Assets

Property and law coexist. Property rights are what the prevailing legal opinions define. They are created by the state and change when the state decides to change them (Bazelon, 1963). Physically, real property is land as well as buildings. In economics, the term "property" is "anything to which value attaches and endures in the time dimension" (Harper, 1974: 17–18) and anything that yields an income to the owner. "Property is an institution" (Denman, 1978: Preface). "Property provides links between an economic system, a legal system, and a political system" (Reeve, 1986: 7). In terms of political economics, conflicting philosophies have created a dichotomy of real property ownership: common ownership and private ownership. It is so vital that "the existence of the institution of property affects our freedom and our well-being" (Denman, 1978:2). Except where otherwise specified, the term *property* in this book means *real property* or *real estate*, as it is commonly used in practice.

Buildings and land as real estate have distinct characteristics from those of other properties. First, real estate, comprising "bricks and mortar," is landed property. It is immovable. Its owners have greater interests in the prosperity of the community where the property is located than they would have if real estate were mobile. Ownership of real estate ties the interests of individual owners to those of a broader community and to the benefits of political stability and economic development. Second, there are no identical plots of land, which attributes definite uniqueness to buildings on land. Third, as real estate is immovable, any neighboring hazards or beneficence would impact on the market value of property, and its maintenance would directly cast positive or negative impact on properties in the neighborhood due to economic externality.

What is a market? One of the definitions is that "it is a group of firms and individuals in touch with each other in order to buy or sell some goods" (Mansfield, 1991:17). A perfect market requires perfect competition, which is defined by four conditions (Mansfield, 1991:220). First, perfect competition demands that the product of any one seller be the same as the product of any other sellers. Second, perfect competition requires each participant in the market, whether buyer or seller, to be so small in relation to the whole market that he or she cannot affect the product's price. Third, perfect competition requires that all resources be completely mobile, that is, each resource must be able to enter or leave the market very readily. Fourth, perfect competition demands that consumers have perfect knowledge of the market situation.

What is a property market? It can be inferred from the preceding definitions as any arrangement by which buyers and sellers deal in rights and interests in land and buildings. Contrasted with the preconditions required by a perfect market, a property market is far from perfect and efficient owing to the nature of real estate. First, properties are heterogeneous. Properties are unique with respect to their structure, age, building material, location, and so on, which contribute to a seller's monopoly position. Second, because of high production cost and high opportunity cost if a property is lying unused, only developers with adequate financial resources can enter into the trade, and only a very small proportion of products of any type will be on the market at any time. It means that transactions are few as compared with the requirements of a perfect market. Third, high transaction cost, incurred either in obtaining knowledge or in legal procedures, is a barrier that deters occupiers moving for the sole purpose of making a gain from price differences. Finally, due to the great heterogeneity and geographically restricted, up-to-date knowledge of a property market, a property trading price may not be an equilibrium price.

Property and the General Economy

The ultimate purpose of a property is to be used by tenants and owners, through whom production and consumption take place. Without proper accommodation, economic and social activities can hardly take place. Nevertheless, having a place does not mean that shelter requirements are completely fulfilled. Inappropriate property can impose adverse effects on the performance and efficiency of occupiers (Fothergill, Mark & Perry, 1987).

Property as a valuable asset can be used as collateral for its owner to raise funds in case of necessity. Property valuation matters, therefore, in the cases of owners intending to make economic investment. If the value of a property falls, its security against fund-raising weakens. An investment scheme consequently may have to be postponed due to limited finances. The same logic applies to a buoyant market where property owners' borrowing positions are strengthened. Therefore, change of property value can accelerate or decelerate, to some extent, the rate of economic growth by its capacity for financial mobilization. In many East and Southeast Asian cities, economic overheating has often been associated with overheated property markets since the 1980s. The burst of property bubbles is often a harbinger of economic recession, when the economic machine grinds to a halt. In Japan, a country with exorbitant cost of land due to a perception of land shortages, high prices of property threatened to halt the economy by raising a barricade against new start-up companies. In spite of that, banks were told not to dump the property on which most of their loans were secured, because banks might have as much as ¥60 trillion of unacknowledged bad loans backed by property (*The Economist*, 13 February 1993). In England, a survey found that 96 property companies borrowed £382 million from the money market in 1971; in 1973, the amount rose to £796 million, leaving a debt to the banks of £2,330 million (Cox, 1984:166). The following property collapse inflicted enormous damage on the general economy through disarrayed financial markets. Too much capital flowing into property investment could ignite and fuel inflation and attract investment into short-term and high-yield property but discourage investment in long-term projects. Rising property value exerts pressure on tenants' overhead, directly affecting the financial balance and performance of the sitting tenants.

Property Investment and Development

Limitation of land supply, durability of buildings, and ability to separate ownership from occupation suggest that property can be an ideal investment medium. Benefits of investment in property take the forms of rental income flows and capital gains when disposed of, if property value appreciates over time. In a property market, investment decisions are made on the assumption that outlay on a property would be rewarded either by obtaining utility derived from exclusive occupation and utilizing it as financial collateral or by receiving continuous rental income through leasing the premise and hopefully by appreciated capital value due to the possibility of market demand surpassing supply in the future.

Political stability is essential to property investment. Long-term property investment requires long-term economic and political stability of the place where the project is located. Not only does political stability provide a basic condition for future income, but it protects the capital value of property from depreciation just because of changing policies. Property is deemed a favorable investment option in a politically stable and economically growing locality. Property investment has a track record of serving as a hedge against inflation. During the 1970s and early 1980s, changes in the value of land and property were positively correlated with the rates of inflation in the United Kingdom (Hollowell, 1982). By contrast, stocks and bond returns appeared negatively correlated with inflation (Radcliffe, 1987). Therefore, properties are particularly attractive in many developed countries as an investment vehicle to financial institutions entrusted with funds, at the same time requiring income flows that are inflation-proof

(MacLeary & Nanthakumaran, 1988). However, property investment is generally not liquid and is characterized by high transaction costs. It requires a considerable outlay of capital relative to the income and savings of most investors. It is risky in terms of market changes in rental value and rental growth, yields on sales, and functional and physical obsolescence.

Because property is a landed premise, it shares the same fate with the local community and relies very much on local prospects. Either as an investment or as an accommodation, property is a product that must be occupied, and then its value is realized. Property supply responds to the final user's demand, which is directly or indirectly related to local economic performance. However, because of a fairly long time gap between conception of a project and its completion, depending on the extent of its complication and building scale, the initial property development decision is based on speculation about future demand. Although property supply is fundamentally stimulated by the final user's demand, property development can be driven in some circumstances by the supply-side, short-term investment motivation. When an abundant amount of funds looks for investment vehicles, property is likely to be chosen among others because of its proven record of inflation-hedging. Relaxing control on monetary supply and private savings for property investment led to a flood of investment in property in the 1970s in Britain (Cox, 1984). This was in anticipation of great profits in the future in the inflationary context. Nevertheless, as this kind of investment may not be completely justified by the user's demand, there is the danger of property value's becoming inflated and then depreciated as a consequence of a "burst of bubbles."

Property development is "an industry that produces buildings for occupation by bringing together various raw materials" (Cadman, 1978:1). These raw materials are land, building materials, finance, labor, public services, and professional expertise. Alternatively, when the outcome is emphasized, property development is defined as "the process by which development agencies, together or on their own, seek to secure their social and economic objectives by the improvement of land and the construction or refurbishment of buildings for occupation by themselves or others" (Byrne & Cadman, 1984:4). Developers are deemed key actors in property development, described as entrepreneurs who provide the organization and capital required to make buildings available in anticipation of requirements of the market in return for profit (Bowley, 1966).

Since it is closely related to the local economy, property development is heavily influenced by cycles in the process of economic growth. Business cycles or business fluctuations, which are identified by the behavior of aggregate economic activity usually measured by changes in the level of real GDP over time, are a remarkable characteristic of the economic development in free market economies (Kydland, 1995; G. Moore, 1983). In many growing economies after World War II and fast growing economies in the East and Southeast Asia in the 1970s and 1980s, business cycles are rather replaced by growth cycles defined in terms of the growth of real GDP relative to a long-term trend of growth (Hall, 1990). Business or growth cycles do not have periodicity, but the same sequence of economic events does repeat over time. Expansions in economic activities characterized by high growth rates are followed by ones with low growth rates.

Cyclical business fluctuations reflecting disequilibrium in the market directly affect supply of, and demand for, property. Although there are various explanations for its wavelike pattern (Klein, 1976; Mitchell, 1941), activities of supply and demand in the property market consequently show a cyclical tendency (Barras, 1979; Ball, 1983). Fluctuations in the property market, affected by the general economy and susceptible to business cycles, are called building cycles. Building cycles do not necessarily synchronize with business cycles. The former lagging behind the latter is more often the case. It is widely believed that the lagging phenomenon is caused by the long process of property development where an upsurge in demand that stimulates property development could have begun to decline following economic downturn when buildings are due to be completed (Barras & Ferguson, 1985; Barras, 1984; Lewis, 1965). The time lag between inception and completion of development projects has strengthened the speculative tendency of property development due to the nature of anticipation in perceiving demand. Therefore, the lag between building cycles and business cycles leads to cycles in property prices that show alternate booms and busts. Building cycles have been studied fairly extensively, and phenomenal property booms and slumps have been covered both sensationally and analytically (Marriott, 1989; Khoury, 1984; Daly, 1982; Sandercock, 1979; Ambrose & Colenutt, 1975). Whitehead (1972) found that the composition of the Glasgow urban land use pattern could be attributed to building cycles. Ball (1996) argued that the rising cost of premises due to property booms facilitated London's suburbanization. Building cycles are also to blame for the role played in restructuring urban form toward an unequal spatial structure. Property slumps precipitate dilapidation of unfavorable urban quarters abandoned by investors, while property booms are often in favor of well-off areas, resulting in social stratification of spatial development. Except for economic cycles that may mislead developers to make wrong predictions of future demand, other uncertainties attached to property development result from change in the political situation, legislation, legal system, and taxation.

Akin to other products, development of property is not purely motivated by the economic rationale and not always driven by cost-benefit calculations. It cannot escape from politics and prevalent social values. Because property development itself can provide temporary construction jobs and stimulate other related sectors, it provides a platform to politicians who try to impress the electorate in a democratic society. Apparent, busy-looking development activities give an image of a booming economy. Therefore, politicians in office may be tempted to mobilize resources within their reach to draw a picture of "cranes in the sky" in order to win popular support. Likewise, not all purchases are economically rational. The populace are living in a society where specific social norms are observed. People in different social groups respect social values that they share. Especially in the class-ridden culture, a higher social class status is often pursued by all means as a main life goal for people in the social mainstream. A fashionable house situated in a prestigious location is a convincing indicator of its tenant's material well-being and thus social position. Therefore, the mentality of "keeping up with the Joneses" underlies the economically irrational bidding.

Property Development within a Macroeconomic Framework

Property development is carried out within a macroeconomic framework and thus is affected by government fiscal and monetary policies. Since public spending, a part of fiscal policy, extracts a sizable amount from the national income, it plays an important role in harnessing the national economy and influencing urban development. An increase of government spending, which seems to have become a trend for many developed countries since World War II (Heald, 1983), is expected to generate multiplier effects to urban construction. Being an effective method of transferring resources from the private sector to the public sector, taxation is an effective political device for redistributing income among social groups in a nation. It is so politically contested that it is blamed as one of the causes of the French and American Revolutions (James & Nobes, 1978). There is a trend in the Western developed countries that taxation as a main revenue resource for government is increasing as a proportion of total national product. Taxes, including social security contributions, represented 50.3 percent of gross national product (GNP) in Sweden, 31.3 percent in the United States, 34.0 percent in the U.K., and 24.8 percent in Japan in 1979 (OECD, 1981). Taxes are collected not only to cover government's expenditure but as a stabilizer to increase or decrease aggregate demand in order to regulate the otherwise free market. Fiscal measures are often employed as a government policy tool to encourage or discourage growth of certain industries by levying more or less taxes, or to the extent of offering subsidies. As far as the impact of fiscal policy on property development is concerned, government spending can be used to build physical as well as social infrastructure to influence and even to reshape the property market. More property development activities would be generated due to the commercial viability of prospective property schemes improved by changing locational parameters. Alteration of the tax regime will affect profitability of property development, where projects with marginal profits would be much more vulnerable to such policy changes.

Monetary policy, as a control of a nation's money supply directly by manipulating its provision or indirectly by measures affecting cost and availability of credit, will raise the level of aggregate demand through increasing money supply and lowering interest rates, thus inducing investment and spending (Hawthorne, 1981). Nevertheless, lax credit control is prone to cause inflation. The easy availability of credit was pinpointed as a main factor contributing to the inflation and then the collapse of the property market of London in the 1970s (Cox, 1984). Since finance plays an essential role in property investment and development, the availability of credit and costs of loan holding will directly affect the decision making of property investors and developers.

PROPERTY ANALYSIS IN A WIDER CONTEXT

Property is for accommodation and investment. Property is an essential component of the urban built environment. The urban built environment is shaped following explicit as well as implicit economic rational, cultural values and political rules as a result of social interactions and mediation. Within the capitalist market system, the property sector is the nexus of social relations, as wealth is stored in real estate. How and why investment is made in property and how buildings are developed under what circumstances are questions intriguing to urban researchers. In order to understand the patterns of urban physical growth and interrelations between urban planning and development, property and its investment and development should be analyzed in a wider context.

There have been numerous investigations into the mechanisms of property market operation. Light has been shed on the property development process by an objective descriptive approach to identify how many functional events occur and how many actors are involved and to disclose how they are connected (Radcliffe, 1978; Barrett, Stewart, & Underwood, 1978; Gore & Nicholson, 1985). Neo-classical economics views the market as a collection of individuals who pursue their goals with preferences. In the process, demand and supply reach a dynamic equilibrium. The neo-classical school focuses on the relationship between market demand and supply and treats it as a key to decode the property market (Balchin & Kieve, 1985; Hallett, 1979; Harvey, 1981). It is assumed that rational behavior of property investors is to seek maximum return in profit from transactions or in utility from owner occupation. Decisions by users to rent or to purchase depend on the current level of rents and prices, personal financial situations, and borrowing conditions of credit. Market prices of property are derived from assessment by potential buyers and sellers. Theoretically, at any moment, there are a maximum price for any property that buyers are prepared to pay and, similarly, a minimum price at which sellers are willing to sell. As long as a buyer's maximum price is above a seller's minimum price, a transaction would occur. The two prices determine a range of price movements. As such, equilibrium in demand and supply is the basic driving force behind price movements in the property market and thus activities of property development. Furthermore, Harvey (1981) stresses that the significance of new supply to the stock is diminished by its relatively small quantity, because of the long time span of buildings.

Neo-classical models rightly emphasize the most important dimension of property: it is an asset, and thus property development is primarily an economic activity. Economic rationality thus explains property investment and development. However, the demand-supply approach wrongly ignores the characteristics of individual actors involved and the significance of their social relationship. It is assumed that participating actors are homogeneous in character and that their interactions are subject to economic rationality. In the real world, not all decisions are economically rational, and social relations among actors may play important roles in their making decisions to develop and invest in property.

Institutional analysis provides a new approach to the interpretation of property in the urban economy. It is found in the belief that economic laws should not be "timeless and placeless" (Witte, 1954:134). A market could be led by mass actions instead of by individual decisions, controlled by management instead of by laissez-faire equilibrium (Commons, 1931). It identifies interactions among actors as a key factor mediating between demand and supply, given the fact that actors have their priorities and constraints (Ambrose, 1986; Adams, 1990; Dunleavy, 1981; Healey, 1992; Krabben & Lambooy, 1993). It emphasizes the role of actors participating in the property market, their behavior, and the framework within which they interact, on the basis that the property market cannot function unless agreements are reached among a variety of actors. A successful project needs, first of all, a developer's willingness to initiate. Then, a landowner agrees to sell land, planners agree to grant permission for development, and a financier is willing to lend. Lack of any one of them will effectively interrupt the development.

According to Goodchild and Munton (1985), landowners and land-ownership patterns have a considerable influence on the spatial layout of development in the United Kingdom. Many landowners are actively involved in the property development process by seeking planning permission themselves and are prepared to market their land plots in order to achieve the best return from land disposal. As such, they often impose their wishes on the type of development to be constructed. The nature of property ownership and character of landholders have cast a strong impact on the profile of London (Jenkins, 1975). Dunleavy (1981) documents that architects and the construction industry exerted considerable pressure on the British central government in shaping the policy for public housing in the 1960s. The imposition of high-rise housing on British cities where terrace housing and tenement apartments are the norm is driven by the two actors in the property development process. The architectural design professionals desired to see social reforms by shaping a new physical environment, stemming from the ideology of the modern architectural movement. The building industry regarded it as a good opportunity to bring boom to their business, whereas the public housing tenants had little influence in the decisions concerning their rehousing.

Neo-Marxist political economics believes that the urban built environment should be a battlefield for value distribution (Harvey, 1985a, 1985b). The total value produced in a capitalist society is distributed in the form of wages, rents, interests, profits, and taxes. For the domain of property, there are tensions between landowners, builders, financiers, and users.

Landowners receive rent, developers receive increments in rent on the basis of improvement, builders earn profit of enterprise, financiers provide money capital in return for interest at the same time as they can capitalize any form of revenue accruing from use of the built environment into a fictitious capital (property price), and the state can use taxes (present or anticipated) as backing for investment which capital cannot or will not undertake but which nevertheless expands the basis for local circulation of capital. (Harvey, 1982:395)

In the struggle for capturing value in land and property development, finance capital uses the built environment as a store of value. One of the factors contributing to rapid urban growth in Venezuela in the 1960s and 1970s was "the relative attraction of property as an investment and store of capital" (Gilbert & Healey, 1985:48). Capital flight and deliberate abandonment of property in areas in urban plight do occur in order to preserve capital value of buildings elsewhere.

The political economics approach widens the understanding of property and the urban built environment by setting property in an overall context of capital flow. Nevertheless, profit and utility are still the basic factors linking demand and supply in the property market, though property transactions are made in an environment shaped by interactions between actors. With a supply-side orientation, the institutional approach highlights two markets in real estate, namely, the investment market and the use market, or two demands, the investors' demand and the final users' demand. Two markets or two demands do not necessarily converge, and then conflicts arise between them. Property supply can be driven by investors' demand, which is more often the case in the short term and in the backdrop of rapid economic growth. When an abundant supply of funds looks for investment mediums, property can be a good option among others because of its proven record of inflation-hedging. Relaxed monetary supply and private savings accessible to the property market would stimulate property buying. Healey (1994) claims there is a tension between a financial orientation and a production orientation toward property development in the British urban renewal process. Financial criteria (i.e., investors' demand) overrun production requirements (i.e., final users' demand). However, this finance-driven investment may not be completely justified by the final users' demand. It is done in anticipation of inflation and future demands in view of expected economic growth. A rational decision to develop or to buy property should consider rental income in the short term and capital appreciation in the long term. Both rental income and capital appreciation would not materialize if eventually there are no final users to take up space.

EMERGENCE OF A PROPERTY MARKET

Real Estate Commodification and Marketization

Under the socialist, centrally controlled economy with predominant state ownership of production means, there were no explicit property markets in the cities of mainland China. The government as the trustee of public assets acted as an omnipotent financier, landowner, developer, and investor for the construction of the urban built environment. No premises were built based on commercial principles. Instead, they were constructed according to plans and subsequently allocated to users of the public sector without financial transactions. Not regarded as economic assets, buildings were considered only as shelters for production and consumption. Apart from planning controls, the government was in full charge of urban construction. Premises were assigned free of charge to urban enterprises, which were mostly state-owned. Governments and their subsidiary enterprises also had a responsibility to supply urban residents and employees with public housing as socialist welfare. The use and allocation of resources were determined by the top down commands from hierarchically structured administrative bureaucracy. Prices, one of the most important signals that the self-regulating market system generates, were set by the central bureaus and bore little relation to demand and supply. This system was flawed in that it did not have inherent mechanisms to encourage efficient production and to manage reasonable consumption. As a result, the country suffered from an inefficient and stifled urban economy.

Free use of production means breeds ills of resource misuse and misallocation. Without price signals indicating the equilibrium of demand and supply, resources are not necessarily allocated to where they are used most efficiently and to where the highest prices are paid. Without the discipline of financial affordability, users are irresponsible with a tendency to procure more than actually needed. Without prices and costs for resource utilization, planned allocation is often abused and causes waste to a great extent, which explains the poor performance of the Chinese planned economy. Planned resource deployment without cost controls does not lead to efficient use of assets.

Along with the progressive reforms towards marketization, it is recognized that land and properties are economic assets rather than just shelters for production and consumption. Commercialization of land and buildings is advocated as a point of departure from the central planning system. Market forces are suggested to play a role in directing resources into the urban built environment in the process of commodification and marketization of buildings. The private sector, eliminated in the 1950s, and other non-state sectors have returned to blend in with the otherwise prevalent public economy because of the economic liberalization. The ensuing state-owned enterprise reforms aim at transforming enterprises from passive production units to businesses responsible for production costs, losses, and profits, in the backdrop of the decentralization that grants enterprises managerial autonomy. If the previous policy of free use of state assets could be justified because both users and owners were parts of the state, which bore losses and collected profits from enterprises, it is no longer apt, as users, whether they are state-owned or non-state-owned, should not be entitled to the mobilization of state assets without financial accounting. With proposed market competition, the practice of free use of land and buildings would give rise to inequality among users. State-users from the public sector might enjoy the benefit of free land and premises, whereas users of the private sector might not. Some users might take more land; some less. The total production cost and thus enterprise performance would be distorted if land cost is excluded. As such, real estate commodification and marketization serve as an essential component of the economic reforms to provide a level field for enterprises to compete. Elimination of land cost from business outlays or overheads distorts efficiency and competitiveness of production, especially for location-sensitive businesses such as shops and hotels whose profitability largely depends on their location.

A Functioning Property Market

Driven by the urban reforms, real estate commodification and marketization gradually come into place, and property development as a new industry in China comes into being. Property development as an economic activity usually contributes substantially to the general national product and employment in countries experiencing rapid urbanization. After many years under the doctrines of Marxism-Leninism, which emphasize narrow-

Table 3.1
Shenzhen Socioeconomic Indicators (1985–1995)

Year	GDP (¥ billion)	Index	Population (million)	Index	Employment (million)	Index
1985	3.9	100	0.88	100	0.33	100
1986	4.2	108	0.94	107	0.36	109
1987	5.6	144	1.15	131	0.44	133
1988	8.7	223	1.53	174	0.55	167
1989	11.6	297	1.92	218	0.94	285
1990	17.2	441	2.02	230	1.09	330
1991	23.7	608	2.39	272	1.27	385
1992	31.7	813	2.61	297	1.49	452
1993	44.9	1151	2.95	335	2.10	636
1994	61.5	1577	3.36	382	2.23	676
1995	79.6	2041	3.45	392	2.45	742

Source: SFNB, 1996.

ing down the gaps between the countryside and cities, China, a late developer, has been developing rapidly its urban settlements since 1980, assisted by a booming economy. The user demand for buildings, thanks to inward foreign capital seeking investment opportunities and gradually liberalized state urban enterprises making business diversification into the tertiary sector, provided a strong stimulus to the newly founded property industry. The released pent-up demand for premises, suppressed by the former planning regime, was also added to the pressure on the market.

Property developers, a new profession since 1949, begin to play a leading role in the construction of the urban built environment. The process of property development, from initiation to transaction, has to follow commercial principles. To forecast market demand and identify buyers and tenants become a part of essential feasibility study for property development, in contrast with the previous practice, where construction was commissioned by government and built for known users. As a forerunner in the national urban reforms, Shenzhen experimented to install market mechanisms in its urban construction in the very beginning of its new town development. It demonstrated that market forces were seemingly working. Its property supply was responsive to market demand, and property development was presumably directed by property prices, which suggested the equilibrium between demand and supply. Shenzhen property stocks multiplied during the period 1985–1995, along with vibrant economic growth (see Tables 3.1 and 3.2). It has been the first time since China adopted socialism in 1949 that property market mechanisms partially replace central plans in guiding the production of the urban built environment. Market forces appear more effective than plans in allocating resources to urban construction. It constitutes a sharp contrast to urban development under the previous planning system, where investment in the urban built environment seemed neglected.

Table 3.2
Shenzhen Property Stocks (thousands of square meters, 1985–1994)

Year	Housing	Index	Offices	Index	Factories	Index	Shops	Index
1985	2387.2	100	343.8	100	556.2	100	548.2	100
1986	3360.9	141	785.7	229	737.2	133	673.9	123
1987	4208.9	176	887.6	258	977.5	176	716.7	131
1988	5496.9	230	1109.2	323	1353.7	243	811.9	148
1989	6710.9	281	1264.2	368	1906.3	343	943.3	172
1990	7509.8	315	1307.8	380	2186.6	393	965.2	176
1991	8422.0	353	1323.3	385	2473.4	445	1077.3	197
1992	9782.0	410	1431.0	416	2783.4	500	1187.3	217
1993	11749.5	492	1489.2	433	3195.8	575	1400.5	255
1994	13814.5	579	1589.3	462	3437.0	618	1799.5	328

Source: SFNB, 1995.

Real estate as assets with investment value appears under the reins of market forces, which seemingly regulate property prices along with changing market situations. Property prices and price changes begin to serve as a barometer to decode interactions between demand and supply. It is remarkable for a country where market prices were absent for 30 years to see economic democracy making inroads into a totalitarian entity. Strong economic growth pushes up property prices, reflecting relative scarcity at a time when supply lags behind demand. Property oversupply drives down real estate prices, which subsequently discourage launches of new projects. In a period of 10 years, Shenzhen properties experienced a substantial appreciation in value and prices ranging from 4 to 18 times for different property sectors (see Table 3.3). The considerable growth in property value and sufficient supply of premises are not a result of planning manipulations but of market orientations, which may be unique to Shenzhen as well as to China in the particular context. The unique situations are characterized by robust economic growth, high inflation, and speculative market behavior.

First, strong demand for property derived from a continuous growth of the economy. Shenzhen's economy had an extraordinary annual growth rate of 43.9 percent on average for the period 1979–1996 (at current prices) (SZTJ, 1997). The figure seems incredible; it is largely due to the fact that the city is a new town development starting from a very small and humble base, with GDP only ¥196 million in 1979, and the rapid economic growth was also amplified by high inflation in the 1980s. Destabilizing inflation reached a two-digit level at 14.4, 28.1, and 25.4 percent for the consecutive years from 1987 to 1989. In spite of these, an economic system liberalized by the reforms should be an indisputable factor attributing to this spectacular performance. High rates of growth have been a remarkable characteristic for the Chinese economy since 1979. An average annual growth rate of national GDP attained 17.6 percent in the period 1978–1996 (at

Table 3.3
Changes in Property Prices (1984–1994)

Year	Housing (multi-story)	Annual Change Rate (%)	Offices	Annual Change Rate (%)	Shops (at Luohu)	Annual Change Rate (%)	Factories (at Futian)	Annual Change Rate (%)
1984	100		100		100		100	
1985	118	18.0	113	13.0	106	6.0	108	8.0
1986	121	2.5	128	13.3	138	30.2	105	-2.8
1987	147	21.5	143	11.7	210	52.2	117	11.4
1988	179	21.8	183	28.0	306	45.7	143	22.2
1989	349	95.0	241	31.7	454	48.4	256	79.0
1990	489	40.1	331	37.3	537	18.3	282	10.2
1991	705	44.2	366	10.6	926	72.4	292	3.5
1992	1061	50.5	603	64.8	1323	42.9	405	38.7
1993	1292	21.8	733	21.6	2130	61.0	497	22.7
1994	1012	-21.7	753	2.7	1996	-6.3	484	-2.6

Source: SFNB, 1995.

current prices) (GTJ, 1997). While Shenzhen is a new town, and its achievement is exceptional, Shanghai, as an old industrial city, by attaining an annual growth rate of 16.0 percent on average in its GDP during 1980–1995 is indicative of the successful market orientation (SSTJ, 1997).

Second, high inflation in the 1980s and early 1990s, when its annual rate on average reached 9.8 percent nationwide (1978–1996), 10.3 percent in Shanghai (1980–1995), and 10.8 percent in Shenzhen (1979–1996), which partly explained the inflated, extraordinarily high nominal growth rates, played a decisive role in boosting real estate value (GTJ, 1997; SSTJ, 1996; SZTJ, 1997). The premise that investment in property serves as a hedge against inflation has been empirically proved by the Shenzhen market. After adjusted by the inflation rates over the period 1984–1994, the real capital gain of Shenzhen properties reached 27 percent for factories, 98 percent for offices, 166 percent for housing, and 424 percent for shops (SFNB, 1995; SZTJ, 1995).

Third, for the existing old cities, a pent-up demand, due to inadequate investment in the past, was a main driving force behind robust growth in property prices. Shanghai witnessed its office rentals increase four times over 10 years from 1985 to 1995, reflecting a trend that the city was resuming its status of an international city in East Asia (SSTJ, 1996). The openness of the Shanghai economy has attracted a great amount of investment from overseas and helped the city regain its previous cosmopolitan atmosphere by an influx of business expatriates. The impact was felt directly by the high-quality housing, which had a value appreciation of 900 percent over 10 years (SSTJ, 1996). The housing market for locals did not have capital gains as high as foreigners' housing, suggesting differences in the purchasing power between two groups. Beijing as a political capital and Guangzhou as a main commercial center in southern China felt the same pressure on the market for offices, whose prices increased 160 and 74 percent during 1991–1995, respectively (C. Y. Leung & Company, 1997). Finally, speculation in property investment, a phenomenon considered related only to the capitalist free market, re-appears in the Chinese property market. It is induced by rapid appreciation of property value occurring since the initiation of property marketization. Short-term speculation plays a positive role by mobilizing finance into the property market, which was in short supply.

Shenzhen's retailing property saw its value appreciate 20 times from 1984 to 1993 before dropping in 1994 (see Table 3.3). This exceptional market phenomenon is attributed to Shenzhen's unique position as an interface between sluggish, inward-looking inland cities and dynamic, outward-looking Hong Kong. It has become a tourist attraction for both inland Chinese and people overseas. Visitors from other Chinese cities came to Shenzhen to taste the dynamism of a market economy, and foreign tourists chose Shenzhen as a convenient side trip in their travel to Hong Kong to peep into a socialist country. Apart from that, Hong Kong residents found Shenzhen an inexpensive place to do shopping because of huge disparities in the purchasing power between two cities. The site value of shop premises rose to capture a share of profits made from the booming retail business due to the burgeoning number of customers.

Housing and office markets experienced a similar buoyant appreciation in value. Against a general backdrop of nationwide housing reforms to phase out free welfare housing, Shenzhen came earlier than other cities to accept the notion of commodity housing. Demand for commodity housing became sustainable over time when city residents were buttressed by enhanced purchasing power because of dynamic and continuous urban economic growth. As for offices, they were taken up by local as well as inward enterprises. Many domestic enterprises flocked to this small new town to explore the opportunities a free market could offer. Inland local governments, because their cities had not yet been open to foreign investment due to either unfavorable geographical locations or an absence of the central government's blessing, set up offices in Shenzhen to expose their localities to the world through the gateway of Hong Kong. As a result, strong demand drove up office prices and rentals.

A Property Market in a Macrosocioeconomic Framework

Fluctuations in the movements of property prices and rentals suggest that market forces are at work according to interactions between demand and supply. Further investigation shows that the property market has also been operating within a broad social and political context. Although Shenzhen, as one of the four special economic zones, is special in its route to modernity because of the exclusive special policies it is entitled to, it still exists and functions within the national socioeconomic framework. Albeit Shenzhen's spectacular growth cannot be disassociated from its geographic and social proximity to Hong Kong, from which much of overseas investment has come, Shenzhen's economy has not been affected much by Hong Kong's changing economic climate because of its economic restructuring.

Although the national economy was not fully market-driven under the cautious gradualist reforms, China's economic performance underwent turbulent fluctuations in the 1980s. There were two brief economic setbacks in the 1980s. The first occurred in 1985/1986, when a central policy of financial austerity had to be implemented to dampen the overheated economy. Inflation has long been considered related to the capitalist market economies and therefore has been perceived as alien to Chinese society since 1949. From 1952 to 1980 an average yearly inflation rate was 1.0 percent (GTJ, 1981). However, inflation, which was not recognized as an inevitable phenomenon associated with fast growing market economies either by the government or by ordinary folks, has been phenomenal since 1978, when integration of the domestic economy with the world market was first attempted. Urban residents saw inflation rates between 1.7 and 2.8 percent from 1981 to 1984 in goods' prices that were controlled by the government. The real inflation in prices was certainly much higher than the official figures (Singh, 1992). Ballooning retail prices in 1985 were a real shock to the whole country. Average urban folks rushed to withdraw cash from their bank accounts in order to change it to goods, whether needed or not. Although the average real income had risen significantly, the fear that high inflation would erode savings was enormous. Furthermore, ever-menacing inflation added another dimension of social resentment to the ordinary Chinese by its effect on wealth re-distribution. Worse was that economic upheavals were complicated by widespread corruption among government officials. All these unprecedented incidences were threatening social stability. In fear of imminent social unrest, the central government took swift action to battle inflation. Public capital investment and money supply were immediately cut to a minimum, and many ongoing construction projects were suspended. The financial austerity brought the property industry to a halt; 804 construction projects were withdrawn, and 130,000 construction workers were made redundant in Shenzhen (Wang, 1991). However, the determination to implement austerity was compromised by a heated debate on whether to adopt a gradual or radical strategy for the economic reforms. Ineffective implementation soon resulted in a re-appearance of money supply relaxation. High growth was again accompanied by high inflation, and again, high inflation intensified the debate on the measures to manage the economy. Unfortunately, the debate on the economic policy finally brought about political confrontation between the two camps, which ended with the 1989 Beijing Tiananmen tragedy. Political turmoil then accounted for the second economic trough of the

1980s. Paradoxically, the political turmoil did not drag the economy into recession. Instead, political reforms to deepen the economic reforms were smothered, and the resultant political confrontation was replaced with a stronger, pragmatic, pro-development stance. Deng Xiaoping's tour to southern China in 1992 sent a clear message to the market that the central government was firmly committed to economic development. A new wave of investment in manufacturing and services, particularly in urban real estate, swept coastal cities. The second property boom soon took place. Apparently, macrosocioeconomic changes affected the property market, and consequently, the property market showed cyclical effects (see Figures 3.1–3.4).

Building cycles due to economic cycles impinged upon the local economy, in view of the close relationship between them and non-synchronization of two cycles (Zhu, 1998). The direct impact of fluctuations in property supply on the economy probably lies, on the one hand, on the notion that shortages of property supply suffocate production schemes or bring higher costs to the use of premises. It is particularly pertinent to fast developing countries, where demand for premises is enormous. Rapid industrialization and urbanization require adequate investment in urban physical structures. On the other hand, excessive capital invested in buildings, which causes oversupply, can be otherwise invested in other sectors productively and thus contribute to the total national output. Either as an investment or as an accommodation, property is a product that must be occupied for its value to be materialized. It is understood that provision of premises cannot be the most critical factor facilitating local economic growth, though a strategy of state-sponsored physical development is often employed to catalyze an economy out of a standstill. However, unavailability of premises and high costs for space occupation must logically impose barriers to incoming users and inhibit growth that could be otherwise realized.

Advent of a Property Investment Market

In the early 1980s, when the economic climate was unfavorable, and private property rights were ill defined, developers could hardly sell their products after completion of development. Buildings had to be held and leased to users. Development capital was thus taken as a hostage, and further development was impeded. High rentals because of the consequent relative undersupply induced users into owner occupation and investors into property investment. High risks resulting from unclear property rights were compensated by high yields from investment. Thereafter, more development activities were carried out with capital released from sales. Examination of the primary market of properties in Nanshan district, one of the three districts of the Shenzhen special economic zone, reveals that

Figure 3.1
Annual New Supply and Take-up in the Housing Market

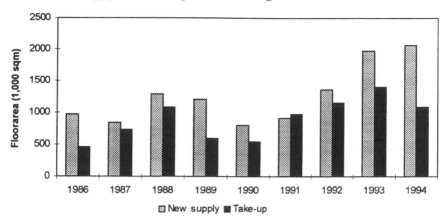

Source: SFNB, 1991–1995.

Figure 3.2
Annual New Supply and Take-up in the Office Market

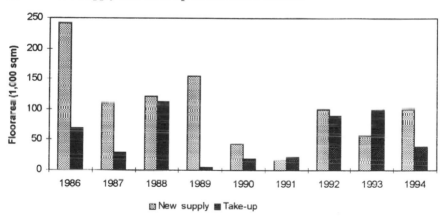

Source: SFNB, 1991–1995.

holding of properties by developers became less over the period 1987–
1996. The share of property sold directly to users as well as to investors
as a percentage of total development rose significantly for offices and factories (see Table 3.4).

The emergence of a leasehold property market has differentiated the
new property market into two submarkets for use and investment and
attracted investors who consider property a worthwhile investment option.

Figure 3.3
Annual New Supply and Take-up in the Industrial Property Market

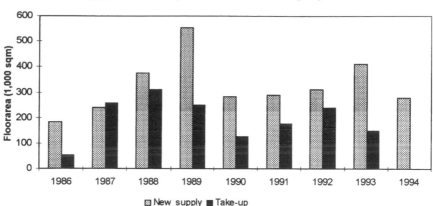

Source: SFNB, 1991–1995.

Figure 3.4
Annual New Supply and Take-up in the Retail Property Market

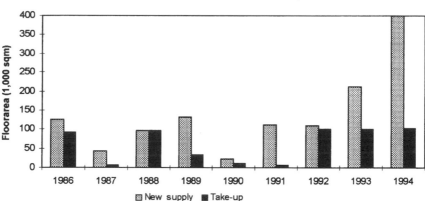

Source: SFNB, 1991–1995.

It facilitates the economy by providing property occupiers with options of freehold and leasehold. The leasehold property market has been active and dynamic since 1993, when the total leased floor areas were 5.18 million square meters; 7.26 million square meters of floor areas were let out in 1994, an increase of 40 percent over the previous year. About 60 percent of commodity factories and offices and a quarter of commodity housing were leasehold (see Table 3.5). Accordingly, the secondary property markets have been active as well (see Table 3.6). The number of transactions

Table 3.4
Property Transactions in the Primary Market, Nanshan District, Shenzhen

Year	Sold (%)	Rented (%)	Vacant (%)
Housing			
1987	77.3	17.6	5.1
1996	80.3	6.7	13.0
Office			
1987	13.4	86.6	0.0
1996	40.7	49.1	10.2
Factory			
1987	35.1	57.5	7.4
1996	81.5	14.5	4.0

Source: SGGJNF, 1997.

Table 3.5
Leased Property Markets

	Housing	Offices	Shops	Factories	Warehouses	Total
1993						
floorsareas (million m²)	2.07	0.59	1.00	1.41	0.11	5.18
rented floorareas / stock	17.6%	39.6%	71.4%	44.1%	n.a.	n.a.
1994						
floorsareas (million m²)	3.25	0.94	0.86	2.10	0.11	7.26
rented floorareas / stock	23.5%	59.1%	47.8%	60.5%	n.a.	n.a.

Source: SFNB, 1995.

between locals increased considerably over the years: from 48.2 percent in 1992 to 86.3 percent in 1994. It indicates that the investment market of properties has shifted from dominance of foreign capital to concentration of local funds.

Investment yields are instrumental in directing capital into real estate holding, while high rentals push tenants to shift to owner occupation. The composition of the Shenzhen secondary market coincides with conventional wisdom that housing and factories are good for owner occupation because of the long-term nature of occupation, while offices are suitable for leasehold due to tenant requirement for flexibility. The circle of property investors is, in general, composed of enterprises, governmental authorities, private individuals, and foreign capital. Local enterprises and foreign capital are two heavyweight players in this nascent domain of investment, especially in the coastal cities. Up to the end of 1996, 23.1 percent of total incoming foreign capital in aggregate, or U.S.$3.7 billion, had been invested in Shanghai's real estate, while there was an amount of U.S.$17.3 billion intended to be invested in property, representing as much as 38.2 percent of the total contractual foreign investment (SSTJ, 1997).

Table 3.6
Transactions in the Secondary Markets by Property Type and Legal Status of Purchasers

Year	Total (sq m)	Locals	Foreigners	Housing	Factories	Offices	Shops
1992	143,340	48.2%	51.8%	n.a.	n.a.	n.a.	n.a.
1993	105,700	76.3%	23.7%	59.1%	36.6%	2.7%	1.6%
1994	176,600	86.3%	13.7%	55.7%	37.5%	3.3%	3.5%

Source: SFNB, 1995, 1994, 1993.

Table 3.7
Foreign Investment in Real Estate, Shanghai (U.S.$ billions)

Year	Capital Intended to Be Invested in Real Estate in the Year	Total Capital Intended to Be Invested in Real Estate in Aggregate by the End of Year	As % of Total Foreign Investment in Shanghai	Capital Invested in Real Estate in the Year	Total Capital Invested in Real Estate in Aggregate by the End of Year	As % of Total Foreign Investment in Shanghai
1993	3.2	5.1	37.2	0.7	1.5	29.4
1994	3.7	8.8	36.7	0.4	1.9	22.6
1995	4.5	13.3	38.8	0.7	2.6	22.6
1996	4.0	17.3	38.2	1.1	3.7	23.1

Source: SSTJ, 1997.

Two-thirds of foreign capital into the Shanghai built environment came from Hong Kong (see Table 3.7).

Fragmentation in the Property Market

The economy in transition has cast its impact on the fledgling property market. Three kinds of dualism are observed in the Shenzhen marketplace. The first is a dual market separating foreigners from locals. Due to great disparities in the purchasing power between local residents and foreign investors, the Shenzhen property market is divided in two, intended to protect local interests against richer foreign investors and users. One market is for local firms and residents, and the other for foreign investors and enterprises. The latter is a relatively small market, in view of Shenzhen as a city actively advocating foreign investment. In Nanshan district, properties purchased by foreigners accounted for 9.8 percent of housing, 15.4 percent of offices, 9.2 percent of shops, and 6.5 percent of factories, in terms of floor area in aggregate up to 1996 (SGGJNF, 1997); 10.2 percent of total commodity properties were owned by foreigners in 1994. Thus, two sets of market demand and supply conditions and thereby two sets of property prices coexist. The division and re-division between two sectors give rise to unearned profit of arbitrage, which invites controversy and undermines integrity of market operations. The local authority has manipulated it by using it as a lever and tool to achieve some intended policy goals. A lax framework of regulations, however, provides ample loopholes for corrupt officials to capture benefits and thus entices corruption.

The second dualism is in the local property market, where two kinds of property exist in parallel: commodity and non-commodity properties. Commodity properties are developed by the developers, who acquire land in the open market and at market rates. The developed properties can be bought and sold in the open market, and owners have full property rights. Non-commodity properties cannot be bought and sold in the open market, because the land plots for non-commodity properties are given at a discount or even free of charge. The land at discount rates for non-commodity properties can be applied directly only to users for their own occupation, with land uses ranging from manufacturing to housing for state-owned enterprise employees. Up to 1994, 42.4 percent of housing, 72.1 percent of offices, 50.5 percent of shops, and 26.7 percent of factories were supplied by developers as commodity properties (SFNB, 1995).

The third dualism involves the largest section of urban properties, housing. Following the second category of dualism, the local housing market is divided into two submarkets: commodity and non-commodity housing. In the commodity housing market, housing transactions are conducted at full market rates. Owners are fully entitled to property rights over premises. Land for commodity housing must be purchased from the market at market rates. Non-commodity housing, is further differentiated into two types: *Fuli* and *Weili* housing. *Fuli* housing is a social welfare provided to civil servants and employees of non-profit-making institutions such as universities and research organizations. It cannot be sold or purchased in the market, and its occupiers have only use rights and thus are not entitled to full property rights. Land for *Fuli* housing is given free to the developers commissioned by the government for development. Therefore, *Fuli* housing prices can be cut substantially because of the exclusion of land costs. In the current market, the cost of land usually accounts for 30 to 70 percent, depending on location, of the total development costs. *Weili* housing, literally meaning housing with small profit to developers, is provided to the employees of state-owned enterprises. Land for *Weili* housing development is given to the appointed developers at subsidized rates. It is the biggest sector in the Shenzhen housing market.

Changing Parameters in the Property Market

Property price and rental gaps between locals' and foreigners' markets have been narrowing over years. For building prices, foreigners paid from 100 to 410 percent more than locals in 1984, depending on the sector. In

Table 3.8
Changes in Property Prices (yuan/square meter) and Rentals (yuan/square meter per month) for Locals and Foreigners (1984–1994)

Year	Price for Local's Property	Index	Price for Foreigner's property	Index	Rental for Local's Property	Index	Rental for Foreigner's Property	Index
				Housing				
1984	507	100	1601	100	8.0	100	32.0	100
1989	1771	349	3514	219	19.9	249	57.2	179
1994	5433	1072	7500	468	38.0	475	64.0	200
				Office				
1984	1160	100	3182	100	8.0	100	15.0	100
1989	2799	241	5336	168	40.6	508	68.7	453
1994	8730	753	9583	301	73.0	913	105.0	700
				Factory				
1984	471	100	965	100	4.0	100	8.0	100
1989	1045	222	1785	185	9.5	237	20.0	250
1994	2360	501	2596	269	25.0	625	28.5	356
				Shop				
1984	680	100	3480	100	18	100	34	100
1989	3088	454	7343	211	48	269	102	300
1994	13570	1996	20600	592	230	1277	300	882

Source: SFNB, 1995.

1994, the price differences between the two markets ranged only from 10 to 50 percent. In the rental market, rental differences between local and foreign tenants changed from 190–400 percent in 1984 to 110–130 percent in 1994, depending on the sector (see Table 3.8). It is largely due to the gap narrowing between the two economies of Shenzhen and Hong Kong, from which most of foreign capital has come. Shenzhen's per capita income accounted for only 3.7 percent of Hong Kong's in 1980. In 1994, Shenzhen's rose to 11.1 percent of Hong Kong's (Census and Statistics Department, Hong Kong, 1995; SZTJ, 1995). The demand from locals was strengthened along with continuous growth of the local economy, as were the property prices and rentals. With deepening reforms toward marketization, the proportion of commodity property to the total property stock has been expanding. According to a survey of Nanshan district, commodity property accounted for 13.9 percent of the total property stock in 1987. The percentage rose to 36.9 in 1996 (see Table 3.9).

PLANNING MANAGEMENT ON URBAN DEVELOPMENT

Urban construction under the planned economic system was directly controlled by the central planners to a large extent. Urban planning should have been in a supreme position to complement economic planning in guiding urbanization. However, because of totalitarianism, the CCP-

Table 3.9
Commodity Properties and Non-Commodity Properties in Nanshan District (1987–1997)

Year	Non-Commodity Building Stock (1,000 sq m)	Commodity Building Stock (1,000 sq m)	Commodity Property Stock as % of Total Stock
1987	1401.1	227.0	13.9
1988	1811.4	376.3	17.2
1989	2348.6	670.9	22.2
1990	3057.0	873.5	22.2
1991	3322.4	1203.9	26.6
1992	3753.6	1477.4	28.2
1993	4392.9	1832.4	29.4
1994	5116.6	2533.5	33.1
1995	5581.3	3026.3	35.2
1996	6003.1	3507.6	36.9
1997	6532.0	3620.4	35.7

Source: SGGJNF, 1997.

controlled government wanted absolute power to manipulate urban development at its whim. Urban physical planning was reduced to being a servant to the paramount industrialization. In the 1960s, urban physical planning was even abandoned. "No urban planning for three years" (*sannian bugao chengshi guihua*) was announced in the 1960 National Planning Meeting (Cao & Chu, 1990). Since the economic reforms, urban planning has been gradually establishing its due status. A new challenge arises as to how urban planning can accommodate market self-regulating mechanisms and coordinate market players toward the goal of orderly urban development. China's urban planning has to reform itself from direct planning controls to indirect planning management.

Development Control Process

Urban planning permission remains a prime control on urban development. According to the Planning Act (1990), urban land use planning is generally composed of two layers—Master Plan and Detailed Plan. The Master Plan is prepared for the next 20 years to draft a strategic structure of urban land uses together with identification of locations for significant urban projects. The Detailed Plan, a kind of zoning with provisions for specific physical controls, is made to guide current development projects. Shenzhen, as a pioneer of market reforms, has been experimenting with a slightly different urban planning system, which comprises three layers—Master Plan, Statutory Zoning, and Detailed Plan (SGGJ, 1997). As a structure plan for urban land uses and development, the Master Plan is the physical interpretation of urban economic development and land use strategies from a macroperspective. There are three components of the Shenzhen Master Plan in a hierarchical fashion, municipal, district, and subdistrict plans. It is a top-down process translating urban development strategies to local levels. The Statutory Zoning is prepared based on the three-layered Master Plans and used for development controls. Land uses and control of development intensity are monitored at this level. The Detailed Plan is a non-statutory document meant for urban design control at a micro local level.

The first Master Plan of Shenzhen was drafted in 1982, when a population of 800,000 by 2000 was envisaged, and a multi-nucleus-and-axes urban structure was formulated. Four years later, in 1986, the population size was revised to 1.1 million by 2000 after the city saw great economic dynamism and market forces at work. The unrestrained dynamism again made planning forecast irrelevant, and the population estimation had to be amended to 1.5 million in 1989. The latest version of the Shenzhen Master Plan was prepared in 1996 for a population of 4.3 million by 2010 in a territory of 480 square kilometers. According to this plan, Shenzhen will serve as the complementary city to Hong Kong, which is undergoing restructuring in a new international setting after China resumed its sovereignty over the territory on 1 July 1997. Shenzhen will also function as the interface between the Pearl Delta region and Hong Kong, in view of the extensive relations between the two regions.

When planning permission is granted based on the plans, the property development process is subject to the government's development control until the building is finally completed and put on sale or for lease. Development control is intended to provide microsurveillance. After land acquisition, *Approval of Architectural Design* (AAD) is the first government supervision, which is mainly concerned with compatibility of building style with its surroundings, access to off-site roads, fire escape passages, and so on. Construction bid can be held subsequently upon receiving the AAD. *Approval of Construction Contract* (ACC) is issued when the authority is satisfied with the winning builder's track record. With the AAD, ACC, developer's financial arrangements, and budget for the development project, *Construction Permission* (CP) will be given, and the project can proceed to the construction stage. Finally, immediately after completion of the construction, *Quality Examination Report* (QER) should be given if the construction is to the satisfaction of the competent authority before the building can be transferred (see Figure 3.5).

Land Acquisition Process

According to rules set by the Shenzhen municipal government, any applicant whose proposed business or development purposes fall into specified categories, such as high-tech and capital-intensive manufacturing, non-commodity housing, cultural, educational, and research institutions, non-commercial public facilities, and other uses deemed applicable by the

Figure 3.5
Development Control Process

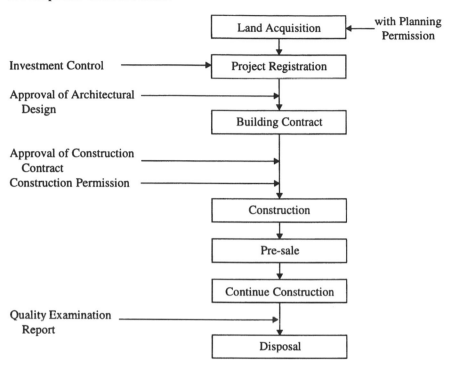

authority, can obtain subsidies from the government in the form of land-use right transfer at a discount. Land prices would be negotiated between applicants and the local land bureau. This process is coined as land-use-right transfer by agreement (see Figure 3.6). The negotiated land prices usually cover at least the costs for green land acquisition from peasants who collectively own the rural land, relocation of sitting tenants, and basic land development, which the government has paid for before it is ready for conveyance. Hence, the government can recover development expenses. This method is also allegedly used in situations where land uses are not so competitive or land parcels are not in desirable locations and thus do not expect a high competition for acquisition.

Except for land users who deserve land subsidies, all applications for land should acquire land plots at market rates according to rules. The market rates for land leases are determined at bidding and auction. Land-use-right sales through bidding are normally applied to property developers who conduct commercial development. The bidding package includes a bid price for the land plot and a development proposal. There

Figure 3.6
Land Acquisition Process (by agreement)

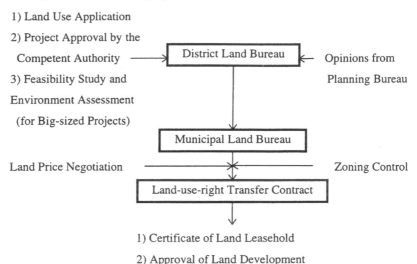

1) Land Use Application

2) Project Approval by the

   Competent Authority

3) Feasibility Study and

Environment Assessment

   (for Big-sized Projects)

District Land Bureau ← Opinions from

Planning Bureau

Municipal Land Bureau

Land Price Negotiation — Zoning Control

Land-use-right Transfer Contract

1) Certificate of Land Leasehold

2) Approval of Land Development

are two kinds of bidding. One is open to all developers as long as they are qualified. Another is restricted to invited developers in order not to incur unnecessary workloads on the bidding organizer (see Figure 3.7). Land-use-right transfer by auction is particularly applied to the situation of a plot in a prime location for commercially profitable uses, where market prices are unknown because few transactions have occurred. It is used to establish a market benchmark for transactions of similar land plots in the near future (see Figure 3.8).

Control of Land Subtransfer

Because of the nature of land state-ownership, local government, on behalf of the state, is the monopolistic supplier in the primary land market. It has been stated that after a land plot is leased to a developer, the land is allowed to lie idle up to only two years. Beyond this limitation, the idle land would be re-possessed by government without compensation. Twenty-five percent of proposed development costs should be materialized apart from land acquisition cost before a land parcel can be subleased. The same rule of 25 percent pay-up is also applied to property presales and subsales. In order to check land speculation and to guarantee some capital gains from land value appreciation collected into the government's coffers, the Shenzhen government introduced the Land Transaction Fee on 13 July 1989. It was a tax on capital gains and was collected on progressive rates from 40 percent up to 100 percent. ¥16.5 million and HK$7.6

Figure 3.7
Land Acquisition Process (by bidding)

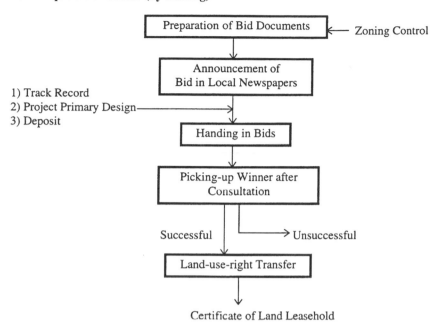

Certificate of Land Leasehold

million had been paid by property owners for the capital gains in property transactions by 1990 (Li, 1991). The state land capital gain tax has been recommended by the central government to be implemented since 1994 nationwide. It is collected progressively on the basis of a tax rate of 30 percent of appreciated land value where the increase is less than, or equal to, 50 percent; 40 percent where the increase is more than 50 percent and less than, or equal to, 100 percent; 50 percent where the increase is more than 100 percent and less than, or equal to, 200 percent; and 60 percent where the increase is more than 200 percent. Shenzhen is somehow exempted from the imposition. Instead, the Land Transaction Fee, is replaced by Land Capital Gain Fee, and its rates are a universal 20 percent on appreciated value after property investors voiced their resentment of the hefty Land Transaction Fee rates.

Participation of Foreign Developers

In the document issued on 28 July 1987, entitled "Policy on Land and Property Market Management" (*Shenzhen Jianshe Ju*, 1990), overseas developers were allowed to practice in Shenzhen, though they were not encouraged into large-scale, comprehensive land and property development. However, visible and invisible obstacles as well as unfathomable political

Figure 3.8
Land Acquisition Process (by auction)

risks were discouraging in the backdrop of long-lasting socialism. The breakthrough of private interests into a system of dominant state ownership was not expected to occur without resistance. The nature of profit-seeking property development by the private sector made government skeptical of its contribution to the welfare of the society, given the long history of egalitarianism. This notion was reinforced by the tendency for monopoly in the nature of land assets. The bitter history of losing sovereignty over territories like Hong Kong and Macao and Shanghai concessions to foreigners was still reminiscent. Therefore, in practice, it was very difficult, if not impossible, for an overseas developer to obtain a business license for sole proprietary operation.

Taxation on Real Estate

Land use fee was first introduced to cities where foreign capital came to invest. Shenzhen as the pioneer in leading the nation passed the *Urban Land Use and Management Regulations* in 1981 and implemented it since 1982 for the management of land used by foreign tenants. Concerned with a speculation tendency of property investment, the Shenzhen authority had imposed a progressive tax on rental income of private properties since 1 July 1985, aiming to curb possible rampant rental increases, which were deemed unproductive to the economy. With the deepening of the economic reforms, it was realized that property should be an essential component of the urban economy and that property investment should be a

Table 3.10
Taxes on Property, Shenzhen (as of 1997)

on Development	on Investment	on Transaction
1. Business tax: 5% of sales income	1. Property tax (for leased property): 12% of rental income	1. Income tax (for private individuals): 20% of net income
2. Urban construction and maintenance tax: 0.05% of sales income	2. Property tax (for owner occupation): 1.2% of 70% value when property purchased	2. Income tax (for enterprises): 15% of net income
3. Corporate tax: 15% of net income (after deduction of costs and taxes)	3. Income tax: 20% of net rental income	3. Urban construction and maintenance tax: 0.05% of rental income
4. Stamp duty: 0.03% of sales income		4. Stamp duty: 0.05% of sales value
5. Land capital gain fee: 20% of appreciated land value		5. Land capital gain fee: 20% of appreciated land value
6. Property ownership registration fee: 0.1% of property value		6. Notarization fee: 0.3% of transaction value
7. Transfer of property ownership registration fee: 0.1% of property value		7. Transfer registration fee: 0.1% of transaction value
		8. Transaction fee: 1.5% of transaction value

Source: Gui et al., 1997.

necessary sector to facilitate the urban market. The fact that property
development was deterred by lack of property investors was instrumental
in educating the policymakers about the usefulness of rental properties.
The progressive tax on property rental income was abolished in July 1987.
Over the years, Shenzhen has developed and refined taxes on property.
There are three categories of taxes regarding their incidence, on development, investment, and transaction (see Table 3.10).

Chapter 4

Gradualist Urban Land Reforms in the Framework of Institutional Change

The gradualist urban land reforms are intrinsically linked with the incremental economic reforms in transitional China. Decentralization has externalized latent localism, which is reflected in the formation of local coalitions. In the process of mobilization of local resources, the land factor was incorporated into local development strategies. Gradualist urban land reforms have been employed as a program to nurture a local property industry operating under new market conditions and to protect local enterprises from harsh market discipline, as they still provide jobs and take social responsibilities that would otherwise be local government's. A local government–enterprise coalition is fostered under the umbrella of gradualist urban land reforms to convert more resources into local development by resisting central government's coercion. Incremental land reforms have also been used as an instrument of positive intervention by local government in the peculiar Chinese political structure for the interests of mayors. Chinese cities in the booming coastal region are formulating an informal local urban regime, during a systematic transition toward socialist market economy, to compete for local growth by capitalizing financial gains from urban land and property development.

INSTITUTIONAL CHANGE AND THE ROLE OF THE STATE

China's economic reforms are a profound change of institutions and transformation of social and economic organizations. "Institutions are the rules of the game in a society or, more formally, are the humanly devised constraints that shape human interaction" (North, 1990:3). "Institutions are relatively stable sets of widely shared and generally realized expectations about how people will behave in particular social, economic, and political circumstances (Weimer, 1997:2). Institutions reduce uncertainty and regulate behavior when human interactions take place. Organizations, whether they are political, economic, or social, behave and perform within a framework defined by institutions that are reckoned as a matrix of formal and informal rules. The formal rules include laws and regulations, whereas the informal rules are norms, conventions, traditions, and customs.

The former is "pulled" by the prospect of future rewards, whereas the latter is "pushed" from behind by quasi-inertial forces. The former adapts to changing circumstances, always on the lookout for improvement. The latter is insensitive to circumstances, sticking to the prescribed behavior even if new and apparently better options become available. (Elster, 1989:97)

A society is organized by the binding power of social institutions, both formal and informal, so as to produce collective benefits through cooperation and coordination (Knight, 1992).

As opposed to economic rationality, social norms are among the determinants of behavior. Rational action is dictated by the pursuit of improvement, whereas behavior guided by social norms is driven by customs and traditions. "[N]orms are sustained by the feeling of embarrassment, anxiety, guilt and shame that a person suffers at the prospect of violating them, or at least at the prospect of being caught violating them" (Elster, 1989:99–100). Code of conduct and social norms are embedded in individuals' minds in a social group in the local cultural context, by which members identify with each other to maintain the stability of the group.

Formal institutions are sanctioned, maintained, and enforced by the state. Informal institutions are controlled by the community and social network. Neoinstitutionist economics believes that institutions define a set of choices for the free market competition and interaction between demand and supply. The performance of an economy is measured by the costs of production and exchange. "It takes resources to transform inputs of land, labor, and capital into the output of goods and services and that transformation is a function not only of the technology employed, but of institutions as well," because "[i]t takes resources to define and protect property rights and to enforce agreements" (North, 1990:61). Transaction costs are partly determined by institutions. Property rights are usually defined by formal statutes. However, "[w]hen legal institutions are weak or incomplete, property rights are informal" (Weimer, 1997:3).

According to neoinstitutionist economics, institutional change is a process of interaction between institutions and organizations (North, 1993; Eggertsson, 1994). Institutional change is regarded as a move to a more desirable set of rules.

Institutions can be seen as a stock of social capital. The stock changes through depreciation and new investments, but changes that occur in the span of a few years tend to be marginal. Although formal rules may change rapidly, enforcement and informal rules tend to change slowly. Many informal rules, such as norms and customs, are not explicitly designed by some authority but evolve spontaneously. (Eggertsson, 1994:21)

Thereby, overall change of institutions is gradual, without entailing significant improvement in human behavior for the immediate future. A cumulative stock of social capital in a form of institutional matrix because of long-lasting inertial traditions makes institutional change marginal, incremental, and path-dependent (North, 1990, 1995). When change occurs, however, it would have long-term implications. Allio et al. (1997) applied three general theories of institutional change to the institutional reforms in Eastern Europe and the former Soviet Union: the economic, the public choice, and the distributional theories. The economic theory considers that institutional change occurs to capture the opportunities for Pareto improvements. The public choice theory regards governments in the former socialist central planning countries as the key actors in the reforms with interests in revenue and electoral prospects that may not be consistent with the Pareto efficiency. The distributional theory takes institutional change as the result of distributional conflict.

A capitalist market economy is based on well-defined private property rights. According to the doctrines of capitalism, private property rights are essential in enabling realization of gains from specialization in production, providing incentives for innovations and safeguarding rewards for enterprising undertakings. Private owners have greater incentives than public owners to enhance the value of production because they must face the result of their behavior, which either increases or decreases the value of their residual claims on assets. Competition is the best way to ensure that goods and services desired by customers are provided at the lowest economic cost. This thinking doubts that government can be good at owning or controlling businesses, as priorities, pressures, and time horizons are entirely different (J. Moore, 1983).

China's economic reforms are changing the economic structure from planning-coordination to market competition. Although the privatization of property rights as a strategy has not been accepted by the political elite who set up the centrally controlled planning regime in 1949, marketization and commodification have been cautiously promoted in order to raise economic productivity. State-owned enterprises are changing from a unit under central planning to an enterprise exposed to market competition with certain degrees of autonomy. Housing provision is undergoing a change from social welfare to commodity. During the process, prices are playing a role in the allocation of resources. Incentives, which used to be political in the past, are gradually becoming economic.

China's economic reforms or institutional changes are basically driven by burgeoning discontent of the masses due to failures of the planned economy in improving people's welfare. Being afraid of losing legitimacy of governance, the party was forced to carry out reforms in order to stay in power. Constrained by the old institutions, the Chinese reform agenda declares explicitly that socialism and a public economy remain the backbone for the country, because, though economic institutions are under reform, political institutions, which used to be the crucial components of the outgoing planned system, are still more or less in place. However, a desire to build a strong economy, which was not achieved by the old system, would probably triumph over conservatism. Pragmatism now prevails in the management of the economy as a result. The salient characteristics of pragmatism implanted in the reform plan suggest that eventual results may betray the original rhetoric. If private ownership and establishment of private property rights deliver goods and ensure fair wealth distribution, the pragmatic reform will probably lead to ownership change, though the rhetoric does not approve.

Property rights, the central issue of institutional change in China, are undergoing a quiet and somehow informal reformation. In large cities such as Shanghai, a large public housing stock is sold to sitting tenants at prices taking account of the number of the buyer's years of working. The formerly public housing is thus privatized, and private property rights, though specifically defined by the authority, as the conversion does not take place under full market conditions, are formally established. Although the formal institutions have not sanctioned the legal conversion of state ownership to non-state ownership for enterprises, informal privatization is undergoing trials, and thus informal property rights are formulated.

The economic reforms have introduced market mechanisms into the economy. It has been acknowledged that though the economic reforms have led to a considerable growth in the national economy, the most significant change should be that market mechanisms have started to play an indisputable role in the operation of the economy. Urban construction and urban land use structure have showed resemblance to those in cities under the capitalist market system. Macropolitical and economic factors have begun to influence price movements in the property market. However, with the transformation from plan to market, an appropriate role of the state has to be found in the management of the economy. Direct state involvement in the economy and society has been a long-lasting institution in China. It is not realistic to expect the role of the Chinese state to be like that of any state under the market economic system. From the notion that institutional change is gradual, the Chinese state may still be actively involved in the development of the national economy (Wang, 1998). Nevertheless, the role of the state will have to change, though gradually, to indirect intervention using state apparatus for the sake of efficient economic management.

According to Ellman (1990), there are three basic models of planning in the economic system: the traditional, Soviet-styled model; the indirectly bureaucratically controlled model; and the regulated market economy model. The planned economic system is a historic reaction to respond to failures of laissez-faire capitalism. Following the Russian model, the Chinese Communist Party set up a socialist, centrally planned autarky with predominant state ownership of the means of production. "The ideal type of command economy is one in which individuals who act do so not as principals but as agents for someone else ... The ideal type of market economy is one in which individuals act as principals in pursuit of their own interests" (Friedman, 1984:5). The ideal type of command economy possibly exists in reality. The defunct Soviet Union economy was such a case. However, the ideal type of market economy—the laissez-faire market—guided by Adam Smith's "invisible hand," has vanished from the reality since the free market forces cannot handle externalities generated from the market on the environment and on long-term sustainable growth. No country in the world is free of state interventions (Zwass, 1987).

Ideology: Market-Critical or Market-Led

Whether laissez-faire or state intervention is an issue for debate, and the debate was intensified when economic stagnation and social stratification were exacerbated in the Western capitalist economies from the mid-1970s after the sensational postwar boom was over. The opening up of developing countries to the international capital gives rise to a new phenomenon of international labor division. Manufacturing in developed countries takes advantage of increasingly attractive production conditions in the developing countries, where cheap labor sites for the manufacturing of industrial products are plentiful because of an inexhaustible reservoir of low-wage labor. International division of production is achieved assisted by the advanced division of production process and communication development (Fröbel, Heinrichs & Kreye, 1980). High-quality services in the developed countries and low-cost production sites in the developing countries have made manufacturing a "borderless" production process. Migration of factories to lower-cost localities has become a trend since the 1980s (Clark & Kim, 1995; Park, 1994; Bauer, 1992; Chng et al., 1988; Lim, 1984). Economic restructuring and consequent social realignment due to the advent of globalization and international division of labor brought the argument to the focus of free market and state intervention again in the countries forced to undergo restructuring. The question is whether social inequalities, arising from social and economic changes and resultant uneven wealth redistribution in the wake of economic restructuring, should be dealt with by market forces or should be addressed by state intervention.

The views critical to market are developed along the lines of market defects and social inequality. With a free capitalist market system, nowadays most developed countries have achieved impressive advancement in economic and social welfare. However, it cannot be denied that many defects are inherently associated with the system of so-called free competition. An absolutely free market system has an inherent mechanism that favors the haves and disfavors the have nots. A substantial section of the populace is not adequately catered to by the market. Poor people lack effective command over market resources. The result is polarization, where the rich become richer and the poor poorer. A perfect free market exists only in theory. In reality, free market competition is bound to be imperfect. There have been numerous market failures. No example can be more illustrative than monopoly. Monopoly virtually halts free entry of competitors into the market, which subsequently brings about tremendous economic inefficiency. Maximization of profits, which is a primary force driving the market, is intrinsically short-term. It tends to utilize natural resources no matter how expensive to the next generation and to the environment. Coming together with the polarization, social instability is prone to occur, which can claim social costs from rising crime rates to large-scale social upheavals. There is no safeguard to minimize social costs within the free market framework. Externality is a general feature of the urban economy. Examples of the externality are environmental pollution caused by manufacturing and enhanced amenities due to the proximity of an urban park. Negative externality is an unintended by-product of urban development. Its adverse effects are not compensated for through a market process and thus would be borne by the community in the absence of public intervention. Without a safeguard to prevent negative enternalities from occurring, the long-term confidence of investors and developers cannot be established. Thus, urban development would be deterred because of that uncertainty. A free market framework does not have devices to internalize those impacts, let alone that many urban goods and services are public goods supplied at a zero price.

Nevertheless, the pro-market views are concerned with fundamental human liberty and economic efficiency. Free market stresses both the social and economic importance of private initiatives and competition, which is deeply rooted in the cultural foundation of capitalist economies. Economic democracy ensured by a free market system is as essential as political democracy to human beings. Individual well-being is evaluated in terms of the fulfillment of personal aspiration. Private individuals should be given the right to seek happiness in their independence. Acting upon market motivation, the private sector is more dynamic and productive than the public sector. Private institutions are more efficient in responding to market incentives than public bodies in delivery of goods and services. Why would the state make wiser decisions than private individuals? The market is the best arbitrator with respect to resources distribution. Therefore, resources can be efficiently utilized to accelerate economic growth, which would eventually benefit all walks of life. Market efficiency is an essential criterion for social policy formulation.

It is unrealistic to make an ideology-free assessment on the two approaches, but a realistic attitude is crucial to judge the course of economic reforms against existing conditions and in situ socioeconomic background. Before we come to understand China's economic reforms, two assumptions have to be made. The market-led approach is understood as intending to pursue economic efficiency by all means, while putting equal social distribution as a secondary consideration. The market-critical approach is recognized as primarily concerned with social equality, or economic development with social and environmental balance. China's institutional change has to recognize that reforms in contemporary China are carried out in the historic context, where the centrally controlled Chinese system has a long history dating back 2,000 years, when Emperor Qin united the country as it is today. The Soviet-styled, state-owned economy did achieve great performance at first, with its freshness presenting a new horizon to people who had long suffered national fragmentation and widespread corruption under the name of free market prior to 1949. However, the rigid control on society as well as on economy soon disclosed a lack of dynamism of the planned economy in encouraging innovation and entrepreneurism. Too much stress on social equality and thereby inefficient resource allocation were to blame for poor economic performance under the socialist planned economy, which finally led to an economic standstill. The market-oriented reforms were more driven by bottom-up popular aspirations than by top-down political decisions. After several political traumas inflicted by the Communist Party, which was obsessed with the Marxist doctrine of class struggle, the policy of economic and technological advancement had to replace the principle of political ideology in order to maintain the authority of the government.

Plan–Market Cooperation

China's economic system prior to reforms was that central authorities determined directly all production decisions throughout the whole economy. Decentralization as the first step for reforms took place to change the system toward one where decisions are made by enterprises at local levels. It is officially maintained that reforms are to transform the socialist, centrally controlled economy to a socialist market economy and to replace direct government plans with indirect state controls. Market orientation is used to improve economic efficiency in production, while the existing state ownership of enterprises and other planning factors, as long as they are not considered detrimental to economic growth, are to be retained.

Therefore, the plan has blended with the market. The economic reforms have come about to liberalize the economy, set individuals free from rigid planning controls, and release abundant initiatives from the ideological cage. The trend is evident in a variety of economic entities that emerged to break the dominance of the state-owned economy. Rapid economic growth is largely attributed to the participation of many non-state sectors like private and collective companies, joint ventures, and foreign investors. How can the state cooperate with non-state sectors in a country where private interests were absent for more than 30 years?

State intervention is necessary for proper functioning of the market (Putterman & Rueschemeyer, 1992). The role of the state has to change from central planner to market regulator. The relationship between the state and the property market and effective state intervention in the property market have to be based on an understanding of the market: its structure, processes, and interaction of actors. There is a belief that the market itself is the best arbitrator to resolve market conflicts (Moor, 1983). It is argued that government intervention often leads to market distortion and thus undermines market performance and economic well-being in the long run (Bradbury, Downs & Small, 1982). Empirical research has shown, for instance, that, rent control undervalues real estate and that tax benefits for new construction discourage renovation (Kinnard, 1994). This market-led ideology is not without flaws in the domain of the urban property sector. Free operation of the property market without state regulation is bound to fail to solve conflicts and achieve desirable social goals. However, a lack of understanding of market forces in the property domain is prone to lead to ineffectiveness in state intervention when tackling market failures. State intervention by utilization of market mechanisms to implement policy goals would be effective because incentive-oriented enterprises tend to respond to market signals (Schultze, 1977).

The state has the discretion to use development control, land use policy, monetary control, and fiscal measures to regulate and manipulate the property market. Monetary policy is defined as the control of a nation's money supply directly by a limitation on its growth or indirectly by measures affecting the cost and availability of credit (Hawthorne, 1981). By making loans less expensive and funds accessible to the property market, government can create a viable environment for property investment where financial risks are offset to a certain degree and thus consolidate demand. Fiscal policy refers to government spending, taxes, and borrowing. Aggregate demand can be stimulated by increasing government spending or by relieving taxes, so that business and households can spend more (James & Nobes, 1978). Taxation is used as a lever to increase or decrease aggregate demand and becomes a key determinant of economic behavior and resource allocation. On the supply side, conventional planning control is used to direct property development, although it has a broader goal of maintaining a balance between economic growth and social and environmental concerns. Government can be an active player in economic production. By strengthening or withdrawing its participation in development, government can effectively adjust the equilibrium in the property market. Infrastructure construction and government projects can improve urban quality and catalyze local demand insofar as the locality is viable. State revenues, which permit local government to take on a positive role in promoting local development, mainly come from taxes and land rentals.

When a local economy is growing or, more precisely, when some indicators are implying that the market will expand, it is interpreted that there will be demand for property and thus undersupply of premises, if property vacancy rates stay low at the moment. Driven by potential profits, developers in the market would come up with proposals to produce what the market demands, unless supply-side constraints, if there are any, prevent it. Developers are automatically motivated by a booming economy where market demand looks certain. However, when the economy is at the other end of the market spectrum, namely, recession, developers in the market tend to be intimidated by the deteriorating situation. With involvement of a large amount of capital, property development becomes highly risky, as the future market is highly uncertain. Apparently, reluctance to invest is paralleled by pessimistic views of the economy.

On the contrary, government has a responsibility to prevent market from overheating and to reverse adverse trends when in recession. The democratic nature of an elected government also has to be concerned with social welfare as well as social justice in wealth distribution. The state should act to maintain a balanced urban development. Gains and subsidies are two scenarios the state would face when the market is in different situations. In a growing economy, the state is in a favorable position to benefit financially or in-kind from the property market. Under fierce market competition, developers are squeezed to give up some profits. Gains to the state may take the form of taxes and "planning gains."[1] Property taxes and various kinds of development charges are state revenues derived from the property market, whereas in a depressed market, the state has to stand up to play a role in reversing the declining trend. In order to achieve that, the state has to deploy public resources and give subsidies to stimulate the stagnant market.

URBAN LAND MANAGEMENT REFORM SINCE 1979

The old land use regime was challenged for the first time in Shenzhen. No sooner had Shenzhen been designated as a special economic zone than its government found itself in a handicapped position, except for the authority given to try experimental policies for the establishment of a pro-market economy. First, grant from the central government for the construction of urban infrastructure was far from adequate to take on large-scale land development. Infrastructure construction was believed fundamental for the competitiveness of a locality to potential investors. "Experience from other export processing zones in Asia has already shown that the lack of sufficient and well-established infrastructure is a major cause of failure" (Wong & Chu, 1985:210). Second, a practical problem arose when overseas investors came to invest in Shenzhen: they were not entitled to free land use as domestic ones were, because the latter were mainly state-owned socialist enterprises. The purpose of setting up the Shenzhen special economic zone (SSEZ) was to build another Hong Kong with characteristics of a socialist market economy by luring as much overseas investment as possible. Its economy was thus expected to deal with privately owned enterprises. Shenzhen has attracted many investment interests from overseas. By the end of 1996, the total contractual inward investment in Shenzhen reached U.S.$23.1 billion, of which U.S.$11.9 billion had been materialized (SZTJ, 1997). Therefore, the commercial relationship between the government as the landowner and private land users as tenants had to be established and legalized.

The issue was how to re-install a notion of land as capital and to strengthen the status of the state as the landowner. For a joint-venture scheme, land should be recognized as an asset, and its owner should be able to claim the property rights in one way or another. Pragmatically, the value of land contributed by Shenzhen partners as a share to joint ventures had to be worked out. In this connection, the first benchmark of a land use fee of HK$5,000 per square meter was established in December 1980, when a plot-sized 4,000 square meter was leased to a Hong Kong developer for an apartment/office project. The lease was to be valid for 30 years, and the developer paid HK$5000/square meter rental in a lump sum. There were up to 10 cases of such leasing by December 1981. Before that, a Shenzhen catering firm together with a Hong Kong investor initiated a joint development named *Bamboos Garden Hotel* in 1979 (*Shenzhen Jianshe Ju*, 1989). It was the first case of land commercialization. The Shenzhen partner provided the land allocated by the Shenzhen government, and the Hong Kong party covered development costs. Upon completion of the construction and the hotel's coming into operation, both parties shared profits based on their terms of agreement. Another creative case was the *Donghu Liyuan* project. It was a residential development of 460 units where the Shenzhen partner provided land, while Hong Kong developers were responsible for all development costs. Profits were divided between Shenzhen–Hong Kong parties at 85 percent–15 percent split after sales. Many joint-property development projects followed this case.

However, this bold experiment did not accord with the law and the Constitution. Only on 1 January 1982 did the belated *SSEZ Land Management Regulation* legalize the practice and declare the end of the era of free land use. In order to strengthen the status of the state as the landowner, all land users were required to pay a land use fee. Categorical rates for land use fee were made known to the public. As such, Shenzhen acted in the vanguard of terminating the old land use regime, which was ostensibly concerned with social equity but, in fact, was gravely inefficient in the economic sense and seriously undermined effective management of land resources. The land use fee introduced on 1 January 1982 was nevertheless received as a heavy financial burden to local land users. The strong resistance from land users was because of the lagging state-owned enterprise (SOE) reforms, which would allow SOEs to retain more profits with some degree of autonomy in managing business and psychological effects as they had been used to the free land use regime. Heavy lobbying from SOE land users pressured the authority to reduce the rates on 1 July 1984, after having been in place two and a half years. It was claimed that the high land use fee had rendered their business unprofitable. However, the land use fee did not constitute a barrier to overseas investors. In facing still more complaints of overcharges on land use from the local land users, the Shenzhen government in 1985 succumbed to the pressure to further reduce the rates to only one-tenth of the 1982 level. Despite the new land use system and compromises made by the government, many land users were still exempted from the imposition of compensatory land use. By 1987, out of 82 square kilometers of land that had been allocated, only 17 square kilometers were levied a land use fee. The income from the land use fee was far behind government expenditure on land development. Land development cost ¥1.7 billion, while only ¥52.5 million land use fees were collected (Zhang, 1993).

The debates on land commercialization lasted so long that impatient Shenzhen reformers decided to let practice move ahead of ideological deliberation. A milestone in China's urban land management was set by the first transaction of land use right in Shenzhen on 9 September 1987, when the Shenzhen municipality sold the use right of a land plot of 5,000 square meters to a local company (*Shenzhen Industrial and Trade Center*, which was ancillary to the *China Aviation Technology Import and Export Company*) at a price of ¥200 per square meter for a lease term of 50 years. Although the land price was settled by behind-closed-doors negotiation, this case set a precedent of land-use-right transfer, even running the risk of violating the national Constitution, whose Clause 4, Article 10 reads clearly: "No organization or individual may appropriate, buy, sell, or lease land, or unlawfully transfer it in other ways."

With a mind to deepen reform in urban land management, on 25 September 1987, the Shenzhen government issued an invitation to bid for another piece of land with an area of 46,355 square meters meant for residential land use. *Shenhua Development Company* won the bid at a price of ¥368 per square meter. Purposely, a third form of land transaction was tried on 1 December 1987, when a plot of 8,600 square meters planned for housing land use was auctioned. *SSEZ Real Estate & Properties Company* won at a price of ¥611 per square meter. This series of land transactions set a precedent for the forthcoming reforms in the management of urban land and finalized the formality of land-use-right transfer.

Having recognized the problem and broken the ideological taboo, on 3 January 1988, the new legislation, the *Provisional Ordinances on Land Management of Shenzhen Special Economic Zone*, was promulgated by the *Guangdong Provincial People's Congress*. It declared that land in Shenzhen should be recognized as a special commodity and that its use right could be leased. Moreover, it said that the rights over leased land could be transferred, assigned, bequeathed, or mortgaged at the lessee's will within a validated term. Later, an amendment to the 1982 Constitution was proposed and approved by the *National People's Congress* on 12 April 1988 that reads: "The right of land use can be transferred in accordance with the law."

Although the urban land management reform has so far been confined only to land-use-right transfer, while land-ownership remains a state monopoly, it will cast a dramatic impact on the urban economy and urban community. First, it will facilitate introduction of market forces into the urban economy as well as into urban development. Second, it is the first step toward the commercialization of land and property development, which allows the state to quit its omnipotent position in physical development and re-establish its role as a regulator. Third, urban infrastructure's will have a designated financial source, so that the problem of under-investment in infrastructure's dragging urban economy behind will be alleviated somewhat by guaranteed income from land sales. Finally, the urban land use pattern will undergo radical changes as market competition replaces administrative allocation. The commercialization and marketization of urban land are to have a profound impact on China's urban landscape.

Therefore, compensatory transfer of land use right has become legalized. The land use right can be transferred to developers or land users for a fixed period after payment of rental in a lump sum. Land use right can be acquired through bidding, auction, or negotiation. Purchasing land use right by bidding and auction is a market allocation, reflecting full market value, while purchasing by negotiation is a market allocation with government subsidies through which local government apparently implements its policy of facilitating targeted industries. The previously implicit land market has become explicit, and property rights are clarified.

GRADUALIST URBAN LAND REFORMS

During the period 1979–1988, the land use fee was introduced in Chinese cities in order to facilitate transactions between the state landowner and foreign land users when foreign investors began to be present. Shenzhen was the pioneer to take it on trial. An informal land market emerged and demonstrated its impact. The 1988 amendment to the 1982 Constitution formally recognized the economic value of urban land, and thus an explicit urban land market was expected to evolve. Although compensatory land use—an imposition of land use fee before the new policy of land commodification has been implemented in 1988—was applied to all land users, mostly land users who were foreign investors paid rentals, while most of SOE land users were exempted from this practice. A huge discrepancy arose between tenants who paid and those who did not pay the land use fee.

Two issues need to be highlighted after a close examination of land allocation between 1979 and 1996 in Shenzhen. First, the legacy of the former land management regime remains effective. In the period 1979–1987, 73.78 square kilometers of land was allocated through administration and free of charge to tenants under the old land management system, and only 15.7 hectares had its use right transferred as experiments. In the period 1988–1996, 24.66 square kilometers of land was assigned to applicants who were allegedly engaged in social, cultural, military, and administrative activities and thus exempted from payment of land rentals. Up to 1996, land by administrative allocation still accounted for 79.5 percent of the total land allocated, a substantial amount because of the historical backlog. The new land use regime does not seem retroactive. Although the land use fee is applied to land users of this category, the coverage is insignificant. Up to 1994, a mere 30.18 square kilometers, one-quarter of total land allocated, paid land use fee (SFNB, 1995). Second, of 27.05 square kilometers that was commercially leased between 1988 and 1996, 91.57 percent was through negotiation, 8.26 percent through bidding, and 0.17 percent through auction. Land allocation according to current market rates (through bidding and auction) was applied to merely 233.7 out of 13,302.7 hectares of the total land supplied, standing at 1.8 percent (see Table 4.1). Given the fact that the rate of property commodification and marketization is much higher than the rate of land commodification, unearned profits, reflected in great discrepancies between buoyant property market prices and discounted land prices, have gone beyond the control of government both as the management authority and as the landowner. As a

Table 4.1
Land Allocation in Shenzhen (1979–1996)

Year	Total (Ha)	Administrative Allocation (Ha)	Compensatory Allocation (Ha)	By Negotiation (Ha)	By Bidding (Ha)	By Auction (Ha)
1979	134.5	134.5				
1980	145.4	145.4				
1981	660.2	660.2				
1982	985.1	985.1				
1983	1663.4	1663.4				
1984	913.9	913.9				
1985	1945.2	1945.2				
1986	167.6	167.6				
1987	772.7	757.0	15.7	10.2	4.6	0.9
total (79-87)	**7388.0 (100.0%)**	**7372.3 (99.8%)**	**15.7 (0.2%)**	**10.2**	**4.6**	**0.9**
1988	1465.9	1239.4	226.5	220.9	4.7	0.9
1989	599.5	401.6	197.9	194.3	3.6	0.0
1990	600.0	396.0	204.0	193.4	10.6	0.0
1991	525.6	156.5	369.1	360.5	8.6	0.0
1992	502.7	71.5	431.2	427.6	3.6	0.0
1993	583.7	47.4	536.3	534.4	1.9	0.0
1994	266.3	93.6	172.7	112.7	56.2	3.8
1995	1034.6	759.7	274.9	235.7	39.2	0.0
1996	336.4	44.1	292.3	197.2	95.1	0.0
total (88-96)	**5914.7 (100.0%)**	**2466.0 (54.3%)**	**2704.9 (45.7%)**	**2476.7**	**223.5**	**4.7**
total (79-96)	**13302.7 (100.0%)**	**10582.1 (79.5%)**	**2720.6 (20.5%)**	**2486.9**	**228.1**	**5.6**

Sources: SFNB, 1991–1997; *Zhongwai Fangdichan Daobao*, 1996, No. 18: 20–21.

result, mechanisms of the land market are not able to be fully established, and integrity of the land marketization is compromised by a dual land market (Zhu, 1994).

Implementation of the new land management system has not been thorough, despite the fact that the free land use has officially ended. A convenient explanation of this gradualist urban land reform is that there is strong resistance from the sitting land users, who have taken free land use for granted. The real reasons are complicated enough and therefore deserve thorough empirical investigations and thoughtful conceptual explanations. It is believed that gradualism in the reforms of the urban land management system does not evolve in a vacuum. It unfolds in the context of transition from plan to market and with profound implications for the formation of urban built form under new urban politics. It develops in association with the re-definition of central–local intergovernmental relations in the reform era and with the advent of localism. In this connection, gradual urban land reforms have become an implicit program to nurture local enterprises and local developers, a plan to foster local government–enterprise coalitions, and an instrument to strengthen local government's position in local development. Rapidly growing Chinese cities are formulating an informal local urban regime during a systematic transition toward a socialist market economy, to compete for local growth by capitalizing financial gains from urban land and property development.

WHO HAS GAINED FROM THE GRADUALIST URBAN LAND REFORMS?

Theoretically, due to changing equilibrium between demand and supply, any appreciation or depreciation in the capital value of property should be attributed primarily to the land where the building stands. Accordingly, the state as the statutory landowner should gain from property booms or suffer from property busts. However, by alienating land leases at subsidized rates in such a large quantity, the landowner does not gain from land sales, at least for a short term. Revenue income to the government as the landowner from sale of land use right is discounted to a substantial degree by the fact that only 1.8 percent of total land allocated during the period 1979–1996 was leased out at market rates (see Table 4.1). Thus, in the context of China's incremental reforms, who has actually benefited from the gradualist urban land reforms?

Developers are in a dominant position during the property development process. They take full profits or suffer whole losses when the market finally delivers the verdict on the completed project. According to the data released by a property consultant firm, property development was portrayed as a very lucrative business with annual profit between 70 and 95 percent. A case study reveals that a state-owned developer, *Shenzhen Development Bank Real Estate Company*, achieved 76.2 percent development profit from a typical project of mixed-use building with retailing, offices, and housing in 1989. The profit was calculated based on a valuation of ¥9.16 million and total development costs of ¥5.20 million inclusive of interests paid on loans and taxes. The land lease was purchased in November 1988 at a price of ¥1,200 per square meter. Building construction commenced five months later and was completed in one year. Upon completion, part of the building was sold immediately, and the rest was retained for the developer's own use (*Shenzhen Jianshe Ju*, 1990).

As far as property investors are concerned, prime factors such as yields from investment, long-term capital growth prospects, and risks are used to measure the performance of property investment before investment decisions can be made. Capital appreciation occurred in all property sectors of Shenzhen to various degrees (see Table 3.3). Total investment yields were very high in comparison with normal investment mediums (see Table 4.2). Property investors in Shenzhen gained handsomely from their investment. An anecdotal story of successful property investment cast a profound influence on luring investment into the Shenzhen property market. The *Shenzhen International Trade Mansion* was presold of 80 percent

Table 4.2
Annual Total Return from Property Investment on Average, 1984–1990
(percent)

	medium-rise housing	high-rise housing	office	factory	shop
locals' market	28.3	20.5	18.5	17.9	42.4
foreigners' market	32.1	21.9	15.4	21.8	20.4

Note: All data are adjusted by the inflation index.
Source: SFNB, 1991.

of floor areas by its developer to a Hong Kong investor in 1988 for HK$77 million. One year later, the same property, after some refurbishment, was sold again to another investor when its capital value appreciated to HK$106 million after deduction of expenditures for improvement. The net annual appreciation rate was 37.7 percent. This case is one of many sensational stories of investment in property in good times.

As for property tenants, rental increase was rather rapid. From 1984 to 1994, tenants faced annual rental increases of 16.9 percent on average for housing, 24.8 percent for offices, 29.0 percent for shops, and 20.1 percent for factories in the locals' market and 7.2 percent for housing, 21.5 percent for offices, 24.3 percent for shops, and 13.5 for factories in the foreigners' market (SFNB, 1991). The rental increases suggested that tenant demand was more than the supply of premises. Tenants did not seem to receive the subsidy embedded in building prices and rentals that the government meant to convey through the cheap land policy. Inward, high-tech industrial tenants reportedly fell victim to high prices and rentals of industrial property in the early 1990s, when government land resource had been almost exhausted after years of transfer to land users and developers (Zang, 1995).

By and large, gains derived from the subsidized land supply materialize in the form of rising rentals, appreciation in capital value, and development profits achieved during the property development process. Land cost is supposed to be a large component in total development costs, especially in a buoyant economic situation where relative shortages of land are persistent. Thus, developers and investors are the prime beneficiaries, while tenants bear rising expenditures for premise occupation. In addition, those land users who self-developed properties for their own occupation unarguably obtained the land subsidy, and those beneficiaries were mostly SOEs. Government as the landlord does not appear to benefit directly from the booming property market. The policy of cheap land seems to drain the coffers of Shenzhen government, as opposed to land income in many high-density East Asian cities, such as Hong Kong and Singapore, being an important source of government fiscal revenues. The parallel supplies of subsidized and commercialized land have created a land market where, on the one hand, land can be obtained at a price much below the prevailing market level, and, on the other hand, land users who do not have access to subsidized land have to compete for land in the open market.

RECONFIGURATION OF CENTRAL–LOCAL INTERGOVERNMENTAL RELATIONS

A bold political decision to initiate a reform process toward a decentralized economy with a mixture of market mechanisms and planning controls inevitably results in a transformation from a closed, socialist autarky to an open, market-oriented economy. In the course of reforms, regional competition intensifies, and economic restructuring and social realignment are localized. A redefinition of relations between the central and local governments is called for, and decentralization as a catchword has been debated both extensively and intensively. Economic reforms have produced considerable benefits to its people and gains in national income. The gradual, incremental and experimental reforms commenced with the rural agricultural sector and then spread to the urban industrial sector. As a means to explore marketization and improve economic efficiency, decentralization is cautiously attempted in a top-down manner, on the one hand, and fervently advocated by the advantaged localities, on the other. Farmers are given more discretion in deciding what to grow and sell produce at prices largely determined in the market. Urban SOEs are getting more autonomy from their supervisory authorities in making their business decisions. Likewise, devolution occurs in the central–local intergovernmental power structure. Decentralization grants more power to local governments in making investment decisions for local growth, which benefits some regions in their development. The consistent growth of extrabudgetary funds since 1978, which are outside central planning, testifies to the extent of decentralization that the localities have gained (Wang, 1995).

From an Ideological Regime to a Developmental State

After many years' preoccupation with ideological battles and political correctness, the Chinese socialist government has finally come to its senses and changed to its predilection for economic development, symbolized by its commitment to reforms. Few people believed that a planned economy, after being 30 years in place, would lead the country to prosperity. The rigid, planned economic system has to be abandoned because of its inefficiency and ineffectiveness. However, a free market system with its cornerstone of private ownership is not expected to replace the existing regime at a stroke. It is insisted that the dominant public ownership of production means and roles of the state in economic management be maintained. The colossal public sector of production is not dismantled as it was in most Eastern European countries, instead it is restructured. The most striking change has been that governments at various levels are much more development-oriented and committed to economic growth than before. The state is giving up its philosophy of class struggle and playing down the tenet of proletariat dictatorship and gradually letting the market take responsibility in the provision of goods to its citizens. A socialist political state is clearly changing to a socialist developmental state (Oi, 1996). Public opinion has it that popular acceptance of government should be established by its successful management of economic development. There are "developmental coalitions deriving political legitimacy from what can be called the nation's collective aspirations" (Bardhan, 1990:5).

The predominant public sector of production built up over the period 1949–1979 made the state a producer rather than a regulator (Auroi, 1992). Since 1979, the state has been converting itself from an economic producer and socialist welfare provider to an advocate for growth, with progressive reforms that are gradually phasing out socialist welfarism. Building an efficient state is pursued with all effort in order for the state to lead development effectively. The view is held that a vast, developing country like China would be in a disastrous state if national government's capacity is limited to act coherently and effectively in national affairs (Rueschemeyer & Putterman, 1992). For the party-led national government, development policies are imperative for its own existence. To work out a development strategy that stimulates economic growth and to expand central revenue income are thus two essential goals of state government, as all of its policy goals for national development cannot be achieved without sufficient revenues collected from local governments. However, the same rationale applies to local governments. Local governments have their own interest in pursuing local development. Local governments treat enterprises within their administrative jurisdictions as one component of the local corporate whole (Oi, 1995; Solinger, 1992; Wong, 1987) and behave like a state "that coordinates economic enterprises in its territory as if it were a diversified business corporation" (Oi, 1992:101). It is the mutual benefits that result in an economic alliance between local bureaucrats and enterprise managers (Huang, 1990). Central–local conflicts thus arise, reflected in the process of fiscal reforms.

Fiscal Reforms: Redefining Central–Local Relations

A well-functioning fiscal system is essential if market is to replace controls (Agarwala, 1992). The current loose fiscal system is the best testimony for a transitional state of the economy where unsettled fiscal relations underlie the central–local conflicts: the national government needs adequate revenues to fulfill its roles in the national affairs whereas local governments require sufficient finance to fund infrastructural projects for local development.

Before 1980, almost all taxes and profits were remitted to the central treasury and then transferred back to local governments according to expenditures planned and approved by the state. Control of revenue resources was one of the very essential components of the centrally controlled planning system (Huang, 1996). Changing fiscal contracts between the central and local governments has been tried and driven by decentralization since 1980. The kernel of the trial is to give enough incentives to localities. The basic framework for a new fiscal system is to classify three types of taxes: central fixed revenues, local fixed revenues, and shared revenues. Central fixed revenues accrue to the central coffers and consist mainly of profits and taxes from the centrally supervised enterprises. Local fixed revenues, derived from the taxes submitted by locally managed enterprises, go to local governments.[2] Local governments are also allowed to claim revenues from investments made locally. Shared revenues, the main source of government income, are divided between the central and local governments following some formulas that vary across regions and periods (Wong, Heady & Woo, 1995). The formula setting has been bargain-plagued, reflective of the scope of central–local conflicts.[3]

Local governments are given some autonomy in managing their economies by decentralized fiscal control. However, in the process, the interests of competitive localities have deviated from the interests of the state. A locality has every incentive to resist pressure and extortion for tax transfer to the center. According to the World Bank (1990:76), tax slippage was pervasive, as about 70 to 80 percent of enterprises were involved. SOEs were the main offenders of tax evasion, with local government as accomplice. Since the outset of the economic reforms, central-local intergovernmental fiscal relations have undergone rough periodical changes It is a struggle between national unity and local growth, between equality in regional development and efficiency in resource allocation. The foremost objective is to strike a fine balance between market domination and planning coordination, which is believed to allow economic efficiency with social equity and thus stability in the transition of the system. This goal is, however, jeopardized by insufficient fiscal revenues controlled by the state. The state's functions in national development have been perceptibly undermined in the areas of the provision of social goods and adjustment of regional disparities in economic well-being and maintenance of macroeconomic stability (Wang, 1994). According to Huang (1996), the central share of consolidated revenues dropped from 66 percent in 1980 to about 45 percent in 1989. Central revenues, as a proportion of GNP, accounted for about 7 percent in 1990. It is considered rather low in comparison with the level for many developed as well as developing countries. For low-income countries, the norm in the late 1970s was 15 percent. For devel-

Table 4.3
Expansion of Extrabudgetary Funds in the Total Budget

Period	Budgetary Funds as % of Total Budget	Extrabudgetary Funds as % of Total Budget
1952-59	90.3	9.7
1960-69	85.0	15.0
1970-79	77.8	22.2
1980-89	53.8	46.2
1990-91	50.6	49.4

Source: *Caizheng Bu*, 1992.

oped countries, it was 24 percent (World Bank, 1988:46). Each local government has been keen to generate "extrabudgetary" revenues for its own purposes in "entrepreneurial" ways. This leads to retention of greater resources at local levels to the detriment of central finances. The scope of local "extrabudgetary funds," which are mainly used to construct local, government-initiated projects, has expanded as the economic basis of local governments expands (Wang, 1995; White, 1991; Blecher, 1991; see Table 4.3).

In order to eliminate tax slippage, which is often at the expense of the central income, a governmental body representing the central government in collecting taxes has been set up in provinces and municipalities since 1995. Before 1995, a unitary bureau collected taxes before dividing them into central and local revenues. Therein the state has strengthened its position in revenue sharing. *Shenzhen Tax Bureau* was split into two units of *National Tax Bureau* and *Local Tax Bureau*. The former is responsible for collection of central taxes, while the latter remains in charge of collecting shared revenues, of which value-added tax is a main component. Although tax subsidies to induce investment can be offered by local government, its extent is limited by the control power of the central government. The case that the share of stamp duty for stock transactions in the Shenzhen stock market taken by the state changed from 50 percent (before 1997) to 80 percent (since 1997) illustrates that the central government still has power.

The Temporary Regulations on the Transfer of Use Right for State-Owned Land (1990), prepared under the *Land Management Act* (1988), stipulates that after deducting 20 percent from the income of land sales as development expenses, 40 percent of the rest should be submitted to the central treasury. Claiming tight margins and even a possible deficit, as land requisition and development costs have been increasing over the years, local government resorts to various tactics to bargain for retention of a higher percentage of land income. Although the issue comes to be understood, and compromises are made by the center to give rebate on the submitted land revenues, local governments are not impressed by the rebate rate. The rate is not universally the same for all localities. It is circumstantial, depending on the bargaining power of local government. The special economic zones and economic technological development zones in the coast cities reportedly receive rebates ranging from 95 to 99 percent (IFTE/CASS and IPA, 1991). In this context, it becomes understandable why local governments are reluctant to transfer land use right in transparent formats of bidding and auction at market rates. Instead, a concealed, thus controversial, land-use-right transfer through behind-closed-doors negotiation is frequently used. Purchasers of land use right pay land rentals at a discount—a reduction of government revenues at the state's expense but able to be recouped by local government's predatory practices. Therefore, land rentals in-kind can be retained for the benefit of a locality.

Advent of Localism

Decentralization has led to the re-emergence of localism in Chinese national politics, that is, competition instead of cooperation among localities. Due to historical reasons, economic development in China was biased toward the coastal areas prior to 1949. The vast hinterland was thus left underdeveloped. During the period 1949–1978, the new socialist government implemented the policy of equality development in regions. New industrial projects were evenly distributed throughout the country in order to diminish existing regional disparities in economic welfare. After three decades of effort, regional economic disparities were reduced, with coastal regions sustaining a modest decline and interior regions having a strong increase in the share of industrial production. However, it had always been debatable to pursue the strategy of equal development with scarce capital evenly invested across regions without consideration of investment performance. Shanghai, during the period 1949–1980, had to remit more than 86 percent of its revenues to the center, with few funds left to finance investment in much needed urban infrastructure (Lin, 1994). The new economic policy has, nevertheless, considerably changed the strategy by shifting the focus from countrywide equality development to economic productivity. Economic efficiency is given priority over social equity, and regional equality is replaced by regional competition. Regional and local factors are given more weight in the decision making of resource mobilization than before. As a result, the coastal regions are brought back into the limelight of investment attention.

Tremendous efforts have been made to transform a highly centralized economy to a partially decentralized system. In spite of the reforms being guided by a framework of gradualism and experimentation, market forces have been playing a role in strengthening some localities' economic capacity due to their existing socioeconomic and geographic advantages. The coastal regions have received more resources in their urban sectors than the inland provinces, where the economic reform policies have not entailed much market-driven investment. Almost all foreign investment-led developments concentrate on the cities along the east coast. Gaps between regions in their economic well-being, narrowed by the policy of equality in regional development under the previous regime, are enlarged again by the market-driven economic reforms (Lakshmanan & Hua, 1987). In terms of output per capita, the ratio of the richest region (Shanghai) to the poorest one (Guizhou) was 8.6 in 1992, and it went up to 11.3 in 1993 (GTJ, 1994, 1995).

Conflicts arose when the central government saw its role undermined by a decline in its revenue income and a consequent increase in government budget deficit, an undesirable by-product of decentralization. Local development and local interests have replaced the national goals with the failure of central planning. Decentralization has delivered more incentives for local growth. In the late 1980s and early 1990s, ample evidence showed that local governments pushed the central government to the limit in granting special policies to localities for offering preferential measures to attract foreign investment (Nolan, 1995; Reich, 1991). Economic transition and inward investment in the background of globalization have redefined localities' position in the process of restructuring the national economy. Localism is instrumentally used as a political strategy to circumvent outmoded structures of central bureaucracies in order for localities to emerge as winners of the regional competition (Goetz & Clarke, 1993).

The primary goal for local governments is thus to mobilize as much revenue as possible in order to finance local development. According to H. Wang (1994:95), local officials have become highly motivated to maximize local revenues, also due to their personal interests. China's local governments have, to a certain extent, become an economic interest group with their own policy preferences. However, in spite of the considerable capacity that Chinese local officials have to pursue their economic goals, their political career advancement is much dependent on discretion of the central authorities. Reshuffling of provincial officials does occur to arrest burgeoning localism, which puts the national economy in danger of becoming geographically polarized. For a long time since its opening to foreign investment, the now prosperous southern province of Guangdong resisted top-down appointment from Beijing and insisted on promoting local cadres. A major political reshuffling of the provincial government took place recently as central government's effort to strengthen its control of the country's richest, but most unruly, province (*Straits Times*, 3 September 1997; 8 January 1998).

GRADUALISM: A PROGRAM TO NURTURE LOCAL ENTERPRISES AND PROPERTY DEVELOPERS

One of the greatest changes brought about by the economic reforms is the changing attitude of local governments toward their jurisdictions. Local governments have assumed the role of a development state seeking an active involvement in the management of the local economy. Native resources are keenly mobilized, and indigenous industries are engaged as main driving forces to expedite local development. Flourishing township-village enterprises in the 1980s were a testimony of bottom-up local development initiatives. Localism has intensified regional competition for resources and markets. Fierce regional competition occasionally evolved to become ugly local protectionism when local government protected local enterprises to pursue local interests and thus to maintain and expand local revenue bases. Strong evidence suggested that "local authorities established, and provided finance for a variety of schemes which promoted the sales of local products" (Goodman, 1994:7). The 1980s "wool war" revealed how far regional conflicts had gone, aggravated by the competitive local interests.[4]

Since the implementation of the new opening-up policy to a wider scope in the latter 1980s, more localities have had access to another avenue for development of their local economies. After well-publicized Guangdong's extraordinary growth, which was principally driven by the inward Hong Kong capital in the 1980s, seeking foreign investment became a fashionable local development strategy. In the belief that foreign capital is searching for sites of low production costs, localities turn the competition for inward investment into a competition for giving more subsidies to lure foreign capital by lowering production costs even below the market clearing level. Cities become rivals in offering tax exemption and reduction as well as land-related preferential treatment in order to attract foreign investment. The opinion that lower production costs lead to more overseas investment prevails. Enrichment of local coffers impoverished by the previous central control of revenues in the name of national interests is directly pegged at the expansion of local economies.

In the early days of the SSEZ, deficient financial capacity of the city government disabled its initiation of large-scale urban land development and cast doubts on the expectation of Shenzhen's becoming a dynamic laboratory testing market mechanisms and serving as the medium between Hong Kong and mainland China, an interface between a capitalist system and a socialist domain. As Shenzhen develops from scratch, a local manufacturing industry has to be nurtured to become an engine to drive the city toward modernity, and a local property industry has to be founded to initiate urban construction and property development to provide enterprises and residents with premises under a new set of market conditions.

Besides a major incentive—15 percent instead of 55 percent enterprise income tax elsewhere for inward as well as for domestic firms—subsidized land supply was added to the package of luring inward capital. Since the informal property commercialization and marketization in the early 1980s, potential value of land and buildings was widely perceived and anticipated to appreciate in time in the background of long-time, pent-up demand for premises. This notion was reinforced by an envisaged tendency of urban land stock toward relative scarcity due to looming rural-urban migrations in great magnitude. It was proven later that the subsidized provision of land is a significant factor in nurturing enterprises. Not only does it reduce initial cost for production, but it awards windfall gains in asset values to enterprises when the property market is established and market demand booms.

Before 1988, when the new legislation abolished the free use of urban land, much land had already been allocated to SOEs without pecuniary payment for occupation. Many land tenants subsequently materialized the potential value of land by forming joint ventures where land was contributed as capital assets. *China Merchant's Steam Navigation* (CMSN), a large Chinese SOE created by an emperor in the Qing dynasty and since then operating in Hong Kong (Hou, 1965), went to Shenzhen in 1979 to develop the *Shekou Industrial Zone*. One of its divisions specializing in land development undertook land leveling of 10 square kilometers with an alleged amount of U.S.$100 million invested in infrastructure, raised from international capital markets (Oborne, 1986:125). Land was transferred free of charge in the first instance. When land development was completed by CMSN, in addition to its own use, some surplus land was subleased to other users at market rates. As the first lessee, CMSN paid only nominal land use fee to the municipal government. It benefited considerably from subsequent property booms because of a large land bank given only at the cost of equipping land with basic infrastructure. Having a large land bank, CMSN could diversify into property development. By March 1984, CMSN had signed 11 contracts with partners for joint-venture property development (Oborne, 1986:123). The success of CMSN in developing a benchmark industrial new town of *Shekou* cannot be detached from its benefits derived from the preferential land provision. CMSN is not an exception. Another large, urban development project with government blessing in the land policy is *Huajiaocheng*, which is a mini-new town of 4.8 square kilometers developed by *Huaqiaocheng Development Corporation* (HDC)—an SOE set up by *China Travel Service (HK)*, another SOE registered in Hong Kong—since 1985. The site was appropriated by the city government and transferred to HDC free in the first instance, though informal agreements on settlement of land rentals between the two parties at later stages might exist. The built-up area of 2.6 square kilometers had been completed with a residential population of 30,000 and 94 enterprises by 1997. From 1986 to 1995, *Huaqiaocheng* submitted ¥950 million taxes to the city government, standing for 2.9 percent of the total fiscal income to the municipal government in the period (SQZGLXB, 1997). Development profits derived from the free land factor obviously helped CMSN and HDC expand and build *Shekou* and *Huaqiaocheng*. Other similar projects include *Nanshan Chiwan Petroleum Logistic Base* of 38 square kilometers (1983), *Wenjindu Industrial Zone* of 6 square kilometers (1983), and *Chegongmiao Industrial Zone* (1987).

Those less profitable and capital-lacking SOEs had to hold their land until the second property boom in the early 1990s, when they could finally capitalize benefits from the land subsidies. Because few land plots were put on sale in the open land market, many newly founded developers, without land reserve at hand but driven by prospective high-profit margins from commodity property development, approached vacant landholders to explore possibilities of joint development. Most of these landholders were SOEs settled in Shenzhen before 1988. Joint development was proposed where developers bore all development costs, and landholders contributed sites. Upon completion, land contributors could claim up to 70 percent of units. The built premise, be it office or housing, was virtually obtained as a gift at the expense of the state, which lost its land revenues. A large land bank held by users or land hoarding accumulated over years to account for one-third of the total land allocated by 1988 has revealed the magnitude of land subsidies passed to SOEs.

Benefiting greatly from the land policy, *Shenzhen Tequ Fazhan Gongsi* (STFG) (SSEZ Development Corporation) has been transformed from a company with only six employees and an asset of four bicycles to a transnational corporation with 6,500 staff and ¥4.2 billion assets in 1994 (SFNB, 1994). During the first property boom in the early 1980s, its development of an area of 80 hectares in the downtown Luohu district earned the company handsome profits. For a three-year period of project development, a gross income of ¥1,260 million from land rentals was reportedly received after incurring development costs of ¥80 million (Zhu, 1996). Growing financial capacities because of huge margins in land development helped STFG expand and up to 1990 its property development had amounted to 5.3 percent of the total floor space of commodity properties in Shenzhen.

In 1984, the *State Economic Commission* and *Ministry of Urban and Rural Construction and Environmental Protection*, in the document *Temporary Measures for Urban Construction and Comprehensive Development Companies*, gave the green light for state-owned development companies to become independent business entities. Thereafter, real estate developers formally registered, though dominated by SOEs, and began to participate in urban development and redevelopment. According to IFTE/CASS and IPA (1991), the rise of property developers has contributed significantly to the profound changes in the landscape of Chinese cities, notably, those cities in the coast region such as Shanghai, Beijing, Xiamen, Guang-zhou, and Shenzhen. Because of the policy control that required that for-eign investment should be made in "productive" sectors—and real estate was not considered "productive"—land and property development mar-kets were not fully open to overseas developers. In order to have a reliable property industry that had the capacity to conduct land and property de-velopment projects to meet the needs of clients in market and also be committed to locality, SOEs in the construction sector were recommended in the first place to initiate a new market-oriented property development industry. The Shenzhen municipal government in 1983 granted full status of developer to eight SOEs for undertaking enterprising activities in land and property construction. A new generation of local developers was thus nurtured to become major players in the arena of urban physical devel-opment, facilitated by the formation of a property market according to market fundamentals of demand and supply. These state-owned devel-opers were given a large quantity of green land free of charge initially, though the Shenzhen government, as a de jure landowner, reserved the right to collect land rentals as soon as developers could make a profit from their commercial undertakings. However, in-kind payments were pre-ferred, such as provision of off-site infrastructure and facilities that oth-erwise were government responsibilities. Industrial estates such as *Shangbu Industrial Zone* and *Liantang Industrial Zone* were built in such a manner. Having held a large land bank that became one of the most valuable commodities in the late 1980s and early 1990s, when the property market was booming and property prices soaring, these developers were in a position to capitalize huge development profits.

Over years, the local revenue base has been established and expanded. In 1979, only ¥17.2 million was collected in local coffers. Fiscal income soared to ¥8.8 billion in 1995 (see Table 4.4). Over a period of 16 years, fiscal revenues of the Shenzhen government increased 510 times. Enter-prises have become a main contributor of taxes and profits. SOEs' profit remittance accounted for 4.7 percent of the city government's fiscal income in 1979. Since 1984, the SOE reforms have changed profit remittance to tax payment. Revenue submission by SOEs rose to 7.9 percent in 1984. The proportion contributed by SOEs further increased to 14.9 percent in 1995 (SZTJ, 1996).

GRADUALISM: A PLAN TO FOSTER A LOCAL GOVERNMENT–ENTERPRISE COALITION

Local governments have to be pro-enterprise in formulating local de-velopment strategies for the interest of localities because of intensive re-gional competition. On the one hand, the incremental institutional change prevents any significant alteration in the state ownership of production

Table 4.4
Shenzhen Budgetary Fiscal Revenue

Year	Total Budgetary Fiscal Income (Million ¥)	Income Taxes and Profit Remittance by State-Owned Enterprises (Million ¥)
1979	17.2	0.8
1980	30.4	0.8
1981	87.8	2.6
1982	91.6	6.9
1983	156.1	18.8
1984	294.4	23.4
1985	628.9	25.5
1986	741.6	52.4
1987	875.2	39.6
1988	1465.2	60.8
1989	2286.7	39.0
1990	2170.4	32.7
1991	2732.9	45.3
1992	4296.0	66.0
1993	6725.1	68.3
1994	7439.9	1315.0
1995	8801.7	1315.2

Note: The data of 1994 and 1995 are not comparable with those of previous years as the statistical formats have been changed since 1994 owing to the fiscal reforms.
Source: SZTJ, 1996.

means. SOEs are maintained as a key player in the local economic structure for a majority of Chinese cities. On the other hand, many socialist characteristics remain attached to SOEs, though they are undergoing transformation toward enterprises operational in market conditions. SOEs were and still are held responsible for the provision of social benefits and welfare to employees and their families. This peculiar transitional situation and SOEs' still significant roles in the local economy leave local governments few options but to make all efforts to keep SOEs alive and make them robust. A coalition between local governments and local industries is thus formed. Local administration endeavors to create a favorable business climate for the indigenous as well as inward investments to prosper. It is possible only when local autonomy is granted by the drive of decentralization.

The SOE reforms are crucial to the success of transition to a modern socialist market economy, because SOEs predominate in the economic structure. Since 1978, the central government has undertaken several steps to reform economic decision making and to improve economic efficiency by separating management from state ownership of enterprises. The chief objectives for the reforms are to install economic responsibility and financial accountability into SOEs and to subject SOEs to hard budget constraints. Due to the gradualist fashion of economic reforms, local governments tend to comply with SOEs' demand for a cushion against the harsh discipline of the market forces. Cheap and even free land is considered one of the protections local governments could offer at their discretion and within their jurisdiction. The move also takes into consideration the fact that SOEs have heavy social responsibilities to carry that otherwise would be government liabilities. Subsidized land supply is deemed a compensation for the social duties SOEs still bear.

Local autonomy allows local governments to exercise tax exemptions and reductions in order to stimulate local economies. Nevertheless, due to rampant localism, it is observed that local tax exemptions and reductions are often given at the expense of the central tax income in the shared revenue (Wong, Heady & Woo, 1995). Some degree of "collusion" between municipal governments and enterprise managers is found when under the central government's fiscal pressure (Broadman, 1995). On the one hand, enterprises receive benefits in the form of tax reductions and discounted land rentals. On the other hand, these gains can, to certain extent, be recouped by local government. Since the 1980s, imposing various ad hoc local fees on enterprises and extending governmental obligations to enterprises such as providing public goods or urban amenities in the domain of public spaces have been a common practice. Those local fees are informal and uninstitutionalized local taxes. According to a survey conducted in the mid-1980s, about 5 percent of enterprise profits were appropriated as fees by local authorities (Tseng et al., 1994). Developers receive the benefit of subsidized land offers and then are subject to fee collections imposed by various local authorities. Over years, fee collection also caught up with property booms to expand its coverage. Local authorities have clearly demonstrated their capability to take part in the distribution of gains from property development. These fees imposed on real estate development reportedly add up to as many as 85 categories and account for 25–30 percent of total development costs, covering items such as greenery maintenance, access road connection, substation installation, and contribution to education funds in the case of Guangzhou, the capital city of Guangdong. Property investment is also infringed upon where local taxes and fees stand at 32–37 percent of rental income (Xu, 1996). In Shenzhen, sundry fees can cost developers who acquired land at market prices 5 percent in development budget (Gong, 1995).

Transfer of land use right at market rates has not been used by most local governments as a norm. Instead, the traditional administrative transfer process is resumed and developers are asked to pay rental in-kind, that is, building infrastructure or social projects and so on. It is reported that over the past few years, Guangzhou has been practicing this kind of transaction for conveyance of land parcels. Developers are responsible not only for the costs of land acquisition and relocation of, and compensation for, existing tenants, infrastructure, and accessory facilities that are to be built within the development area but also for some infrastructure projects and public utilities such as roads, parks, schools, post offices, and local police stations near the development site. These projects are carried out as a payment to the local government for using land without paid transfer of land use right (IFTE/CASS & IPA, 1992). Thus, land income that is supposed to accrue to the central government is retained in the form of local built environment.

As such, new relations are developed under the framework of gradual transformations between local governments and enterprises within the jurisdiction. This spontaneous and informal institutional change aims at enriching local interests. A local government–enterprise coalition is established to benefit both parties, whereas interests of the central state are compromised. The tentative and thus indecisive change in the central–local intergovernmental fiscal relations has left ample room for bargaining within which the coalition, an informal institutional change, is formed with an absence of formal institutional endorsement. Local developers grow and expand with the facilitation of local government, and then in due time the beneficiary companies pay back to the city in a form of commitment to the projects with high risk and low profit but great significance to the government, such as high-tech industrial parks. Developers are sometimes persuaded to take unprofitable social projects that are useful for the community. For instance, *Chengjian Group* spent ¥8 million to renovate *Binghe* residential estate in order to give the city a face-lift because of its strategic location, but without commercial profits. Profitable, state-owned developers are occasionally cajoled to sponsor social projects with national significance such as donations to poor provinces or to sponsor some projects to alleviate poverty on behalf of municipal governments.

GRADUALISM: AN INSTRUMENT OF ACTIVE INTERVENTION IN LOCAL GOVERNMENT

Under the old, centrally controlled system, the economic and political interests of local governments were suppressed by the central government power of revenue appropriation and expenditure setting (Tseng et al. 1994). Local governments were hardly reckoned as politically independent entities. Local government roles are now redefined by a new political structure. An accountable local government seems to appear to serve the locality. However, mayors cannot be fully responsible to municipal citizens due to an undemocratic political structure where the top officials in all levels of government below the central state are appointed and assessed by the bodies at upper levels. It is so not only because of political reforms lagging behind the economic transformation but also as a measure attempting to curb ever-growing localism. Municipal governments are only partially responsible to the local constituency because mayors' mandate is given by the upper-level governments rather than by the local people. This governance system will continue unless political reforms are called upon.

On the one hand, the officials employed in the development state have to be development-minded. They need to legitimate their positions by their performance in office and pave the way for the progress of their political careers. On the other hand, their accomplishments are assessed by the government bodies at upper levels who are not local residents living in the local constituency. Visible physical accomplishments look more convincing to non-residents than invisible, but real, benefits to residents. Landmark-style projects can obviously serve as conspicuous achievements affiliated with the local leaders in charge. During Shanghai's renaissance in the 1980s, the adopted form of grand bridges over the Huangpu River instead of tunnels underneath by the mayor clearly indicates that the former is more visible and impressive, despite more expensive, than the latter. Frequent reshuffling of mayors in important localities has caused a sense of anxiety among local chiefs to deliver what can appeal to supervisory authorities. Reshuffling has become more frequent than before due to the reconfiguration of the central leadership and consequent political alliances. Local chief officials now typically have a short tenure. The first two mayors of Shenzhen, Liang Xiang (1981–1985) and Li Hao (1985–1991), each held the position for five to six years in the 1980s. However, after ten years of making Shenzhen a heavyweight, important city in the 1990s, change of local leadership turned out to be more frequent than in the 1980s, when the city was not so significant in its economic strength. The third and fourth mayors, Zeng Liangyu (1991–1993) and Li Youwei (1993–1995), each served two years in office. The current mayor, Li Zhibing, commenced his term in 1995. There is an urgency for mayors to set up a short-term agenda to accomplish development schemes. Within the term of mayorship, one needs to convince one's superiors for the second term or promotion. Quantitative, instead of qualitative, urban changes are pursued as a result.

The notion that market mechanisms should play a role in the management of urban development has been well accepted by local government. But the nature of the development state determines that government plans cannot be totally discarded in favor of market actions. The growth-oriented local governments have to find an instrument to transmit government plans to market actions. The policy of subsidized land provision seems an effective instrument to guide market agents in implementation of the local government's or, more precisely, the mayor's plans. Given the situation that many local governments are weak financially, granting subsidies or waiving taxes has become the only means by which the authorities could impact on urban development. The land factor has thus been utilized by mayors to the full extent to fulfill their visions under the auspices of the gradualist urban land reforms.

The road project of Binhai Avenue, one of the city's east-west thoroughfares, was proposed for construction without any hesitation, clearly for its visual impact rather than utilitarian function, as east-west transportation was no more a problem than north-south traffic flows. While affordable housing, for example, is a more urgent and a tougher issue for the government to tackle, the modernist expression of its seafront section and the speediness of its construction prompted the mayor to give the Binhai Avenue project priority over others. Its construction was partly financed by proceeds from sales of land plots along this expressway. Municipal leaders are keen to maximize the impact of limited resources on the city profile by investment in conspicuous projects at strategic locations. The newly built, modernist *Diwang Commercial Center* in Luohu frequently appearing on governmental brochures as a symbol for 1990s Shenzhen evidently reveals the importance of the image of buildings for the municipality.

Due to remarkable expansion of Shenzhen after its designation as a special economic zone, Luohu, the city center for the defunct Baoan County and a major retail cluster for the new SSEZ, was reaching its limits of capacity. It has been a dream for consecutive city governments to build a new city center that can reflect a new image of the city. The new city center is expected to become a landmark symbolizing the success of special economic zones and accomplishments of the SSEZ municipal government. Futian has been identified and planned as the future new downtown since 1986, when rich Hong Kong businessmen were wooed personally by the city leaders to participate in this scheme. *Hopewell China Development Corporation* was approached about its development. The consequent negotiations reportedly progressed to such an extent that 30 square kilometers of land would be appropriated from the farmers and contributed to the proposed joint development as a share by the government, and *Hopewell* would invest HK$2 billion to land development. Thereafter, the developed land would be leased to market for further property development. Although the scheme was dropped before it reached the final stage, the enthusiasm and determination of the city government were unambiguously demonstrated.

In 1996, this grand project was again put on the city government's agenda. An international competition was held in August 1996 for the new city center design. Four architectural design firms from France, Hong Kong, Singapore, and the United States were invited to participate in the competition. Following the selection of final plans, the government declared four incentives to promote the new downtown development. All of them are land- or property-related. First, developers could enjoy a 30 percent discount in prices for land acquisition. Second, local and foreign housing markets would be unified in the new downtown so that price differences between two markets would be eliminated in favor of local housing developers. Third, no capital gain tax would be imposed on the first transaction of new properties. Fourth, special property mortgages would be arranged and offered to property purchasers by domestic finance institutions (*Zhongwai Fangdichan Daobao*, No. 17, 1996). Although the property market was not buoyant at the moment, and oversupply of buildings was looming, the city government remained determined to push for the new city center development. Eighty-five out of 160 hectares of developable land have been leased at negotiated and thus low prices to six big Hong Kong developers of repute.

To develop a manufacturing industry of high technological and capital intensity has been one of the initial objectives of top priority to any mayor of the Shenzhen municipality. It has not been successful for the primary reason that Hong Kong, the chief source of inward investment, is not an economy of high-tech industries. High costs of land and labor have made Hong Kong's manufacturing uncompetitive. Access to Shenzhen and other places in Guangdong with ample land and labor has facilitated the economic restructuring of Hong Kong, which can transfer its manufacturing to the mainland. Inward industrial capital is obviously beneficial to Shenzhen with creation of jobs and access to the international market through expatriate Hong Kong managers. In the 1990s, however, Shenzhen is becoming less competitive than other localities in the Pearl Delta region, as the latter can offer cheaper land and labor. Industries are observed moving out of Shenzhen to destinations of lower costs. Shenzhen is forced to climb one rung higher in order to stay relevant.

Indigenous tech-entrepreneurs from universities and research institutes in inland provinces are targeted and invited to Shenzhen to take part in the adventure. Science and Technologies Park (1.02 square kilometer) is proposed to spearhead the development of high-technological industries. Subsidies in premises are to be provided, because high land and property costs already constitute a prohibitive constraint to proprietors' potential investment schemes with high initial capital cost and long-term risks. A developer was appointed to conduct the development of industrial land as well as properties and expected to provide factories at affordable prices to tenants. Its financial feasibility is ascertained by government offerings of green land at a discount and of permission to develop commodity housing for the market of foreigners. The development market for foreigners' housing has been monopolized by a few state-owned developers. The controlled supply vis-à-vis buoyant demand has pushed up housing prices and thus profits. This linkage—profitable housing development compensating for unprofitable provision of industrial properties—shows that land resources are being effectively mobilized to implement the government policy of industrial development.

Daizi kaifa is a special land development scheme with unique financial deals between land developers and the local government. Under this scheme, land developers are invited to carry out land development to make sites ready for further building construction without payment in advance or in arrears. Instead, they are paid in-kind, that is, the use right of a proportion of land when the development is completed. It is believed to evade the central control of monetary supply, which is meant to curb excessive local capital investment and constrains the local coffers. For the land developers, land provision can be secured by participating in the scheme, as can the property development license, which has been strictly controlled in Shenzhen since the 1992/1993 property boom. As such, they can carry out speculative property development in the future. Local government likes to have as much land as possible developed and thus ready to capture any development opportunity that arises. Rapid conversion of green land to developed land, or expeditious urbanization, can thus be claimed as credits to the incumbent mayor. Risks are, however, effectively transferred from the governments to the land developers. The government's hasty action is questionable to the interest of the local community. The tendency of property oversupply would worsen, and land values would be undermined as land-use-right transfers in such circumstance are most likely underpriced. Property oversupply would destabilize the local property market and thus the city's long-term growth. It serves only the city government's short-term interests for fast growth. Discounted sale of land in order to speed up urbanization is shortsighted and to the detriment of the local community.

NOTES

1. "Planning gain" is professional jargon that refers to various innovative charges or benefits provided by the applicants pursuing planning permission by the local planners in Britain in the handling of development applications. As Simpon (1984:7) puts it: "[p]lanning gain is the practice by which local authorities persuade developers to carry out work or provide amenities not required for their own schemes." Planning gains can be realized only in the circumstance of high development pressure, where private developers are willing to provide a less remunerative, but socially desirable, use as part of a scheme, such as land donated for road improvements, provision of infrastructure, environment works, and inclusion of affordable residential units in a commercial project (Byrne, 1989).

2. State-owned enterprises in China are categorized in two groups: central enterprises (*zhongyang qiye*) and local enterprises (*difang qiye*). For central enterprises, one of the state ministries or departments assumes administrative supervision and takes responsibility for the organization of finance and management, whereas the same rests with local authorities for local enterprises.

3. The task of defining a sharing formula has proven difficult.

For the 1980–84 period, revenues from the shared taxes were allocated to provide 80 percent to the centre and the remaining 20 percent to local governments. In 1985 the sharing system was redesigned to address the problem of surplus and deficit provinces. . . . Although the exact formulas differed, the basic principle was to agree on a contract between centre and provinces for sharing tax revenues, with a view to giving maximum incentives to provinces for revenue collection by allowing them to retain a relatively high share of marginal revenues beyond the levels agreed. (Agarwala, 1992: x)

Another problem is that contracts are often fixed in nominal amounts. Even growth rates in tax revenues are allowed for; these rates are moderate and generally fixed in nominal terms. Thus, the revenue-sharing formula creates an inherent tendency for revenue that goes to the center to decline relative to local revenue and to GDP.

4. In order to promote local growth, local governments make every effort to invest in industries that process and add value to local raw materials, even to the extent of blocking commodity transactions in the free market. The "wool war" erupted as the result of ugly local protection in the 1980s. The governments of main wool-producing areas (Gansu, Qinghai, Xinjiang, and Inner Mongolia) were anxious to expand their own wool-processing industries as a means of increasing their income. Most of the local wool production would have to be retained in order to satisfy local processing capacity, regardless of the low production efficiency at the locality. Thus, the flow of local raw materials would have to be restricted to other regions, although manufacturers in other regions could offer high prices to purchase due to their higher production efficiency. The result was the emergence of a succession of commodity wars over such things as wool, silk, and cotton whereby local government, production units, and merchants competed for supplies (Watson & Findlay, 1992).

Chapter 5

Formation of a Local Property Development Industry

The pace and scale of Shenzhen urban development have been unprecedented in China's urban history. Much of the credit has to be attributed to the nascent local property industry, which itself is the product of the economic reforms. The two factors—property commodification and marketization as well as state-owned enterprise reforms—have germinated a local property industry with facilitation of inward foreign capital, in the context of the country in transition from a static and rigid planning system to a dynamic, market-oriented economy. Nevertheless, the gradualist economic reforms and piecemeal, state-owned enterprise transformation complicate the evolution of a fledgling property industry that has developed its unique characteristics in the transition between plan and market.

PROPERTY MARKETIZATION: AN INCUBATOR FOR A NEW PROPERTY DEVELOPMENT INDUSTRY

A very important precondition for the formation of a new, market-oriented property industry is the revival of commodification and marketization of land and properties. The initial goal of attracting foreign capital and manufacturing operations into Shenzhen pushed the municipal authority into changing to marketization instead of adhering to the extant socialist planning in the management of the economy. Investment from overseas, mainly Hong Kong, was capital from free markets. Lacking an institutional framework for the economic reforms, the Shenzhen government was forced to be pragmatic. New situations of foreign investment and consequent use of land and premises led the Shenzhen government to the frontier of change in the land use system to accommodate new users.

The market economy requires that land and premises be commodities circulated in the market. The subsequent move was reckoned as a bold, but necessary, action in the reform movements toward a socialist market system, when the Marxist ideology regarding land as public assets was still considered an official doctrine. This fundamental change of land commercialization was later proven crucial in setting urban China in motion toward a new era of urban development. Most Chinese cities suffered a syndrome of underinvestment in the urban built environment, due to the ill-prepared plans that gravely ignored the connection between urban performance and quality of infrastructure. It was the first time since 1949 in urban China that market forces played a role in urban development, albeit partially. Instead of being free goods assigned by government previously, prices of premises as commodities emerged and began to be adjustable in the emerging market.

In the capitalist market system, city government is chiefly responsible for the provision of urban infrastructure and social projects, while the private property industry decides development of individual buildings within a statutory framework, whereas the development of socialist cities was entirely a matter of the state, because the state owned all the production means. When China was under the socialist, centrally-controlled system with predominant state ownership prior to 1980, no property industry and formal property markets existed in Chinese cities. All land and property development was carried out by either governments on behalf of users or occupants themselves for their own use. There was no profession of real estate developers, and construction was carried out by state-owned construction companies at the command of government.

The grand economic reforms since 1979 have been transforming the whole society toward market orientation along with separation of state ownership and user leasehold of production means. Emergence of private industries, foreign-local joint ventures, and non-state-owned enterprises is a significant change in the China's economy in transition (Zhu, 1996). As a result, a quasi market is created, and demand becomes market-driven. When the SSEZ was officially inaugurated in 1979, an area of 327.5 square kilometers was appropriated for the newly established SSEZ government as territory. The whole territory consisted of green land used for agricultural farming, except for a central area named Luo Hu, functioning as a marketplace for the region. Infrastructure construction to equip land for urban use was the first compelling task for the new government, which was handicapped by inadequate finance. What was granted to the SSEZ authority was the right to develop market mechanisms and to explore external resources. Economic decentralization and special policies are instrumental for Shenzhen to nurture a market environment where market-guided enterprises can operate.

The opening up of Shenzhen as a special economic zone caused a sen-

Table 5.1
Overseas Investment (OI) in Shenzhen

Year	Committed Investment (Million US$)	Actual Investment (Million US$)	OI Related Jobs Created	Percentage in Total Employment
1979	29.8	15.4		
1980	271.2	32.6		
1981	863.6	112.8		
1982	180.3	73.8		
1983	334.5	143.9		
1984	645.6	230.1		
1985	1026.5	329.3	25000	11.0
1986	513.6	489.3	33300	12.9
1987	648.9	404.5	64700	20.0
1988	487.4	444.3	85400	20.5
1989	489.0	458.1	133700	25.1
1990	693.4	518.6	148100	26.7
1991	1151.6	579.9	188900	29.1
1992	2517.7	715.4	222300	31.3
1993	4977.4	1432.2	225600	28.9
1994	2986.5	1729.6	266600	32.4
1995	3596.5	1735.5	307400	34.6
1996	1680.0	2422.4		
total	23093.7	11867.6		

Source: SZTJ, 1986–1997.

sation in the world. The potential of a huge domestic market and low labor cost constituted a great pull factor to draw inward investment from overseas (see Table 5.1). In 1980, Shenzhen had an economy of ¥270 million in GDP, providing 26,500 jobs. By the end of 1990, the economy expanded substantially to ¥23.1 billion in GDP with employment of 405,100 workers (SZTJ, 1992). Most of the favorable policies granted to foreign investment are also applied to inward domestic investment and make Shenzhen equally attractive to domestic enterprises. SOEs elsewhere were subject to an enterprise income tax at 55 percent, while that rate was only 15 percent in Shenzhen. It helped to draw a large number of SOEs from inland provinces to settle in the SSEZ, facilitated by the ongoing SOE reforms. By the end of 1987, 2,658 enterprises (318 of them engaged in real estate development) had come to Shenzhen to conduct their production from other provinces, with pledged investment of ¥6 billion and actual investment of ¥1.7 billion (see Table 5.2). These inward domestic enterprises contributed 70 percent to total industrial output in 1987 (Liu, 1988). By the end of 1989, the number of domestic enterprises increased to 3,900, coming from 28 provinces. A total investment of ¥9.5 billion had been pledged, and 3.6 billion actually materialized (Park, 1997: 109). These investments were obviously translated into substantial demand for land and buildings. Many premises were needed to accommodate production, the workforce, and workers' families. Over years, the new prop-

Table 5.2
Total Investment by Inward Domestic Enterprises in Shenzhen

Year	1979	1980	1981	1982	1983	1984	1985	1986	1987
Actual Investment (¥ million)	12.2	13.2	27.3	77.0	108.1	158.0	560.6	493.8	250.5

Source: Liu, 1988: 237.

Table 5.3
Shenzhen Urban Physical Development

Period	79 - 82	83 - 86	87 - 90	91 - 94	total (79-94)
Floorarea Constructed (Million sq m)	1.95	13.04	15.63	21.90	52.52
Capital Investment into Built Environment (¥ Million)	967.8	7,116.8	14,934.3	55,482.0	78,610.7

Sources: SFNB, 1995: 179; SZTJ, 1996.

erty industry seemed responsive to the ever-increasing demand from users as well as from investors (see Table 5.3).

BACKGROUND: STATE-OWNED ENTERPRISE REFORMS

The reforms of SOEs in their operation and ownership, intended to substitute a market-oriented system for the mandatory planning one, are crucial to the success of economic modernization, because SOEs dominate the Chinese economic structure and control essential industrial sectors. Since 1978, the central government has undertaken several steps to change the business decision-making process and to improve economic efficiency by separating management from the state ownership of enterprises. The objectives of the SOE reforms are to instill economic responsibility and financial accountability in SOEs and to put SOEs under hard budget constraints.

In the traditional, centrally planned economy, the state as the owner of its enterprises extracted almost all surplus from firms. Since the government controlled most surplus, enterprises had to be assigned funds for purchasing the supplies allocated to them under the central plan. When the reform programs were initially unfolded, giving SOEs greater autonomy and more incentives for production was first attempted. Market elements, though modest in scale, were introduced to the operation of SOEs in order to stimulate production. Profit retention was tried so as to establish a link between economic benefits and enterprise performance. Under the scheme, SOEs were allowed to have freedom of manufacturing products demanded by the market and to retain a portion of profits (3 percent in 1979) in excess of required delivery upon the successful accomplishment of state-set plans (Su & Zhao, 1997). Retained profits could assist enterprises to expand production needed by the market and to improve workers' welfare. In the experiment in Sichuan Province, for example, 65 percent of the extra profit was collected by the state, 28 percent was retained by enterprises and 7 percent was paid to workers as a bonus (Aram & Wang, 1991).

However, the profit target setting involved intensive bargaining between supervisory authorities and enterprises (Lim, Cai & Li, 1996). Every enterprise naturally wanted to maximize the retention of profit, while the state intended to do the same because it needed sufficient revenues to carry out national development projects and to maintain a "soft" budget to assist less profitable and loss-making enterprises. Apparently, the state lost this "tug-of-war," as enterprises were in a better position to bargain for profit retention. With the dwindling of revenue income to the state, profit remittance was replaced with taxes in 1983 in order to guarantee stable revenues to the state. Enterprises were to remit 50 percent of profits to government and to pay an income tax at 55 percent for the other 50 percent of profits. In the following year, corporate income taxation was unified at 55 percent income tax for whole profits plus 15 percent for the Infrastructure Development Fund. Shenzhen, as a special economic zone, had lower taxation on enterprises: 15 percent for income tax, 15 percent for Infrastructure Development Fund (imposed since 1987 and abolished in 1993), and 10 percent for State Budget Adjustment Fund (imposed since 1989 and abolished in 1993).

In 1987, the contract-responsibility system was put on trial for the purpose of separating management and ownership of enterprises. The state remained the owner of enterprises and contracted out SOEs to individual managers at an agreed amount of profit remittance to the state. By 1988, 80 percent of large- and medium-sized SOEs had been under the contract system (Yuan, 1988). "The main purpose of these measures is to reduce government intervention in the running of SOEs and to make them financially independent, and to introduce profit rather than plan fulfillment as the indicator of enterprise performance" (Fan, 1994:138). It strengthened the incentive mechanisms and granted greater autonomy to enterprises. Government grants were replaced by repayable bank loans and interest. SOEs were required to purchase premises according to their needs as well as their affordability. In the process, state budget constraints were somewhat hardened.

In spite of those efforts to transform SOEs, about 34 percent of SOEs within the state budget did not make a profit in 1994, with a total loss of ¥33.42 billion, while only 10 percent of SOEs had a loss in 1985 (Jiang,

1995; Perkins, 1995). Although Shenzhen was a new city without historical burdens, 29.3 percent of SOEs affiliated with the municipal government had a loss. The losses reached ¥414 million in 1995 (Zhu & Yuan, 1997). Many reforming measures on enterprise management, taxation, labor, and capital markets have been only halfheartedly implemented due to political and fiscal constraints as well as resistance from vested interests (Perkins, 1995). The national share of industrial output accounted for by SOEs fell from 43 percent in 1993 to 34 percent in 1994. The overall productivity of SOEs was improving, but at a much lower rate than that accomplished by non-state enterprises (Hope, 1996).

In 1994, a spate of potentially far-reaching reforms was launched, including enactment of the Company Law (July 1994), which establishes the legal status of the corporation system. The earlier efforts in the SOE reforms were strengthened with the promulgation of more managerial autonomy to SOEs in 1992 (Iskander, 1996). In 1993, the document *The Decision on Issues concerning the Establishment of a Socialist Market Economic Structure* presented an agenda for creating a modern enterprise system. In early 1994, the State Council announced the "10,000–1,000–100–10" SOE reform experiment, which introduced new accounting methods to 10,000 SOEs, new state asset valuation methods to 1,000 SOEs, corporation to 100 SOEs, and comprehensive reform to 10 cities. Many SOEs have since completed transformation toward limited liability companies, resulting in about 170 companies listed on the Shanghai Stock Exchange and 110 listed on the Shenzhen Stock Exchange (Broadman, 1995; Iskander, 1996).

Many problems still need to be solved for the success of the SOE reforms. The reforms have so far failed to carry out necessary tough measures of imposing hard budget constraints on SOEs to replace the prevalent soft budget constraints.[1] SOEs have a certain, but not complete, degree of autonomy. Enterprises are still under the control of government in the areas of selection and appointment of managers. Property rights over SOEs are actually exercised by numerous hierarchical governmental bureaus, with the state as a distant owner in the background. Enterprises are now concerned with profits and losses but are not entirely responsible for them. Division of revenues after deduction of taxes between bureaucracies and enterprises remains unsolved. If SOEs have losses, the state still has to help them out by direct subsidizing or a delay in loan repayment. This is deemed one of the major potential threats to China's economic prosperity. Attempts to impose hard budget constraints have proved very difficult to execute, as SOEs have a large number of surplus workers (Hu, 1996). Due to various reasons, many SOEs are not making profits (Koo, Li & Peng, 1993; Wang, 1998). A hard budget would drive many of those loss-making SOEs to bankruptcy. No government can afford to face massive bankruptcies, as large-scale unemployment would be too great a social risk. "Although direct subsidies to state enterprises from the budget have been declining in the 1990s, aid through preferential access to credit—quasi-fiscal subsidies—has risen" (Hope, 1996:14). It was reported that SOEs could still obtain planned allocation of investment finance, while enterprises of other ownership did not appear to have easy access to bank finance.

One of the major characteristics of China's SOEs is that enterprises have heavy "social burdens" to carry: providing an array of social services such as housing, education, hospitals, and social security (pension, accident, and health insurance) to their employees, services normally supplied by government in a free market system. A glimpse at the issue of retirees reveals how enormous this social obligation borne with SOEs: retirees account for 25 percent of the total number of urban workers in 1997. About 20 percent of SOEs' capital assets are buried in social projects. Housing for employees costs enterprises an extra 35 to 40 percent of total wages, and the cost for medical care accounted for 12 percent of total wages (Liu, 1997). Government feels that it is its duty to keep loss-making enterprises alive because their social value is higher than their economic value determined by the prices of their output.

The incentive for enterprise managers to invest in the long-term value of firms has not been established. On the contrary, an absence of clear private property rights has led to excessive leakage and gradual decapitalization of SOEs through an increase of wage and benefit payments, evident in the discrepancies between productivity growth and wage increases. The slow and incremental SOE reforms are implicated by an involvement of a web of issues that are interrelated. Changing the structure of SOEs involves concomitant reforms in the financial market, tax regime, legal system, housing, and land markets. Another reason is that government bureaucrats have vested interests in maintaining the existing system of control over enterprises. Competition by bureaucrats in a rent-seeking environment leads government officials to extend subsidies to their subordinates regardless of investment benefits.

Successful SOE reforms should hinge on the establishment of a new system of enterprise governance, the provision of a new social security net, and thus a labor market and a housing market detached from "work units." A new direction for the SOE reforms has been demonstrated in that modern enterprises can be established through the "corporatization" of SOEs, that is, conversion of SOEs into shareholding companies through implementation of the new Company Law (Tseng et al., 1994). In this new framework, a system for the management of state-owned assets by state holding companies, state asset management companies, and enterprise groups will be formed. Taxes and SOEs' profits remittance are separated by the establishment of *Guoyou Zhichan Jingyin Gongsi* (GZJG) (state assets management corporation) under the *Guoyou Zhichan Guanli Wei-*

yuanhui (state assets management committee) in municipal government: taxes go to government and profits to state assets management corporations. Three GZJGs of different specialties have been set up in Shenzhen since 1987 (SQZGLXB, 1997). However, there are still an absence of penalties for business failures and room for corrupted officials to intervene in enterprises for personal interests. Soft budget constraints and a compliant banking system are currently the greatest obstacle to the progress of SOE transformation.

FOREIGN CAPITAL INTO REAL ESTATE

Foreign investment, which was expelled from China in 1949, when socialist China was founded, has been wooed again since the country decided to depart from central planning and is expected to revamp the stifled Chinese economy with new technologies and modern management. However, in the inception of change of direction, the matter of foreign capital into real estate was highly sensitive in the political arena, and thus the authority's attitude was ambiguous. There was a consensus that Chinese cities were backward in their physical infrastructure; therefore the urban economy was impeded from proper functioning by poor urban facilities. It was imperative to direct more investment into urban land and buildings to atone for the past negligence. Foreign capital could be a useful source for the task. Nevertheless, a bitter history of foreign concessions in Chinese coastal cities such as Shanghai and Xiamen was still reminiscent of the painful experience of losing sovereignty over territories. The lingering memory of the preliberation foreign occupation made it politically unacceptable to grant foreigners landed interests in a socialist country. The legitimacy of the Chinese Communist Party was partly earned by its stout objection to the presence of foreign trading in China, branded as oppression of foreign imperialism. Economically, investment in real estate was regarded as unproductive and speculation-prone.

Only in the late 1980s, was foreign capital permitted into development of industrial property for own use, because manufacturing was prioritized as one of the pillars of the Shenzhen economy. The pace of inward industrial investment was hampered by the tardiness of local building construction due to shortages of development capital. In the first governmental directive concerning foreign capital in properties, entitled *Policies on the Management of Land and Property Markets*, released on July 1987, foreign developers were still officially disallowed to develop commercial land and building projects (*Shenzhen Jianshe Ju*, 1991). However, while the central government was concerned with political correctness, local governments were pragmatic in seeking inward capital into land and properties in their jurisdictions. Many Chinese cities faced a daunting task of renovating dilapidated, old towns, and Shenzhen needed to develop a new town with up-to-standard infrastructure and sufficient buildings to accommodate social and economic activities. Handicapped by the initial financial inadequacy, the Shenzhen government was not financially capable of carrying out this mission. Various forms of participation had to be tried, instead of sole government sponsorship, which was the norm elsewhere. Market-oriented developers had to be found to initiate urban physical development before the city could embark on a long journey to prosperity. Foreign investment was flowing into Shenzhen to take advantage of low production cost and tax relief. Domestic investment was also foreseen to be sparked by the inward capital because of Shenzhen's being in the vicinity of Hong Kong—a gateway to the world market. Equipped with the given autonomy, Shenzhen contrived an initiative to make use of foreign capital in urban construction. It took the form of a joint venture between foreign development capital and local land assets. If it was politically wrong, according to the extant ideology, to engage foreign developers in land and property development as sole proprietors, it should be innovative and acceptable to involve foreign capital in urban construction. Land as a valuable asset was rediscovered.

The first incidence of market-guided property development with an involvement of overseas capital occurred in the hospitality industry. After three decades of isolation from the world and concomitant, perennial political turbulence, China's opening up and liberalization symbolized by the SEZs intrigued the world. Many overseas tourists who had been deterred from visiting China by politically related difficulties were then able to make the trip. Being close to China, Hong Kong was a convenient gateway to the mainland. Due to its proximity to Hong Kong, Shenzhen became an ideal destination for tourists intending to spend a few days to view the scenes of socialist China—a world supposedly diametrically opposite to the capitalist West. Spurred by a high potential of quick returns, given the severe shortage of hotels and other entertainment facilities, the adventurous Hong Kong capital penetrated Shenzhen to make the first mark of foreign interests in Chinese real estate since the nationalization of properties in the 1950s. The joint venture of *Bamboo Garden Hotel* was materialized by Hong Kong funds, which covered all development costs, including expenses for land requisition and compensation for existing land tenants and the land contributed by the Shenzhen partner (*Shenzhen Jianshe Ju*, 1989).

The first spate of real estate development occurred in the catering industry and was stimulated by curious tourists swamping into the poorly furnished city, and the second wave of property development hit the marketplace in the emerging sector of commodity housing, which caught the attention of Hong Kong developers. Being a city of refugees who fled from political persecution under the Communist regime on the mainland, Hong Kong has close family ties with neighboring Guangdong. The traditionally strong blood ties among the southern Chinese create a housing market with great potential for profit. It is a housing market for the Hong Kongers' relatives who are living in Guangdong. Shenzhen is perceived as an ideal location for such housing for two reasons. First, Shenzhen is a convenient place for family reunions because of its proximity to Hong Kong. Second, huge price differences between Hong Kong and Shenzhen housing units constitute a strong inducement for investment, as an outlay of investment in Shenzhen housing accounts for only a fraction of that in housing on the other side of the border. In 1981, there were five Hong Kong-based property companies in cooperation with Shenzhen partners developing housing estates (Wong, 1982).

Shenzhen Tequ Fazhan Gongsi (STFG) (SSEZ Development Corporation)—a state-owned company—was immediately set up and appointed in charge of comprehensive physical development to participate in joint ventures with Hong Kong developers. On 4 September 1980, an agreement was reached to develop two office buildings of 20 stories. STFG joined the scheme with a provision of 1.2 hectares of land, while Hong Kong partners provided a development fund of HK$60.2 million. Upon completion, STFG retained the retail space on the ground and first floors, as well as 58 percent of net profits from sales of office space, and the rest, 42 percent, went to the Hong Kong partners. By the end of 1983, this type of joint development for housing, shops, offices, and hotels had aggregated to 36 contracts with a pledged capital inflow of HK$5.88 billion and a total land area of 86 hectares (Zhang, 1993). As a result, Shenzhen experienced the first property boom in its history. Adventurous overseas capital into real estate accounted for 43.2, 50.0, and 30.3 percent of the total capital construction investment for 1980, 1981, and 1982, respectively.

These development activities were made possible only when the state land was passed to STFG as development assets. In the first instance, land-use-right transfers from government were made to state-owned STFG on lease of 30 to 50 years free of charge at the time for STFG to undertake "six connections and leveling" (connections of electricity, water, sewers, drains, access roads, and telecommunications to sites, as well as site leveling), which equipped raw, green land with basic infrastructure. The Shenzhen government only charged nominal rentals for the raw land leasing in the form of revenue remittance by STFG as a state-owned enterprise. The rest of the profits were retained by STFG as financial assets for further development. With the same arrangement, *Hopewell China Development (Shenzhen)* proposed to invest HK$2 billion in developing a new town of 30 square kilometers in Futian, Shenzhen. *Luen Sing Enterprise* planned a scheme of HK$2.4 billion to develop a cultural and educational center with 6 square kilometer along Houhai Wan and a 26-hectare industrial estate in *Wenjindu* (Wong, 1982). The joint ventures in Shenzhen property development set a precedent in the history of Chinese socialist urbanization that urban development can be conducted based on the commercial principle of profitability. A survey revealed that eight joint ventures in real estate had made handsome profits, with an average development profit rate of 75.6 percent, better than all industries examined (Oborne, 1986:153).

Foreign capital in the property sector was no doubt crucial for Shenzhen's initial urban construction. Nevertheless, experience and expertise in dealing with property development that Shenzhen developers acquired and built up with their Hong Kong partners were more important for the growth of a fledgling industry. As perceived, property development is a business full of risks and uncertainties. The City Center Redevelopment Project has taught developers that a long-term commitment to property development must be accompanied by the strategies of dealing with rapidly changing situations, which are often the case for countries like transitional China. The project, undertaken by the joint-venture developer *Xinghuacheng*, was to redevelop Shenzhen's original city center, the central district of Luohu. Luohu used to be the sole commercial and retailing core before the Shenzhen special economic zone was endorsed. Although the new central area had stretched into neighboring areas along with substantial expansion of the city itself, the old core of Luohu remained a prime focus of retailing.

The joint venture was set up in 1982 following the norm at the time between a Shenzhen state firm and a Hong Kong partner on a common perception of the area's huge commercial potential, with total expected investment of HK$150 million within a time frame of 30 years. On 12 April 1983, the project named *Huacheng* was launched officially by both Mayor Liang Xiang and the Hong Kong general manager, and the budget for redevelopment was raised to HK1.7 billion. The Shenzhen party contributed the site of 20 hectares as a share for the joint scheme. Both parties shared the expense for displacement of existing residents and shops. According to the agreement of 30 years' cooperation, which was divided into three phases, for the first 10 years the Hong Kong developer should take 75 percent of net profits and Shenzhen 25 percent. Both parties would get equal shares of proceeds from transactions in the second 10 years, and in the third decade the Shenzhen partner would have 75 percent and Hong Kong 25 percent of profits.

Building conditions and environmental quality were much improved with demolition and refurbishment of buildings at key locations. McDonald's, an icon of American commercial culture, was erected at a strategic location, seemingly to symbolically usher in the capitalist market. However, soon the developer felt the pressure of rising costs for resettling displaced tenants. Rapid appreciation of capital value of all properties citywide caused a rippling impact on the buildings to be demolished. The market value of the affected buildings had increased to a new height, and compensation for resettlement was correspondingly demanded at a higher level. Although the sitting tenants could not legally claim higher compensation, as they did not own the land and buildings, the notion of property use right made them nominal owners. Therefore, the redevelopment project was claimed financially unsustainable if the original renewal plan was maintained. An immediate response to inflated development costs was to change zoning by raising plot ratios in line with commercial viability and investors' expected yields. Nevertheless, any revision to the approved zoning had to be concerned with two fundamental issues. The first was that environmental amenity would be undermined by increasing building density. The second was that the capacity of infrastructure in the area had reached its limits. An unexpected increase in density would implicate the proper functioning of the central area and thus socialize the cost. If infrastructural capacity could be expanded, liability for the cost should not rest solely with the city government. According to the convention, developers who benefited from zoning alterations should make a financial contribution to the city. Thus, the joint venture was at an impasse. The lesson was learned that unexpected change of market variables, which is typical for a transitional economy, should be taken into account for a long-term project.

Partnership is a common practice for property development and investment that require substantial funds. The scheme of *Wenjindu Industrial Zone* provided a good opportunity for Shenzhen developers to learn to hedge against unfavorable consequences. Located close to the *Wenjindu Customs*, the *Wenjindu Industrial Zone* scheme had a geographical advantage in luring Hong Kong manufacturing to migrate to Shenzhen. The partnership was formed for a 30-year commitment without much deliberation and elaboration. The joint venture went well in the 1980s, when new factories were built and sold promptly. The industrial property development lasted until half of the earmarked land was utilized, then the scheme virtually ceased when the Hong Kong party stopped pumping money further, while the property market was still booming. The joint-venture contract was signed following the norm that development finance was the responsibility of the Hong Kong partner, while the land was provided by the Shenzhen party. It was reported that the Hong Kong businessman had cash-flow problems in his mainline business, and thus his Shenzhen development had to be postponed.

It was in the interest of Shenzhen to maintain the momentum of property development. An argument broke out across the border. Shenzhen blamed Hong Kong for not inputting development finance as much as the contract required, whereas Hong Kong claimed that its move was justified, as the contract was valid for 30 years and did not specify a timetable for fund inflow. Obviously, the latter had the upper hand over the former, if the contract was to be observed. The predicament originated in the naïveté and inexperience of the Shenzhen developer. However, the deadlock had to be broken in the interest of the city. Shenzhen government officials, interviewed by the author, declared that they were prepared to refer to the "international convention," which allegedly allowed government to acquire not-yet-developed land for development of public facilities such as schools, parking lots, and so on. Knowing this intention, the Hong Kong partner was reportedly furious and granted an interview to a Hong Kong newspaper to attack Shenzhen's breach of the joint agreement. The accusation would have complications for the image of the Shenzhen government, which might have contributed to a lack of confidence that was already deeply rooted in the mind of foreign investors about poor interference of the Chinese government. Therefore, this lesson was learned at a huge cost.

Foreign capital has played an essential role in the first stage of Shenzhen development toward the establishment of a good showcase of a socialist market system. Those early adventures have given examples of how projects should be handled, and thus it is not exaggerated to claim that the first generation of local developers is hatched by the inward Hong Kong developers. Market forces started to demonstrate their influence on the course of urbanization. However, most foreign capital was invested in projects of the consumption sectors, with short-term projection for profits, such as hotels, shops, offices, and apartments in prime locations where existing urban infrastructure was fully exploited. Few foreign developers were interested in projects for long-term production. In comparison with that early adventurous capital, foreign developers who arrived later in the early 1990s were more speculative.[2] Moreover, the impact of foreign capital on the local property market has declined from its prime time, 1979–1983, when funds from overseas accounted for 31 percent of the total capital investment, to the recent period of 1992–1996, when they took only 16 percent (SZTJ, 1997). Therefore, homegrown developers were needed to be groomed for taking on large, long-term projects.

STATE LAND AS FREE ASSETS

Land and property development became the first test for the SSEZ to show how an urban economy could be built up under a socialist market system. Foreign capital's role in urban construction was limited to partnership because of dominant state ownership of real estate and ambiguous property rights over land leasehold. The city government with scanty financial resources was challenged by an enormous task of urban construction. It became imperative to nurture a local property industry with the capacity to undertake urban land and property development required by partially market-regulated, rapid economic growth. The property industry itself will be a significant contributor to the local economy and help to shape an efficient urban physical environment.

After 30 years of building up the socialist economy, state-owned construction enterprises were seen as the only plausible candidates to be nurtured as property developers operated in an emerging property market. Strong demand for buildings was generated by an unprecedented vibrant economy, thanks to dynamic market performance. Viability of property development at the time was guaranteed by the situation that Shenzhen was the only city in the country exposed to inward investment on a large scale. Clearly demonstrated, enthusiastic investment interests from both abroad and inland made property development almost a risk-free business. A substantial amount of capital required up front hindered, nevertheless, any local SOE from initiating the process of property development. SOEs were weak in capacity for financial mobilization, because they had not been molded as real, independent enterprises by the old, state-controlled management structure. A pragmatic, nurturing measure had to be conceived to break this impasse. Land, a state asset within the reach of local government, was thus used as initial capital offered to the developers-to-be. The recipients did not pay for the asset transfer or paid only rentals for utilizing state assets at a nominal rate in the form of enterprise revenue remittance. The initial free transfer of state land to SOEs reflected the characteristics of gradual institutional change. Although SOEs were on the track of reforms to become independent and autonomous enterprises, the close relationship between government and SOEs forged under the central planning system, where free land was an institution, remained instrumental. Thereafter, a favorable condition was presented to the state-owned developers to grow and expand.

Although the Shenzhen government, representative of the state as the de jure landowner, reserved the right to collect rentals from land given initially free of charge as soon as state-owned developers could make profits on their development business, there were no legal constraints guaranteeing the obligation. Alternatively, developers were often required or persuaded, depending on their status in the process of SOE reforms, to pay land rental in-kind, that is, building off-site infrastructural facilities that would otherwise be government liabilities or carrying out low-profit development such as industrial estates. Several industrial estates, such as the *Shangbu Industrial Zone*, were built in such a manner.

In the course of learning to conduct property development in the market environment where market demand and prices prevail, Shenzhen developers have accomplished several milestone-projects of significance to the city landscape. Development expertise, which has been built up gradually over years, is so crucial that it determines the fate of a project in a market where customer preferences begin to dominate. The ITC Mansion is such a case to demonstrate how a nascent property industry is learning to develop a project to maximize output. Many provincial and municipal governments in China wanted to have offices in Shenzhen to handle outward investment from their provinces to Shenzhen and to attract inward investment to their inland cities. Having perceived this demand for offices, the state-owned developer *SSEZ Real Estate & Properties* initiated developing an office building named ITC Mansion in October 1982. Despite 38 prospective tenants turning up with down payments for the intended office space, the developer was still two-thirds short of development costs. Development finance constituted a major obstacle, on the one hand. On the other hand, after a visit to Hong Kong to survey design of similar buildings, the developer realized that the original building design did not have a proper combination of tenants to maximize the value of the building and to make best use of the location. Its architectural design was subsequently revised to reflect new ideas by adding a shopping center at the ground floor and a rotating restaurant on the top. The height of the building increased to 53 floors from its original 38 floors for the purpose of enhancement of prestige. The revision turned an otherwise purely office block into a visual and functional focus in the central area where it was located. The alterations, however, exacerbated the problem of shortage in development finance. Having seen that the housing market was booming at that time, the developer conceived a remarkable strategy of developing housing using the down payments with an intention to multiply the capital, in the faith that housing could be quickly built and sold at great profit margins. It succeeded. Profits made from the housing development were used to finance the ITC Mansion project, and it was completed successfully. The ITC Mansion has become a 1980s landmark of Shenzhen.

After several years in the field, the development capacity of these developers has expanded, along with dynamic growth of the local economy. With growing demand for buildings and strengthening of the market orientation of the property sector, more state-owned enterprises, following their forerunners, diversified into the property business. The number of developers reached 28 in 1987. The SOE reforms attempted a new profit-sharing formula in order to give SOEs incentives to improve production so as to stimulate the economy. The new arrangement provided SOEs with the means to invest in fixed assets, which had been strictly controlled by central planning previously. After a proportion of after-tax profits was submitted to the state as dividends paid to the owner of SOEs, the rest could be retained and invested at enterprises' discretion. Some developers were able to venture into the arena of property investment. *SSEZ Real Estate & Properties* has retained properties in prime locations for long-term investment since the late 1980s, convinced by sustainable tenant demand for space at good addresses. This move is a significant enhancement of the property market, as it enriches the mode of supply. Besides freehold, an option of leasehold assists business start-ups by easing off business outlays.

Properties were commercialized as commodities whose prices were determined by market forces, but land as the most important component in property development was monopolized and undervalued to a considerable degree. The profit margins, created by the difference between market prices of properties and undervalued land through non-market allocation, have produced a new generation of state-owned developers in the backdrop of a strong, growing economy liberalized by marketization. The profit margins supposedly collected by the state as the landowner were mobilized by the local government to breed locally based developers. Some of them have later become heavyweight players in the Shenzhen marketplace. A conservative assessment estimates that development profits would be between 70 and 95 percent in the 1980s (Zhu, 1994:1619). Profitability rose when user demand was rising. State-owned property developers have contributed substantively to the construction of the Shenzhen built environment. In 1991, there were 109 developers, and 79 of them were SOEs, representing 72.5 percent. In 1994, the number of developers increased to 337 where 207 were SOEs, accounting for 61.4 percent. The development of properties by 30 of the largest public developers amounted to 70.1 percent (1993) and 64.8 percent (1994) of the total (SFNB, 1994).

The gradual process of strengthening land commercialization "privatizes" the land value, and the resultant high profitability of property development is instrumental in the formation of public developers in transitional Chinese cities. The land factor will further facilitate the growth of developers who have connections with local government, together with other forms of indirect assistance from government such as postponement of taxation, preferential access to land loans, and tolerance of bad loans by the state banking system. Nevertheless, the land issue will also complicate the property market when the economy enters the next stage of marketization. By 1987, 76.8 square kilometers of land had been allocated to SOEs, of which 19.8 square kilometers, or a quarter of the total, remained vacant. The vacant land increased to 38.7 square kilometers in 1992, held by developers as well as users. A large land bank in the control of developers has been built up. Payment of land use fee covered 7.2 percent, and land rental covered 0.2 percent of the total land allocated in 1987. Up to 1994, land use fee coverage rose to only 25.3 percent, and payment of land rental covered 17.5 percent of the total land assigned (SFNB, 1991, 1996).

NEW DEVELOPMENT ENTERPRISES EXPOSED TO MARKET COMPETITION

Despite occasional fluctuations and stagnation, Shenzhen's economy has been robust, and the city has achieved sound socioeconomic progress. Its

GDP in 1990 (¥17,167 million) was 64 times as much as that in 1980 (¥270 million). Such a spectacular phenomenon in economic performance should be attributed to the liberalization policies, which allow market mechanisms to direct urban economy, and to the SOE reforms, which free enterprises from the "planning cage." Without a doubt, Shenzhen is exceptional in that it was one of only four special economic zones in the whole country and was able to attract much inward investment both from overseas and from inland provinces with preferential policies.

After profit taxation replaced the practice of revenue remittance, SOEs were able to retain more profits after certain conditions were fulfilled. From 1982 to 1984, state-owned manufacturing enterprises retained 55.2 percent of profits for further investment as well as for improvement of employees' welfare. Since the tax reform, enterprises retained 70 percent of profit after taxation on average (Bei, 1990). In Shenzhen, due to special policies to encourage modern SOEs to compete in the market with foreign enterprises, SOEs were allowed to retain more profits than their counterparts in inland cities. In 1990, the proportion of profits held by SOEs in Shenzhen was 73.7 percent of the total. In 1995, it rose to 87.6 percent (He, 1997).

Many enterprises have prospered to the extent that their managers can consider business diversification in order to make good use of burgeoning assets. Profits made by SOEs have grown exponentially over the years. The enterprise profits accumulated by SOEs under the control of Shenzhen Investment Management Corporation were only ¥51 million in 1980. They swelled to ¥5.1 billion in 1995. The second property boom in the short history of Shenzhen during the period 1988–1993 presented an irresistible pulling factor to drive these companies into real estate. In a period of five years, the prices of housing and shops increased 6 times, offices 3 times, and factories 2.5 times (SFNB, 1995). The longtime dominant position of property industry in neighboring Hong Kong further reinforced the perception of investment in real estate as "never going wrong." The prevailing belief in southern China is that wealth should be saved in the form of land and properties. Market opinions have it that Shenzhen will follow in Hong Kong's footsteps, as Shenzhen already bears some resemblance to Hong Kong in its urban landscape. Opinions became convinced that real estate should be a lucrative investment after the market witnessed a tremendous appreciation in property value. With autonomy in business operation in the course of SOE reforms, profitable SOEs began to spin off subsidiaries to venture into the property industry. Applications for setting up property development firms flooded the competent government offices. In order to control the development market, the government issued ad hoc licenses to many applicants valid only for the project for which the applicant put up the application, and upon completion the development company would be defunct or apply again for a license.

Table 5.4
Number of Developers in Shenzhen

Year	Total	With a Full License	With a Single Project License
1987	28	n.a.	n.a.
1988	58	n.a.	n.a.
1989	107	n.a.	n.a.
1990	86	43	43
1991	109	44	65
1992	138	44	94
1993	188	63	125
1994	337	117	220
1996	396	117	279

Source: SFNB, 1991–1997.

The number of developers mushroomed: 8 in 1983 and then 107 in 1989. It increased to 188 in 1993, before it finalized at 396 in 1996 (see Table 5.4). The ownership of these new development enterprises is, however, ambiguous: they are neither state-owned nor privately owned. Compared with normal SOEs, they have more autonomy in business operation, less controls by planning quotas, and less social responsibility for their employees. They may be controlled by the mother companies regarding business scope, and financial losses and profits. The most fundamental change is that they are not entitled to soft budget constraints from the state and thus face greater competition. Being latecomers, these developers do not have land-related benefits, which were given to those early developers before the 1988 new land use legislation. Without a land bank at hand, they have to compete in the open land market in order to acquire land plots for property development. A large quantity of land was, however, already assigned to the early developers and land users before 1988, and since a disproportionate amount of land has been leased to land users directly through negotiation since 1988, land available on the open market has been scant. In contrast with a provision of 2,044 hectares of land to users through negotiation between 1988 and 1994, only 35.8 hectares of land were supplied to the open market for bidding and auction where new property developers could compete (SFNB, 1996).

A fierce competition was clearly displayed in the 1990s land-bidding events. It was unambiguously demonstrated by three land-bidding competitions in 1991. The first bid was held on 6 August. A total of 2.6 hectares subdivided into three plots were competed for by 26 developers. The average land price was bid up to ¥1,875 per square meter of floor area allowed by the predetermined plot ratio (*Shenzhen Fangdichan Shichang Kuaibao* [Shenzhen Real Estate Express], 12 August 1991). One month later, a second land bid was publicly announced and held on 26 September. A total of 3.25 hectares in five plots attracted participation of 47 developers, resulting in 19 bidders at least and 31 bidders at most hunting for each single plot. The strong competition apparently drove the land prices up, reaching ¥2,914 per square meter on average, an increase of 55 percent over the last benchmark (*Shenzhen Fangdichan Shichang Kuaibao* [Shenzhen Real Estate Express], 2 and 12 October 1991). Being afraid of an imminent overheating of the property market driven by the escalating land prices, the Shenzhen authorities put financial restrictions in place in order to cool down the heated land chasing by reducing the number of participants. The new measures increased bid deposits from ¥200,000 to ¥1 million, which were to be expropriated in case of any failure and fault, and the period by which payment for land acquisition should be cleared was reduced to 20 days from two months. The new regulations effectively made fewer developers qualified for the third bid of 2.75 hectares of four land pieces. Only 20 developers participated, and the winners obtained their land at a price of ¥2,674 per square meter on average (*Shenzhen Fangdichan Shichang Kuaibao* [Shenzhen Real Estate Express], 2 November 1991).

The primary land market was not responsive to demand from the development market, as much land was still allocated to land users directly with explicit subsidies. The latecoming developers without a land bank had to resort to poaching on the secondary land market, which was composed of hoarded land allocated to SOE users for their production as well as for their employees' housing construction under the former land management regime. These land hunters were joined by single project-based developers who were not eligible for acquiring land from the open market due to lack of a track record. Developers without a full license accounted for half of the total number of registered development companies in 1990. This ratio rose to 70 percent in 1996 (see Table 5.4).

An active, but covert, land market has been created as a black, secondary land market. Before the land management reforms are to be completed, these land users are the virtual landowners, though without legal status. The hidden, secondary land market is much larger than the primary land market. Although the new urban land use system has been in place since 1987, its implementation has been lax, and the rules have not seemed retroactive to the earlier allocated land. In spite of an existing regulation that rules out any commercial transaction of land designated for own production and employees' welfare housing uses, the secondary land market still exists because of government's hidden agenda to assist the loss-making SOEs. The ongoing SOE reforms still put unprofitable enterprises under protection. Government has been subsidizing these enterprises, to weather tough times and has not imposed any rental on land uses.

Despite Shenzhen being a new town without a historical burden of loss-making SOEs on the brink of bankruptcy, some SOEs are not in a position of making profit due to poor management and structural weaknesses. The booming property market has turned land into a very precious commodity.

Table 5.5
Capital Construction Investment by Source (percent)

	State	Local Government	Foreign Capital	Bank Loans	Local Enterprises	Others	Total
1979-1983	8.7	9.7	31.0	29.3	18.1	3.2	100.0
1984-1988	1.4	13.9	15.5	20.4	36.7	12.1	100.0
1989-1993	0.1	11.2	18.0	23.6	34.4	12.7	100.0
1994-1996	0.0	14.4	18.2	16.1	35.6	15.7	100.0
up to 1983	8.7	9.7	31.0	29.3	18.1	3.2	100.0
up to 1988	2.5	13.3	17.7	21.6	34.1	10.8	100.0
up to 1993	0.7	11.7	17.9	23.1	34.3	12.3	100.0
up to 1996	0.3	13.3	18.0	19.2	35.0	14.2	100.0

Source: SZTJ, 1997.

The unprofitable SOEs would be bailed out temporarily if they could divert currently vacant land plots into market to capture the potential value. Schemes of joint development are invented in this circumstance: a joint property development between profitable SOEs' capital and loss-making SOEs' landholding privilege. Single project-licensed developers with development capital solicit those land occupiers for joint development deals. Developers cover all development costs, and land occupiers contribute sites. Normally, completed buildings are split from 50–50 to 30–70 between developers and land contributors. If it is still profitable for the developer after shedding such a big proportion, it is because the land cost, which is not taken into account, constitutes a large share of total development costs. Higher benchmarks for property price are set by the joint development because of relatively high costs for the developer. However, profit margins are cut significantly, and developers would not have much room to maneuver if the prevailing market prices come down unexpectedly.

WHO BUILT THE CITY OF SHENZHEN?

Not like urban construction and investment in infrastructure under the central planning system, where government was the only developer, Shenzhen's urban physical development has involved many actors: the state, the local government, foreign capital, local enterprises, domestic private individuals as tenants and investors, and banks. Local enterprises, foreign capital, and local government are three principal builders of the Shenzhen city. Up to 1996, local enterprises contributed 35.0 percent, foreign capital 18.0 percent and local government 13.3 percent to the total investment in urban properties and facilities, indicated by the data of Capital Construction Investment[3] (see Table 5.5).

Induced by the first property boom, which was basically caused by the sensation of Shenzhen's opening to the world, foreign capital led invest-

Table 5.6
Property Development and Capital Construction Investment by Period (percent)

Period	Jan. 79 - June 83	July 83 - Dec. 87	Jan. 88 - June 92	July 92 - Dec. 96	1979 - 1996
Floorarea Built during Each Period as % of Whole Period 1979 - 1996	3.5	20.7	30.2	45.6	100.0
Capital Construction Investment during Each Period as % of Whole Period 1979 - 1996	1.1	6.3	19.2	73.4	100.0

Source: SZTJ, 1997.

ment into commercial properties, which were inadequate at the time in coping with prospective inward investment. Foreign capital then receded to a less prominent position, replaced by local developers in ascendance, until the second property boom starting from the early 1990s when it revived its interests in property. Local enterprises, after their investment capacity was strengthened by greater profit retention and preferential fiscal policies, have become a leader in investment in the built environment. At the outset of Shenzhen's construction, the role of the state was already marginalized. Its financial contribution continued to decline dramatically until 1993, when it ceased to allocate any grant to the Shenzhen government. The Shenzhen local government was crippled by a lack of strong fiscal support from the central government. It strengthened its position and gathered momentum only when its fiscal base was slowly established and expanded. Responsibility has been assumed since then in the investment in urban infrastructure and social facilities.

Although there were about 400 development companies in 1996, many of them were small and insignificant in terms of the volume of development undertaken. The top 30 developers produced 70.1 percent of total floor space; the top 50 ones, 85.1 percent in 1993 (SFNB, 1993). These big development companies are usually state-owned involving foreign capital in the form of joint venture. They have controlled a large share of the property development market, and their development behaviors cast great impact on the whole market. Because of enhanced purchasing power along with substantive economic growth and property established as a good investment medium, presale as a method of raising development finance has become accepted by the market. The up-front payment for property purchases usually amounted to 20–40 percent of property development finance.

About half of the property in floor area constructed during 1979–1996 was built during 1992–1996, the period of the second property boom in Shenzhen history. Seventy percent of capital investment was made in the same period, which meant that much improvement in infrastructure was made recently when local government fiscal strength was enhanced (see

Table 5.7
Percentage of Gross Domestic Product Contributed by Construction Industry and Invested in Built Environment

Period	1980-1983	1984-1987	1988-1991	1992-1995
% of GDP Contributed by Construction Industry	22.8	14.3	8.4	11.9
% of GDP Invested in Built Environment	65.9	52.4	35.1	36.8

Source: SZTJ, 1996.

Table 5.6). The construction industry has become a pillar of the Shenzhen economy, and a substantial amount of capital has been invested in the built environment (see Table 5.7). Economic cycles or, rather, growth cycles[4] are clearly revealed by the activities of the construction industry, indicated by changes in its contribution to GDP and in amounts of capital invested in buildings and infrastructure.

NOTES

1. The concept of soft budget constraints is introduced by Kornai (1986) to explain the behavioral differences between a capitalist firm and a production unit in a centrally planned economy. A capitalist firm that fails to cover its costs out of current revenue (or, in the case of borrowing from outside sources, out of expected future income) is ultimately forced to exit the market. In a centrally planned economy such an exit threat is nonexistent. As long as a firm has access to implicit or explicit subsidies from government, there are no incentives to cover the costs of production or behave as a cost minimizer. The forms of soft budget constraints include following cases. First, the two-tier pricing system is an example of a soft budget that offers large profit margins to those SOEs able to obtain most of their inputs at below-market prices and sell part of their output at free market prices. Second, explicit subsidies come from government budgetary funds. Third, firms may enter into political negotiations about the level of effective taxation, lobbying for tax exemptions and reductions in tax rates. The contract responsibility system offers ample opportunities for selective tax waivers and discretionary taxation. Fourth, as the banking system takes on a larger role in the financing of investment, soft loans become a way of keeping loss-making SOEs afloat.

2. Cautiously seeking foreign capital for land and property, the Shenzhen government launched site sales experimentally in the Hong Kong market in 1989. As a means of raising funds for infrastructure construction, the nature of the auction is a presale of land use right. The acquisition of land use right in advance entitles the purchasers to the right of developing property on the site purchased. According to an observer, all the winners of the land bidding were not developers in their own right. Obviously, Shenzhen, as a low-cost locality for property development, was used a marketplace for business diversification. This kind of capital was purely speculative in nature.

3. Capital construction investment (CCI) is investment in new projects, including construction of a completely new facility or an addition to an existing facility. It includes construction of plants, mines, railways, bridges, harbors, water conser-

vation facilities, stores, residential buildings, schools, and purchase of machinery and equipment, vehicles, ships, and planes. CCI and technical upgrading and transformation (TUT) are two major components of investment in fixed assets. TUT covers renewing, replacing, and rebuilding existing fixed assets.

4. In many growing economies after World War II and particularly fast-growing economies in East and Southeast Asia, economic cycles are rather replaced by growth cycles defined in terms of growth of real GDP relative to a long-term trend of growth (Hall, 1990). Growth cycles do not have periodicity, but the same sequence of economic events repeats over time. Expansion in economic activities featured by high growth rates are followed by those with low growth rates.

Chapter 6

Conclusion: Implications of Gradualist Land Reforms

The gradualist urban land reforms are meant to change the Chinese urban development system through increments and experimentation. The party's rhetoric insists that state ownership should be maintained, and thus subsidies are given to the loss-making SOEs, hoping they would be rescued and become healthy thereafter. However, the incremental change has many undesirable implications. A dual land market is created, threatening to corrupt the nascent land market. Building cycles occur in China's cities, but with characteristics related to a transitional economy. Rampant rent-seeking tests that corruption of an incomplete market is inevitable. More-over, urban planning is facing a challenge to keep a balance between rigidity and flexibility in the transitional economy. Marketization, though partial, is playing its role in shaping the land use structure. "Groping for stones to cross the river" was a pragmatic strategy for the initial economic reforms, where new organizations played in an old system. Further reforms would, nevertheless, need a new institution to set up rules for market players.

DUAL LAND MARKET

The practice of gradual urban land reforms, that is, parallel supply of land at both subsidized and market prices, has resulted in a dual land market. On one hand, land can be obtained at negotiated and thus sub-sidized rates to an extent much below the prevailing market prices. On the other hand, land applicants who do not have access to land subsidies have to compete in a much contested open land market. Land allocated through negotiation has been overwhelming and out of proportion to land

Table 6.1
Subsidized Land Release

Year	1988	1989	1990	1991	1992	1993	1994	1995	1996
Land Leased Through Negotiation as % of Total Commodity Land Supply	97.5	98.2	94.8	97.7	99.2	99.6	65.3	85.7	67.5

Source: SFNB, 1991–1997.

released at market prices (see Table 6.1). The legacy of the old land management system also aggravates land market conditions, as the new measures of land commodification policy do not seem to apply to the land allocated to users before 1987, which amounts to 7,372 hectares, or 47.6 percent of the total usable land stock in the SSEZ territory. Land subsidies are offered for two apparent reasons: giving incentives to end users in order to encourage direct investment and thus to promote local growth and providing land subsidies as a protective cushion to SOEs for their stable transition to fully fledged players exposed to market competition without large-scale bankruptcy destabilizing a society where its citizens have paid heavily for perennial social changes. The implicit policies in the hidden agenda are to retain land-related benefits in the locality and for the mayor to use cheap land as a tool to implement what can enhance his or her political career.

Price disparities between two modes of land provision have produced enormous pressure on the government to release cheap land. The pressure is intrinsically built in the land acquisition process to pursue potential gains from price differences between two land submarkets. An abundant supply of subsidized land contracts commercial land supply, which pushes commercial land prices upward. The consequent widening gap between two prices provides sufficient motivation to land applicants to claim subsidized land for whatever reasons. It leads to a vicious spiral of ever greater pressure on the provision of non-commercialized land. Despite the compensatory land use regime having been in place, as much as 79.5 percent of land allocated was through an administrative process, 18.7 percent was provided through negotiation at a discount, and only 1.8 percent was assigned in the open market at full market rates by 1996. Thus, it gives rise to a disproportionate dual land market composed of a very tiny, primary, open land market and a large land reserve in users' and developers' hands, which later becomes a secondary black land market.

Overclaim of subsidized land was evident in mounting land hoarding from 3,305 hectares in 1988, to 3,873 hectares in 1992 (see Table 6.2). Land hoard accounted for 36.1 percent of total land allocated by 1988, when the free land use regime was officially abolished. However, land hoarding did not abate thereafter. It still stood at 34.1 percent in 1992. Industrial land

Table 6.4
Commodity Housing Market Indicators (1984–1994)

Year	Price Index for Locals' Market	Yield Index for Locals' Market	Price Index for Foreigners' Market	Yield Index for Foreigners' Market
1984	100	100	100	100
1985	118	103	111	100
1986	121	120	133	97
1987	147	138	153	95
1988	179	125	176	93
1989	349	71	219	82
1990	489	56	270	72
1991	705	45	361	65
1992	1061	47	461	44
1993	1292	41	531	38
1994	1012	47	468	43

Source: SFNB, 1995.

in 1994, rising from 4.5 percent in 1993. It further rose to 13.0 percent in 1995 and 1996, when there was 12.9 percent more housing under construction. The office market confronted the same problem. Office vacancy stood at 10.2 percent in 1996, and there was 12.9 percent more under construction (SGGJNF, 1997). Because of poor sales markets, developers were compelled to hold unsold properties and ventured into leasing markets that saw yields declining due to relative oversupply (see Table 6.4).

Nevertheless, high vacant rates do not necessarily mean supply's outstripping overall demand. Vacant housing and offices have accumulated partly because developers' supply does not match market demand. On the one hand, for example, there is a huge demand for affordable, low-income housing. On the other hand, development enterprises have an inclination to develop high-standard apartments, expecting great profit margins. The price of local commodity housing apartments rose to ¥655,000 a unit (at ¥550 per square meter) in 1993, while the average annual income of a local household in 1995 was ¥24,552 (SZTJ, 1996). Although the government is promoting Shenzhen as a complementary city to Hong Kong and trying to attract service industries and offices to settle in the city, Shenzhen is still a predominantly industrial city. Many office functions are production-related and thus in the low end. Many of those tenants cannot afford normal office spaces located in the central business district; instead, they make do by converting housing and factories to offices. The conversion of Shangbu industrial zone into commercial and office functions, though illegal, was a spontaneous market response to the market supply gaps.

Property shortages and gluts have unambiguously demonstrated that the property market in the transitional Chinese cities is highly inefficient. The inefficiency results from the remaining soft budget constraints that state-

---

Table 6.2
Land Supply and Land Hoarding

Year	Land Supply in Aggregate (ha)	Land Developed in Aggregate (ha)	Land Hoard (ha)
1979	424.5	290.0	134.5
1980	569.9	380.0	189.9
1981	1230.1	550.0	680.1
1982	2215.2	870.0	1345.2
1983	3878.9	1040.0	2838.9
1984	4792.8	1790.0	3002.8
1985	6738.0	4760.0	1978.0
1986	6905.6	4760.0	2145.6
1987	7678.6	5800.0	1978.6
1988	9144.6	5840.0	3304.6
1989	9744.6	6010.0	3734.6
1990	10344.6	6934.0	3410.6
1992	11373.0	7500.0	3873.0

Source: SFNB, 1991–1994.

had been provided generously all the time, in accordance with the official policy of promoting investment in manufacturing. Similarly, an unequivocal phenomenon of land hoarding occurred to the industrial sector. Since 1981, a large proportion of industrial land had been held unused, reaching 10.6 square kilometers or 56.4 percent of the total, in 1990. The new regime of land commodification did not improve the situation of land wastage. Land hoarding constituted a large land reserve controlled by landholders in comparison to the primary land market managed by the government land bureau. Without an effective new institutional framework and monitoring measures, the land reserve is ready to leak into the secondary land market. Joint development schemes are the cases of illegal land transfer in the secondary market. Leassees of subsidized land benefit, to a great extent, by capitalizing the price differences—an arbitrage of two submarkets.

Land undersupply in the open market resulted in an upsurge in land prices. Commodity properties experienced unprecedented increases in prices. The prices of commodity housing increased 6.2 times within a period of five years (1988–1993). The proportion of land value to the final capital value of property reveals the impact of land price on the final price of buildings. Take commodity housing, for example; the ratio of land to property values was 0.35 in 1987 and 0.39 in 1990. Then it escalated to 0.54 in the middle of 1991 and to 0.64 in September 1991. It was reported that the ratio would reach as high as 0.76, according to an inference based on the last land-bid prices (*Shenzhen Fangdichan Shichang Kuaibao* [Shenzhen Real Estate Express], 1 February 1992). This phenomenon shows a simple fact of demand considerably outstripping supply. A survey revealed that industrial land use density increased considerably over the years. The actual plot ratio of industrial land in aggregate increased to as much as 3.5 times in 1986 and further to 5.1 times in 1990 as that in 1983 (Zhu, 1993). Rising land use density suggests that genuine land users might be squeezed out by the speculative land banking. With the existence of an ample industrial land stock, industrial land was, however, becoming less accessible and probably more expensive than otherwise for the final tenants. Land hoarding also suggested unavailability of land due to lack of infrastructure that the local government expected land leassees to construct.

The incomplete land reforms do not assist the installation of land market mechanisms to guide efficient utilization of land resources. Instead, the dual land market corrupts the integrity of land marketization. Inequality in the land market discourages improvement of economic efficiency in property development. Favoritism or protection to SOEs does not necessarily warrant the expected results. More often than not, it renders inefficient utilization of discounted resources by the recipient. A straw poll carried out by the author revealed that 55.6 percent of manufacturing respondents indicated that, among three factors, cheap premises were the least important incentive, behind labor costs and tax reductions, while the rest saw it the second least important factor. On the whole, premise subsidies derived from subsidized land provision were ranked lowest in terms of significance by the respondents. Of sampled users 88.9 percent thought their premises not expensive at all, which implied that they could pay more for the same building. In the office sector, all users did not regard the prices paid for space as too high. In other words, all surveyed office users would be prepared to pay more for their occupied space (Zhu, 1994).

In comparison with their counterparts elsewhere, Shenzhen developers captured a greater profit margin in property development due to land as a major factor provided at artificially low prices. It may be intentional, as described previously. However, an unintentional effect fell on tenants who obtain premises from the open market. A relatively small market for commodity properties, owing to a small commodity land market, gave rise to a tight market of rental premises. As a result, tenants faced a market where rentals always increased. During the period 1984–1990, there were annual rental increases on average of 6.4 percent for housing, 22.1 percent for offices, 12.2 percent for shops, and 13.8 percent for factories (SFNB, 1991). All these increases were adjusted by the inflation index. By and large, the benefits derived from cheap land were retained in the form of rising rentals, capital appreciation, and development profits. Real tenants did not benefit from the cheap land policy.

Another unintended consequence of the lopsided dual land market is that it has contributed to the oversupply of commodity housing in 1990s Shenzhen. The joint development schemes—partnerships between SOEs with land and SOEs with capital—set up a tight profit margin for the

Table 6.3
Shenzhen Property Vacancy Rates and Yields in 1989

	Housing	Office	Factory	Shop
Vacancy Rate (%)	2.8	1.1	0.8	2.2
Yield (%)	12.4	17.4	15.4	23.5

Source: SFNB, 1991.

developers who contribute the capital and undertake the project, because of a large slice given to the land partner. Thus, high sale prices had to be maintained, although demand for commodity housing was weakening when it approached 1995/1996. Because of the imperfection of the property market, the unwillingly maintained high prices sent out a false signal to the market and stimulated further supply, which finally resulted in over supply.

BUILDING CYCLES: CHARACTERISTICS OF THE CHINESE TRANSITIONAL ECONOMY

Ironically, building overconstruction is seemingly descending up booming Chinese coastal cities for the first time since 1949. Un ment in urban premises and infrastructure was a constant prob ing many Chinese cities in the post-1949 era, characterized by of shortages. Interactions between demand and supply in 198 suggested that property demand was approaching the supp gressively as time went by. Property vacancy rates reached at the end of 1989, while yields, a measure of property formance, stood at extraordinarily high levels (see Tabl

It is argued that in a buoyant market, property sup demand is a normal market phenomenon. It is calle which is not considered unusual because of a delay ception and product completion. However, unrespc different from normal lagging. Due to reasons s' infrastructure, which made sites not ready for pr tight credit because of monetary control in fear c erty supply was not responsive in the late 198 surge in property demand. Property demand with a presence of continuous appreciation i decline in property vacancy rates. Between of properties increased between 3.5 and 1 erage for various sectors. However, since looming property oversupply after fou boom, which saw commodity property r vacant commodity housing accounted

owned property industry still enjoys and inequality between the developers with access to land subsidies and those without. Subsidies in the form of low land prices and soft budget constraints have led to economic irrationality of some property development enterprises. High-price benchmarks for commodity housing were set up by the developments whose land was obtained from the open land market where land prices were pushed up by each bidding event. Land prices were bid up by the reckless state-owned developers in the background of diminishing land supply. In 1988, a development company won a land bidding by offering the highest price. But after second thought, it figured out that no profits could be made given such a high land cost. Therefore, it had to default on the deal by losing ¥500,000 deposit (IFTE/CASS & IPA, 1992). It happened again in 1991, when a public developer won all five plots presented in a bidding event by offering unreasonably high prices but eventually failed to pay up. Consequently, four land plots were taken back, and ¥2 million deposit was forfeited (Zhang, 1993). This reckless behavior and irrationality in the estimation of bid prices clearly point to the remaining soft budget constraint—a characteristic inherited from the previous centrally planned regime. It has been dealt with by the ongoing SOE reforms but has not been solved because of the concern with possible threatening social unrest caused by the resultant massive layoff. These developers do not suffer due damage caused by misjudgment and mismanagement, because financial losses are ultimately taken by their supervisor—the local government. Therefore, the loss is socialized.

Artificially low land costs and soft budget constraints have also led to unjustified high risk-taking behavior of state-owned property developers. State developers have a penchant for delays in land rental payment. Arrears of payment for land acquisition accounted for 54.4 percent of contracted sum, accumulating to a few billion yuan (Zhen, 1995). Tolerance in allowing payment delays has effectively made land a discounted factor in the development process. This practice actually passes a part of development risks to the landowner—government. If a project does not show profits, then cashing of land costs would be postponed indefinitely until the enterprise could deliver. All risks and losses are absorbed by the government. However, profits are "privatized," as any development profits would be taken by developers to a large extent. Thus, developers are induced to take on as many property development projects as they can. The soft budget constraints have made developers insensitive to the market mechanism of scaling down prices to the clearing level in order to cut losses. Instead, developers are keen to keep good accounting records by not cutting prices. High property prices are maintained, but there are few market transactions.

The false market signals triggered a capital flight into real estate. Local enterprise funds into real estate have been increasing in proportion, the

Table 6.5
Capital Construction Investment in Shenzhen (percent, 1979–1996)

Year	State	Local Government	Foreign Capital	Bank Loans	Local Enterprises	Others	Total
1979-83	8.69	9.74	30.97	29.31	18.09	3.19	100.00
1984-91	0.76	11.43	23.33	21.81	31.96	10.71	100.00
1992-96	0.01	13.81	16.45	18.29	36.14	15.30	100.00

Source: SZTJ, 1997.

highest among all investors since 1984 (see Table 6.5). In the 1990s, more enterprises were accumulating capital to embark on the stage of business diversification. The central taxes of infrastructural development fund and national budgetary adjustment fund, both imposed to curb the deficit in the central budget in 1987 and 1989, respectively, have been canceled since 1993 in order to give more financial power to SOEs. It was estimated that up to ¥10 billion had been put into real estate as investment by SOEs in Shenzhen (Li, 1997; Guo, 1997). A survey of 31 Shenzhen SOEs reveals that 13.4 percent of ¥12.14 billion financial assets were invested in real estate. Only 62.7 percent of long-term investment was committed in companies' mainline business undertakings, while as much as 32.8 percent was diversified into real estate. For their investment in inland cities, 60.2 percent of the total ¥176 million were put into bricks and mortar (Shen, 1995). The survey has also found out that many SOEs diversifying into real estate were trying to make up for the losses inflicted in the mainline business. It has raised concerns that too much money into real estate causes a glut in the property market and unsold properties make SOE investments unproductive. These enterprises' life would be jeopardized, and SOE reforms would be further delayed.

SHORT-TERMISM AND RENT-SEEKING

Due to the existing political structure where mayors are appointed in a top-down process and there are ambiguous property rights over land assets, short-termism is prevalent in the preparation of urban development plans and in the implementation of urban master plans. Without a statutory status, urban, long-term planning objectives are often compromised and interrupted by mayors' short-term projects. Vicious competition between localities and unjustified offers of subsidized land lead to short-term local gains but long-term national losses. The strategy of land released to land users that is undervalued serves as a tool to achieve short-term urban growth. By 1994, of the 155 square kilometer total land stock that the Shenzhen special economic zone had, three-quarters had been released from the government holding, rising from 42 percent in 1986. The local government's financial resources are diminishing when urban land as the

Table 6.6
Property Values in Nanshan Compared with Those in Luohu (where property values = 1)

Housing			Factory			Shop		
1984	1990	1994	1984	1990	1994	1984	1990	1994
0.71	0.64	0.79	0.90	0.81	0.85	0.71	0.52	0.78

Source: SFNB, 1995.

most precious resource for the locality is exhausted. Long-term land asset management is sacrificed for the benefit of the incumbent government.

In spite of the tacit agreement between government and developers who receive land benefits for contribution to the urban public domain, investment in urban infrastructure and facilities, a long-term objective for the urban prospects, has not been as adequate as expected. Having materialized the benefit, developers are reluctant to part with the profit in hand. Even in some circumstances developers have to be coerced to fulfill the tacit agreement. The provision of subsidized land has become a drain on government revenues, which are critical for the Shenzhen government to play the leading role in the development of physical and social facilities.

Investment in urban infrastructure and facilities not up to the standard required by overall urban expansion is reflected in the increasing gaps between locations in terms of property values. Property prices vary in a marketplace because of many known and unknown, general and specific reasons. Location is a main explanatory factor accounting for property price variations, though how a good location is perceived is an exploratory topic in the field of property research. Nevertheless, accessibility of a location is regarded as one of the main factors contributing to property value. Accessibility to locations within an urban territory is differentiated by the spatial disparities of infrastructural quality. Improvement in urban infrastructure will be eventually reflected in the enhancement in property values. It is found that, by comparison, values of properties in Nanshan were declining relatively to those in Luohu during the period 1984–1990 (see Table 6.6). Being a district where the city center is located, Luohu has benefited from proximity and agglomeration of investments over the years, and thus the quality of the best location in Shenzhen has been farther improved, whereas infrastructural investment in Nanshan, a district farthest away from the city center, is not adequate as perceived by the market. Properties in good locations are more contested than those in not-so-good locations. Urban land development was not up to the extent expected. When releasing raw land to applicants at a discount, the government hoped the recipients would equip the land and develop buildings thereafter. Only since 1990, when fiscal revenues started to consolidate, has the government played a larger role in managing urban development. Five years' fiscal income in the period 1991–1995 accounted for 77.2 percent of the total government revenue income in the whole 17-year history (1979–1995) of the SSEZ. Thus, Shenzhen government was able to raise its share in the capital construction investment from 11.43 percent (1984–1991) to 13.81 percent (1992–1996). Infrastructural quality, measured by the property or land value, has improved in Nanshan since 1990 (see Table 6.6).

It may be legitimate to offer land subsidies in order to guide the market with government schemes and to infuse government plans into market actions. Local government may capitalize one or two benefits by making use of this strategy. However, it is achieved at the expense of land market corruption, which would have a long-term negative impact on the local economy. Short-term expedients could harm long-term planned urban development. The transitional urban land market is certainly not economically efficient, evident in the allocation of a considerable amount of land undervalued. The principle of equality, if the socialist market economy needs to be established, is gravely violated. The dual land market would destroy the integrity of the land market and undermine the management of the property market. Recent development has suggested that excessive subsidies and protection to SOEs should be to blame for property over-supply and rigidity of property prices in facing declining demand. The property markets in Beijing, Shanghai, Shenzhen, and other booming cities are thus plagued. Soft budget constraints, lack of market discipline, and subsidized land supply are the factors held responsible. These issues will be exacerbated by intensified urban development in many land-scarce Chinese cities, if mechanisms of the land market are not strengthened.

Gains derived from land subsidies not only have been taken by developers but have been siphoned off by corrupt government officials. Rent-seeking behavior of government officials is observed in the game of property development, and it is partly to blame for the release of subsidized land disproportionate to the total supply and for the overinvestment in high-standard housing. Rent-seeking means that one is better off by doing something that makes everyone else worse off (Tullock, 1993). It usually refers to manipulation of governments in order to obtain rents while other people's interests are harmed (Krueger, 1974; Rowley, Tollison & Tullock, 1988). Beihai, which used to be a small and tranquil city in Guangxi Province, was the destination of numerous property developers in 1992, when feverish land speculation brought it into the limelight. Land value appreciated many times over a very short period. In the process, officials in control of land supply demonstrated a classical case of rent-seeking. Government officials in charge of land supply, whether directly or indirectly, are a chief factor in this land scam; 123 officers were implicated, and a total of 110 million in bribes and illegal commissions were involved. Ten special development zones were set up, of which only two were approved by the central and provincial governments. The city master plan recommended urban land development to reach to 14 square kilometers by 1991, 90 square kilometers by 2000, and 161 square kilometers by 2010, having considered the potential of urban economy and land supply conditions. However, 154.26 square kilometers of land had been leased out by August 1994, far more than the amount supposedly controlled by the urban land use plan (Zhen, Wang & Ba, 1997). The case of Beihai is not an exception. In 1994, in courts 20,186 government officials nationwide were accused of corruption (*Beijing Review*, 27 March–2 April 1995, p. 6).

PLANNING DILEMMA IN A FAST-GROWING TRANSITIONAL ECONOMY

To have legal authority to supervise urban development, planning needs to be rigid in its procedure and implementation. However, an economy in transition has uncertainties, and planning needs to be flexible in dealing with unexpected issues. Coupled with the absence of an effective legal structure under the current institutional environment, the Chinese economy in transformation has put urban planning in a dilemma. Rigidity does not serve the ever-changing urban economy, whereas flexibility encourages rent-seeking and corrupts the market.

Shangbu industrial zone is a case to demonstrate how traditional planning was not adequate to cope with rapid development of a transitional economy. Located in Futian district, Shanbu industrial zone was one of the first major projects developed in the early 1980s. Its construction started in 1982 with 144.8 hectares in size and was planned to build 2.2 million square meters of standard industrial buildings designated for the electronics industry. The construction was completed in 1985. When completed, the site was on the fringe of the city, which had only 469,800 residents. The total population was projected to 3 million by the year 2000, and everything else was planned according to this perimeter in the city's first draft of plans. But the development of Shenzhen has proved much faster than expected. The urban population had already reached 3.35 million by 1994.

Due to rapid growth of the economy and resultant urban expansion, Shangbu industrial zone found itself in the middle of the city's built-up proper, and Shangbu's land use for industries soon proved inapt. The designation of Futian as a new city center for the near future further enhanced the value of the site, which now seems underused. When Shenzhen entered its second decade of development, many new tertiary functions had found their way to the city, such as banking, stock exchange, retailing, and so on. The amount of vacant land preserved in prime locations for expansion of service industries was underestimated. Shangbu thus became a target penetrated by such activities due to its good location and its suitable, multistory, standard industrial buildings. On the other hand, land was becoming more expensive around Shangbu. Industrialists found it too expensive to accommodate their workers in the vicinity of factories. Dormitories on the city fringe were available at much lower prices. Therefore, time and cost incurred in long-distance commuting, as well as rising opportunity cost of occupying the site for industrial usage, prompted factory managers to relocate production outward. As a result, the high-potential land value had spontaneously driven changes of land use to as high as 70 percent of the area by the end of 1995. During this market-driven process, commercial activities penetrated this industrial area. The use of buildings was converted, though illegally, from industrial to office and commercial use. Because the environmental capacity of Shangbu was not planned to suit commercial and office land uses, the change of land use created huge traffic congestion in the area. In addition, land values are illegally appropriated by the land users, instead of by the landowner—government.

Clearly, the land market is functioning, and market forces are responsible for the formulation of urban structure. As a challenge to urban planners, planning in the new era has to consider how to incorporate the flexibility into land use planning that recognizes the land market mechanisms; how to cope with market pressure for land use changes; and how to work out a contingency plan to deal with rising problems, such as changing land values derived from changing land use, infrastructure expansion, and so on.

CONCLUSION: ROLE OF CITY GOVERNMENT UNDER INSTITUTIONAL CHANGE

China's urban economic profiles have been altered profoundly by the economic reforms. The SOE reforms are changing urban enterprises into independent business units responding to market signals. Non-state sectors are growing and making inroads into the urban economy once dominated by SOEs. Coastal cities are leading the urban China toward a socialist market system. The reforms are ultimately changing the roles of urban government as well from an omnipotent organizer of production and consumption to an economic regulator and social redistributor. During the process, the legacy of central planning is still powerful, and lingering authoritarianism has transformed Chinese governments at every level to a stout advocator and facilitator for economic growth.

Decentralization has granted local governments the residual claimancy to fiscal revenues and thus provided local governments with strong incentives for pursuing local prosperity. The urban reforms have been so far successful in stimulating the urban economy by embracing participation of a wide range of interests. However, the urban reforms have not institutionalized a framework within which long-term, sustainable urban growth can be maintained. Equality in the allocation of urban resources has not been observed, and land and property markets are far from efficient.

The cheap land policy may have bailed out loss-making SOEs and thus saved jobs for workers. However, inefficient enterprises cannot be rescued forever. Getting rid of inefficient SOEs will improve the economy because resources will be used more efficiently, and thus more healthy jobs will be created. Transfer of state land at a discount to state-owned developers may play a positive role in nurturing a locally based property industry that has contributed substantively to the development and re-development of Chinese cities. But again, the cheap land factor misguides beneficiary developers and distorts property markets. The unique building cycles in Chinese cities and current oversupply of commodity properties indicate that subsidized land supply is a chief culprit for the looming property bust.

Furthermore, provision of land subsidies has become a drain on local government revenues, which are critical for local government to build adequate physical and social facilities. The leakage of land revenues away from the primary landowner—state and local governments—will be aggravated when values of properties rise dramatically due to rapid economic growth. The ongoing urban land reforms have to continuously strengthen market mechanisms and limit undue planning interference. Market inefficiency caused by partial land marketization, unique property cycles because of soft budget constraints, and leakage of capital gains in land from government have suggested that expedient measures for short-term goals would not lead to establishment of long-term stability of local growth. Commitment of local government to long-term local growth has to be built into the forthcoming new institution. The goal is to form a well-functioning land market compatible with operations of a market economy, whether it is socialist or capitalist. Only when land allocation conforms to market competition would utilization of land resources be efficient. The old urban land use system as an institution was incorporated into the centrally controlled economy where SOEs were key components. While SOEs are under a slow and incremental change, and everything else related is held back, well-performing enterprises are dragged down by loss-making ones. Progress in economic welfare is eroded by ill-fated bailouts. The self-destructive cycle needs to be broken, and new organizations need a new institutional environment.

The most important principle in a market economy is spontaneous order maintained by a legal system and clear definition of property rights (Buchanan, 1979). "Market without divisible and transferable property rights are a sheer illusion" (Nutter, 1974:223). Markets cannot exist without clearly defined property rights, and marketization needs protection of property rights. Therefore, marketization is a political commitment. An institutional change is required to clarify property rights over enterprises and state land assets. It is timely to call for political reform to address the

Table 6.7
Growth of Land Value in Selected Developing Cities

City	Period	Location	Land Price Increase Per Annum (%) (Fixed Prices)	Increase of GNP Per Capita Per Annum (%)
Teheran	1940-60	Average of 18 Districts	10.0	6.2
Tel Aviv	1951-71	Average of 4 Districts	21.0	5.9
Seoul	1953-66	Average of all land in City	18.7	4.6
Jamaica	1965-71	Average of All Urban Land	17.0	3.8
Mexico	1939-58	Average of 2 Districts	15.0	3.7
New Delhi	1959-67	Middle-class Residential District	17.0	0.5

Source: Darin-Drabkin, 1977, Table 4.1, p. 77.

ownership of assets and equality in the land market, if a sustainable local development is pursued.

Land is a medium where wealth is stored. Land constitutes a great part of the wealth in any politically stable and economically prosperous society. Land value changes across time and space. In a rapidly growing economy, land value rises with intensifying competition for land use and investment when a buoyant economy needs land to carry out production and consumption. Limited supply of land in general and of land at specific locations makes urban land supply relatively scarce against demand. Capital-seeking investment in land complicates the land market where land value does not simply reflect an equilibrium of users' demand and owners' supply. When an enormous amount of capital, coming from both abroad and home, seeks investment options, property would be contested by the pursuit of short-term capital gains rather than by the demand from end users. From a historical perspective, it is observed that land value appreciation is usually faster than GDP growth in developing countries (see Table 6.7). During the period 1955–1988 in Japan, it was estimated that the ratio of urban land value on average to GNP rose from 1.00 to 1.29. The ratios of the whole urban land and residential land in six main cities to GNP were widening more rapidly from 1.00 to 2.68 and 3.48, respectively (OECD, 1992). Empirical evidence has tested that urban land value in a rapidly urbanizing country would be highly likely to have substantial appreciation. The phenomenon reflects rising demand from both end users and investors who purchase property at a premium, expecting that future growth in the economy would justify the investment.

In a high-density setting, as most of China's cities are categorized, land would be more contested than in a low-density environment, and thus investment in land would be more speculative. Whatever the causes, land value will rise, sometimes dramatically. As the landowner, government should be able to situate itself in a position to capture capital gains from land value growth. Examples from Hong Kong and Singapore, two high-density cities in East Asia and Southeast Asia that have experienced rapid economic development in the last three decades, show that income from land sales constitutes an important part of government revenues. Hong Kong's land system is of public ownership, similar to mainland China's, while in Singapore, government owns about three-quarters of the land. Over the period 1961–1987, income from sales of land leases accounted for 15.4 percent of government revenues in Hong Kong (Gui, 1988). Singapore government secured 22.4 percent of revenues from land leasing during 1984–1998 (Government of Singapore, 1984–1998).

"Groping for stones to cross the river" as a pragmatic strategy, generated from a special historic situation, served China reasonably well. Under this framework, China's economy has achieved good progress. However, without formal institutional change, the reform process has been full of risks. The power to legitimate the results of reform experiments is held in the central government, which assesses the experience through a political process, depending on whether it is politically convenient to do so. Rule breaking as a result of conflicts between old institutions and new organizations is hard to avoid, but reformers have to bear the responsibility for breaching old rules. It is a highly risky affair, by the evidence of many political casualties in the previous two decades. Therefore, the partial reforms have not presented incentives to the full, nor have rewards been adequate. China's urban economy in the new millennium will have to change its track. Unambiguous property rights over assets have to be clearly defined. Government should build up its financial capability to act as a true development state. Marketization of urban land and property development will have to carry on further to lead China's urbanization.

Bibliography

IN ENGLISH

Adams, D. (1990) Meeting the Needs of Industry? The Performance of Industrial Land and Property Markets in Inner Manchester and Salford. In P. Healey & R. Nabarro (Eds.), *Land and Property Development in a Changing Context*. Aldershot: Gower, 113–127.

Agarwala, R. (1992) *China: Reforming Intergovernmental Fiscal Relations*. Washington, D.C.: World Bank.

Allio, L. et al. (1997) Post-Communist Privatization as a Test of Theories of Institutional Change. In D. L. Weimer (Ed.), *The Political Economy of Property Rights—Institutional Change and Credibility in the Reform of Centrally Planned Economies*. Cambridge: Cambridge University Press, 319–347.

Ambrose, P. J. (1986) *Whatever Happened to Planning?* London: Methuen.

Ambrose, P. J. & B. Colenutt. (1975) *The Property Machine*. Harmondsworth & Baltimore: Penguin.

Aram, J. D. & X. Wang. (1991) Lessons from Chinese State Economic Reform. *China Economic Review*, 2(1), 29–46.

Auroi, C. (Ed.). (1992) *The Role of the State in Development Processes*. London: Frank Cass.

Balchin, P. & J. Kieve. (1985) *Urban Land Economics*. London: Macmillan.

Ball, M. (1996) London and Property Markets: A Long-Term View. *Urban Studies*, 33(6), 859–877.

Ball, M. (1983) *Housing Policy and Economic Power—The Political Economy of Owner Occupation*. London: Methuen.

Bardhan, P. (1990) Symposium on the State and Economic Development. *Journal of Economic Perspectives*, 4(3), 3–7.

Barras, R. (1984) The Office Development Cycle in London. *Land Development Studies*, 1(1), 35–50.

Barras, R. (1979) *The Business Cycle in the City of London*. London: CES.

Barras, R. & D. Ferguson. (1985) A Spectral Analysis of Building Cycles in Britain. *Environment and Planning A*, 17, 1369–1391.

Barrett, S., M. Stewart & J. Underwood. (1978) *The Land Market and Development Process—A Review of Research and Policy*. Occasional Paper No. 2. Bristol: School of Advanced Urban Studies, University of Bristol.

Bauer, J. (1992) Industrial Restructuring in the NIEs—Prospects and Challenges. *Asian Survey*, 21, 1012–1025.

Bazelon, D. (1963) *The Property Economy*, New York: Random House.

Beijing Review. (1986) No. 10, 10 March, p. 14.

Bertaud, A. & B. Renaud. (1994) *Cities without Land Markets—Lessons of the Failed Socialist Experiment*. Washington, D.C.: World Bank.

Blecher, M. (1991) Development State, Entrepreneurial State: The Political Economy of Socialist Economy in Xinju Municipality and Guanghan County. In G. Write (Ed.), *The Chinese State in the Era of Economic Reform—The Road to Crisis*. Armonk, N.Y.: M. E. Sharpe, 265–291.

Bowley, M. (1966) *The British Building Industry: Four Studies in Response and Resistance to Change*. Cambridge: Cambridge University Press.

Bradbury, K. L., A. Downs & K. A. Small. (1982) *Urban Decline and the Future of American Cities*. Washington, D.C.: Brookings Institution.

Broadman, H. G. (1995) *Meeting the Challenge of Chinese Enterprise Reform*. Washington, D.C.: World Bank.

Buchanan, J. M. (1993) Property as a Guarantor of Liberty. In C. K. Rowley (Ed.), *Property Rights and the Limits of Democracy*. Hants: Edward Elgar, 1–64.

Buchanan, J. M. (1979) *What Should Economists Do?* Indianapolis: Liberty Press.

Buck, J. L. (1930) *China's Farm Economy*. Chicago: University of Chicago Press.

Byrd, W. A. & Q. Lin (Eds.). (1990) *China's Rural Industry: Structure, Development and Reform*. New York: Oxford University Press.

Byrne, P. & D. Cadman. (1984) *Risk, Uncertainty and Decision-Making in Property Development*. London & New York: E. & F. N. Spon.

Byrne, S. (1989) *Planning Gain: An Overview*. London: Royal Town Planning Institute.

C. Y. Leung & Company. (1997) *Property Times: PRC Markets*. Hong Kong: C. Y. Leung & Company.

Cadman, D. (1978) *Property Development*, London: E. & F. N. Spon.

Census & Statistics Department, Hong Kong. (1995) *Hong Kong Annual Digest of Statistics*. Hong Kong: Census & Statistics Department.

Chan, K. W. (1994) *Cities with Invisible Walls—Reinterpreting Urbanization in Post-1949 China*. Hong Kong: Oxford University Press.

Chang, C. & Y. Wang (1994) The Nature of the Township-Village Enterprise. *Journal of Comparative Economics*, 19, 434–452.

Chang, S. D. & R. Y. W. Kwok (1990) The Urbanization of Rural China. In R. Y. W. Kwok, W. L. Parish, A. G. O. Yeh & X. Q. Xu (Eds.), *Chinese Urban Reform—What Model Now?* Armonk, N.Y.: M. E. Sharpe, 140–157.

Chen, K. (1992) Crossing the River While Groping for Planted Stones: A Public-Choice Analysis of China's Economic Reform. Unpublished staff seminar paper no. 21, Department of Economics and Statistics, National University of Singapore, Singapore.

Chng, M. K. et al. (1988) *Industrial Restructuring in Singapore: For ASEAN–Japan Investment and Trade Expansion*. Singapore: Chopmen.

Clark, G. L. & W. B. Kim. (1995) Asian NIEs in Transition. In G. L. Clark & W. B. Kim (Eds.), *Asian NIEs & the Global Economy—Industrial Restructuring & Corporate Strategy in the 1990s*. Baltimore: Johns Hopkins University Press, 252–278.

CND. (1998) State-Owned Enterprises for Sale at Bargain Prices. *Global News*, No. GL98–133, 30 September.

Commons, J. R. (1931) Institutional Economics. *American Economic Review*, 21, 648–657.

Cox, A. (1984) *Adversary Politics and Land: The Conflict over Land and Property Policy in Post-war Britain*. Cambridge: Cambridge University Press.

Daly, M. T. (1982) *Sydney Boom and Sydney Bust—the City and Its Property Market 1850–1981*. Sydney: George Allen & Unwin.

Darin-Drabkin, H. (1977) *Land Policy and Urban Growth*. Oxford: Pergamon.

Denman, D. (1978) *The Place of Property—A New Recognition of the Function and Form of Property Rights in Land*. Berkhamsted: Geographical Publications.

Dong, F. (1992) *Industrialization and China's Rural Modernization*. New York: St. Martin's Press.

Dunleavy, P. (1981) *The Politics of Mass Housing in Britain, 1945–1975—A Study of Corporate Power and Professional Influence in the Welfare State*. Oxford: Clarendon Press.

The Economist. (1992) When China Wakes. *The Economist*, 28 November.

Eggertsson, T. (1994) The Economics of Institutions in Transition Economies. In S. Schiavo-Campo (Ed.), *Institutional Change and the Public Sector in Transitional Economies*. Washington, D.C.: World Bank, 19–50.

Ellman, M. (1990) Socialist Planning. In J. Eatwell, M. Milgate & P. Newman (Eds.), *Problems of the Planned Economy*. London: Macmillan, 13–21.

Elster, J. (1989) *The Cement of Society—A Study of Social Order*. Cambridge: Cambridge University Press.

Fainstein, S. S. (1994) *The City Builders—Property, Politics & Planning in London and New York*. Oxford: Blackwell.

Fan, Q. (1994) State-Owned Enterprise Reform in China: Incentives and Environment. In Q. Fan & P. Nolan (Eds.), *China's Economic Reforms—The Costs and Benefits of Incrementalism*. London: Macmillan; New York: St. Martin's Press, 137–156.

Fothergill, S., S. Monk & M. Perry. (1987) *Property and Industrial Development*. London: Hutchinson.

French, R. A. & F. E. I. Hamilton. (1979) Is There a Socialist City? In R. A. French & F. E. I. Hamilton (Eds.), *The Socialist City—Spatial Structure and Urban Policy*. Chichester: John Wiley & Sons, 1–21.

Friedman, M. (1984) *Market or Plan?* London: Centre for Research into Communist Economies.

Fröbel, F., J. Heinrichs & O. Kreye. (1980) *The New International Division of Labor*. Cambridge: Cambridge University Press.

Fung, K. I. (1982) The Spatial Development of Shanghai. In C. Howe (Ed.), *Shang-*

hai: Revolution and Development in an Asian Metropolis. New York: Cambridge University Press, 269–300.

Fung, K. I. (1981) Urban Sprawl in China: Some Causative Factors. In L. J. C. Ma & E. W. Hanten (Eds.), *Urban Development in Modern China*, Boulder, Colo.: Westview Press, 194–221.

Gilbert, A. & P. Healey. (1985) *The Political Economy of Land*. Hants: Gower.

Goetz, E. G. & S. E. Clarke (Eds.). (1993) *The New Localism—Comparative Urban Politics in a Global Era*. Newbury Park, Calif.: Sage.

Goldstein, S. & A. Goldstein. (1990) Town and City: New Directions in Chinese Urbanization. In R. Y. W. Kwok, W. L. Parish, A. G. O. Yeh & X. Q. Xu (Eds.), *Chinese Urban Reform—What Model Now?* Armonk, N.Y.: M. E. Sharpe, 17–44.

Goodchild, R. & R. Munton. (1985) *Development and the Landowner: An Analysis of the British Experience*. London: George Allen & Unwin.

Goodman, D. S. G. (1994) The Politics of Regionalism—Economic Development, Conflict and Negotiation. In D. S. G. Goodman & G. Segal (Eds.), *China Deconstructs—Politics, Trade and Regionalism*. London: Routledge, 1–20.

Gore, T. & D. Nicholson. (1985) The Analysis of Public Sector Land Ownership and Development. In S. Barrett & P. Healey (Eds.), *Land Policy: Problems and Alternatives*. Aldershot: Gower, 179–202.

Government of Singapore. (1984–1998) *The Budget for the Financial Year, 1984–1998*. Singapore: Government of Singapore.

Granick, D. (1990) *Chinese State Enterprises—A Regional Property Rights Analysis*. Chicago: University of Chicago Press.

Gray, J. (1982) Conclusion. In J. Gray & G. White (Eds.), *China's New Development Strategy*. London: Academic Press, 289–310.

Hall, T. (1990) *Business Cycles—the Nature and Causes of Economic Fluctuations*. New York: Praeger.

Hallett, G. (1979) *Urban Land Economics—Principles and Policy*. London: Macmillan.

Hamer, A. M. (1996) Chinese Urban Land Management Options during the Move to Market. In J. S. Lee, W. B. Kim & H. N. Jung (Eds.), *The Land Reform Process in the Post-Communist Countries*. Seoul: Korea Research Institute for Human Settlements, 13–73.

Harper, F. A. (1974) Property and Its Primary Form. In S. C. Blumenfeld (Ed.), *Property in a Humane Economy*. LaSalle, Ill.: Open Court, 1–22.

Harvey, D. (1985a) *The Urbanization of Capital*. Oxford: Basil Blackwell.

Harvey, D. (1985b) *Consciousness and the Urban Experience*. Oxford: Basil Blackwell.

Harvey, D. (1982) *The Limits to Capital*. Oxford: Basil Blackwell.

Harvey, J. (1981) *The Economics of Real Property*. London: Macmillan.

Hawthorne, J. (1981) *Theory and Practice of Money*. London: Heinemann.

Heald, D. (1983) *Public Expenditure—Its Defense and Reform*. Oxford: Martin Robertson.

Healey, P. (1994) Urban Policy and Property Development: The Institutional Relations of Real Estate Development in an Old Industrial Region. *Environment and Planning A*, 26, 177–198.

Healey, P. (1992) From Shipyard to Housing Estate: The Transformation of the

Urban Fabric. In P. Healey et al. (Eds.), *Rebuilding the City: Property-Led Urban Regeneration*. London: E. & F. N. Spon, 145–173.

Healey, P. (1991) Urban Regeneration and the Development Industry. *Regional Studies*, 25, 97–110.

Hollowell, P. (Ed.). (1982) *Property and Social Relations*. London: Heinemann.

Hope, N. C. (1996) Opening Remarks. In H. G. Broadman (Ed.), *Policy Options for Reform of Chinese State-Owned Enterprises*. Washington, D.C.: World Bank, 13–16.

Hou, C. M. (1965) *Foreign Investment and Economic Development in China, 1840–1937*. Cambridge: Harvard University Press.

Hou, L. (1996) Land Use System and Urban Development in the Transitional Period: The Case of Shanghai. *The Symposium of Rural-Urban Transition in the Planning and Development of Mega-Urban Regions in China*, 12–15 December, Guangzhou, China.

Hou, L. & M. Zhao. (1995) *Rural Industrial Development in Shanghai: A GIS-Based Study*. In proceedings of "Planning in a Fast Growing Economy"— Third International Congress of the Asian Planning Schools Association, September 22–24 1995, School of Building & Real Estate, National University of Singapore.

Howe, C. (1981) Industrialization under Conditions of Long-Run Population Stability: Shanghai's Achievement and Prospect. In C. Howe (Ed.), *Shanghai— Revolution and Development in an Asian Metropolis*. Cambridge: Cambridge University Press, 153–187.

Howe, C. (1978) *China's Economy—A Basic Guide*. New York: Basic Books.

Hsueh, T., Q. Li & S. Liu. (1993) *China's Provincial Statistics 1949–1989*. Boulder, Colo.: Westview.

Hu, X. (1996) Reducing State-Owned Enterprises' Social Burdens and Establishing a Social Insurance System. In H. G. Broadman (Ed.), *Policy Options for Reform of Chinese State-Owned Enterprises*. Washington, D.C.: World Bank, 125–148.

Huang, Y. (1996) *Inflation and Investment Controls in China*. Cambridge: Cambridge University Press.

Huang, Y. (1990) Web of Interests and Patterns of Behaviour of Chinese Local Economic Bureaucracies and Enterprises during Reforms. *The China Quarterly*, No. 123, 431–458.

Imbroscio, D. L. (1997) *Reconstructing City Politics—Alternative Economic Development and Urban Regimes*. Thousand Oaks, Calif., London & New Delhi: Sage.

Institute of Finance and Trade Economics, Chinese Academy of Social Sciences (IFTE/CASS) and Institute of Public Administration (IPA). (1992) *Urban Land Use and Management in China*. Beijing: Jingji.

Iskander, M. (1996) Improving State-Owned Enterprise Performance: Recent International Experience. In H. G. Broadman (Ed.), *Policy Options for Reform of Chinese State-Owned Enterprises*. Washington, D.C.: World Bank, 17–90.

James, S. & C. Nobes. (1978) *The Economics of Taxation*. 2d ed. Oxford: Philip Allan.

Jenkins, S. (1975) *Landlords to London—The Story of a Capital and Its Growth.* London: Constable.

Jiang, Q. (1995) State Asset Management Reform: Clarified Property Rights and Responsibilities. In H. G. Broadman (Ed.), *Policy Options for Reform of Chinese State-Owned Enterprises.* Washington, D.C.: World Bank, 91–100.

Khoury, S. (1984) *Speculative Markets.* New York: Macmillan.

Kinnard, W. N. (1994) Transfer of Ownership Rights via Rent Control. In J. R. DeLisle & J. Sa-Aadu (Eds.), *Appraisal, Market Analysis, and Public Policy on Real Estate.* Boston: Kluwer Academic, 347–380.

Klein, P. (1976) *Business Cycles in the Postwar World—Some Reflections on Recent Research.* Washington, D.C.: American Enterprise Institute for Public Policy Research.

Knight, J. (1992) *Institutions and Social Conflict.* Cambridge: Cambridge University Press.

Koo, A. Y. C., E. H. M. Li & Z. Peng. (1993) State-Owned Enterprise in Transition. In W. Galenson (Ed.), *China's Economic Reform.* San Francisco: 1990 Institute, 33–80.

Kornai, J. (1986) The Soft Budget Constraint, *Kyklos,* 39(1), 3–30.

Krabben, E. & J. G. Lambooy. (1993) A Theoretical Framework for the Functioning of the Dutch Property Market. *Urban Studies,* 30, 1381–1397.

Krueger, A. O. (1974) The Political Economy of the Rent-Seeking Society. *American Economic Review,* 64, 291–303.

Kydland, F. E. (Ed.). (1995) *Business Cycle Theory.* Aldershot, U.K. & Brookfield, Vt.: Edward Elgar.

Lakshmanan, T. R. & C. Hua. (1987) Regional Disparities in China. *International Regional Science Review,* 11(1), 97–104.

Lassar, T. J. (1990) *City Deal Making.* Washington, D.C.: Urban Land Institute.

Lewis, J. P. (1965) *Building Cycles and Britain's Growth.* London: Macmillan.

Lim, D. (1984) Industrial Restructuring in Singapore. Asian Employment Programme Working Papers, Bangkok: ILO-ARTEP.

Lim, J. Y., F. Cai & Z. Li (1996) *The China Miracle—Development Strategy and Economic Reform.* Hong Kong: Chinese University Press.

Lin, Z. (1994) Reform and Shanghai: Changing Central-Local Fiscal Relations. In H. Jia & Z. Lin (Eds.), *Changing Central–Local Relations in China—Reform and State Capacity.* Boulder, Colo.: Westview, 240–260.

Lipson, E. (1946) *A Planned Economy or Free Enterprise—the Lessons of History.* London: Adam & Charles Black.

Lü, X. & E. J. Perry. (1997) The Changing Chinese Workplace in Historical and Comparative Perspective. In X. Lü & E. J. Perry (Eds.), *Danwei—the Changing Chinese Workplace in Historical and Comparative Perspective.* Armonk, N.Y.: M. E. Sharpe, 3–17.

Ma, L. J. C. (1981) Introduction: The City in Modern China. In L. J. C. Ma & E. W. Hanten (Eds.), *Urban Development in Modern China.* Boulder, Colo.: Westview, 1–18.

MacLeary, A. & N. Nanthakumaran (Eds.). (1988) *Property Investment Theory.* London: E. & F. N. Spon.

Mansfield, E. (1991) *Microeconomics: Theory/Application.* 7th ed. New York: W. W. Norton & Company.

Marriott, O. (1989) *The Property Boom*. London: Abingdon.

Mitchell, W. (1941) *Business Cycles and Their Causes*. Berkeley: University of California Press.

Moor, N. (1983) *The Planner and the Market: An Examination of the Role of the Planner in the Development Market*. London & New York: George Godwin.

Moore, G. (1983) *Business Cycles, Inflation, and Forecasting*. 2d ed. Cambridge, Mass.: Ballinger.

Moore, J. (1983) *Why Privatise?* London: Conservative Political Centre.

Murphey, R. (1953) *Shanghai—Key to Modern China*. Cambridge: Harvard University Press.

Naughton, B. (1995) *Growing out of the Plan—Chinese Economic Reform, 1978–1993*. Cambridge: Cambridge University Press.

Naughton, B. (1988) The Third Front: Defense Industrialization in the Chinese Interior. *The China Quarterly*, 115, 351–386.

Nolan, P. (1995) Politics, Planning, and the Transition from Stalinism: The Case of China. In H. J. Chang & R. Rowthorn (Eds.), *The Role of the State in Economic Change*. Oxford: Clarendon, 237–261.

North, D. C. (1995) Five Propositions about Institutional Change. In J. Knight & I. Sened (Eds.), *Explaining Social Institutions*. Ann Arbor: University of Michigan Press, 15–26.

North, D. C. (1993) Institutional Change: A Framework of Analysis. In S. E. Sjostrand (Ed.), *Institutional Change—Theory and Empirical Findings*. Armonk, N.Y., & London: M. E. Sharpe, 35–46.

North, D. C. (1990) *Institutions, Institutional Change and Economic Performance*. Cambridge: Cambridge University Press.

Nutter, G. W. (1974) Markets without Property: A Grand Illusion. In E. G. Furubotn & S. Pejovich (Eds.), *The Economics of Property Rights*. Cambridge, Mass.: Ballinger, 217–224.

Oborne, M. (1986) *China's Special Economic Zones*. Paris: OECD.

OECD. (1992) *Urban Land Markets—Policies for the 1990s*. Paris: OECD.

OECD. (1981) *Revenue Statistics of OECD Member Countries*. Paris: OECD.

Oi, J. C. (1996) The Role of the Local State in China's Transitional Economy. In A. G. Walder (Ed.), *China's Transitional Economy*. Oxford: Oxford University Press, 170–187.

Oi, J. C. (1995) The Role of the Local State in China's Transitional Economy. *The China Quarterly*, No. 144, 1132–1149.

Oi, J. C. (1992) Fiscal Reform and the Economic Foundations of Local State Corporatism in China. *World Politics*, 45(1), 99–126.

Pagano, M. A. & A. Bowman. (1995) *Cityscapes and Capital—the Politics of Urban Development*. Baltimore & London: Johns Hopkins University Press.

Pannell, C. (1992) The Role of Great Cities in China. In G. E. Guldin (Ed.), *Urbanizing China*. Westport, Conn.: Greenwood, 11–39.

Park, J. D. (1997) *The Special Economic Zones of China and Their Impact on Its Economic Development*. Westport, Conn.: Praeger.

Park, S. O. (1994) Industrial Restructuring in the Seoul Metropolitan Region: Major Triggers and Consequences. *Environment and Planning A*, 26, 527–541.

Perkins, F. (1995) *Productivity Performance and Priorities for the Reform of*

China's State-Owned Enterprises. Economics Division Working Papers 95/1, Research School of Pacific and Asian Studies, Canberra.

Putterman, L. (1993) *Continuity and Change in China's Rural Development—Collection and Reform Eras in Perspective*. New York: Oxford University Press.

Putterman, L. & D. Rueschemeyer (Eds.). (1992) *State and Market in Development—Synergy or Rivalry?* Boulder, Colo., & London: Lynne Rienner.

Radcliffe, R. (1987) *Investment: Concepts, Analysis and Strategy*. Glenview, Ill.: Scott, Foresman & Company.

Reckinger, J. D. et al. (1991) The Government's Perspective on the Land Development Process. In P. W. Nyden & W. Wiewel (Eds.), *Challenging Urban Development—An Urban Agenda for the 1990s*. New Brunswick, N.J.: Rutgers University Press, 166–179.

Reeve, A. (1986) *Property*. London: Macmillan.

Reich, R. B. (1991) *The Work of Nations—Preparing Ourselves for 21st-Century Capitalism*. New York: Alfred A. Knopf.

Rowley, C. K., R. D. Tollison & G. Tullock (Eds.). (1988) *The Political Economy of Rent-Seeking*. Boston: Kluwer Academic.

Rueschemeyer, D. & L. Putterman. (1992) Synergy or Rivalry? In L. Putterman & D. Rueschemeyer (Eds.), *State and Market in Development—Synergy or Rivalry*. Boulder, Colo.: Lynne Rienner, 243–262.

Sandercock, L. (1979) *The Land Racket—the Real Costs of Property Speculation*. O'Connor, Australia: Silverfish Book.

Schultze, C. (1977) *The Public Use of Private Interest*. Washington, D.C.: Brookings Institution.

Shen, G. (1990) Rural Enterprises and Urbanization: The Sunan Region. In R. Y. W. Kwok, W. L. Parish, A. G. O. Yeh & X. Q. Xu (Eds.), *Chinese Urban Reform—What Model Now?* Armonk, N.Y.: M. E. Sharpe, 158–179.

Sik, O. (1967) *Plan and Market under Socialism*. White Plains, N.Y., & Prague: IASP and Academia Publishing House of the Czechoslovak Academy of Sciences.

Simpson, I. (1984) *Planning Gain: The Implications for Planning in the UK*. Strathclyde Papers on Planning. Glasgow: University of Strathclyde.

Singh, I. (1992) *China: Industrial Policies for an Economy in Transition*. Washington, D.C.: World Bank.

Sit, V. F. S. (Ed.). (1985) *Chinese Cities—the Growth of the Metropolis since 1949*. Hong Kong: Oxford University Press.

Solinger, D. J. (1992) Urban Entrepreneurs and the State: The Merger of State and Society. In A. L. Rosenbaum (Ed.), *State & Society in China—The Consequences of Reform*. Boulder, Colo., & Oxford: Westview, 121–141.

Straits Times (Singapore). (1998) Political Reshuffle Soon in Guangdong. 8 January.

Straits Times (Singapore). (1997) China Reshuffles Party Leaders to Root Out Regionalism, 3 September.

Tang, W. S. (1994) Urban Land Development under Socialism: China between 1949 and 1977. *International Journal of Urban and Regional Research*, 18 (3), 392–415.

Taylor, J. R. (1988) Rural Employment Trends and the Legacy of Surplus Labour, 1978–86. *The China Quarterly*, 116, 736–766.

Tseng, W. et al. (1994) *Economic Reform in China—A New Phase*. IMF Occasional Paper 114. Washington, D.C.: International Monetary Fund.

Tullock, G. (1993) Rent Seeking. In C. K. Rowley (Ed.), *Property Rights and the Limits of Democracy*. Hants: Edward Elgar, 1–98.

United Nations. (1991) *Small Town and Rural Human Resources Development to Reduce Migration to Large Cities*. New York: United Nations.

Wang, H. (1994) *The Gradual Revolution*. New Brunswick, N.J.: Transaction.

Wang, S. (1995) The Rise of the Regions: Fiscal Reform and the Decline of Central State Capacity in China. In A. G. Walder (Ed.), *The Waning of the Communist State—Economic Origins of Political Decline in China and Hungary*. Berkeley: University of California Press, 87–113.

Wang, S. (1994) Central–Local Fiscal Politics in China. In H. Jia & Z. Lin (Eds.), *Changing Central–Local Relations in China—Reform and State Capacity*. Boulder, Colo.: Westview, 91–112.

Wang, W. Q. & Y. Cheng. (1995) *The New Tendency of Housing Development in China*. In proceedings of "Planning in a Fast Growing Economy," Third International Congress of the Asian Planning Schools Association, 22–24 September, School of Building & Real Estate, National University of Singapore.

Wang, X. (1995) *An Overview of Housing Reform in China*. In proceedings of "Planning in a Fast Growing Economy," Third International Congress of the Asian Planning Schools Association, 22–24 September, School of Building & Real Estate, National University of Singapore.

Wang, X. Q. (1998) *China's Price and Enterprise Reform* London: Macmillan.

Wang, Y. & A. Murie. (1996) The Process of Commercialization of Urban Housing in China. *Urban Studies*, 33(6), 971–989.

Wang, Y. & S. Zhang. (1995) *A Study on Urban Pattern of the Changjiang Delta*. In proceedings of "Planning in a Fast Growing Economy," Third International Congress of the Asian Planning Schools Association, 22–24 September, School of Building & Real Estate, National University of Singapore.

Watson, A. & C. Findlay. (1992) The "Wool War" in China. In C. Findlay (Ed.), *Challenges of Economic Reform and Industrial Growth: China's Wool War*, Sydney: Allen & Unwin, 163–180.

Weimer, D. L. (1997) The Political Economy of Property Rights. In D. L. Weimer (Ed.), *The Political Economy of Property Rights—Institutional Change and Credibility in the Reform of Centrally Planned Economies*. Cambridge: Cambridge University Press, 1–19.

White, G. (1991) Basic-Level Government and Economic Reform in Urban China. In G. White (Ed.) *The Chinese State in the Era of Economic Reform—the Road to Crisis*. Armonk, N.Y.: M. E. Sharpe, 215–242.

Whitehead, J. (1972) Building Cycles and the Spatial Pattern of Urban Growth. *Institute of British Geographers Transactions*, No. 5–6, 39–55.

Witte, E. F. (1954) Institutional Economics as Seen by an Institutional Economist. *Southern Economic Journal*, 21 (October), 131–140.

Wong, C. P. W. (1987) Between Plan and Market: The Role of the Local Sector in Post-Mao China. *Journal of Comparative Economics*, 11, 385–398.

Wong, C. P. W., C. Heady & W. T. Woo. (1995) *Fiscal Management and Economic*

Reform in the People's Republic of China. Hong Kong: Oxford University
   Press.
Wong, J. & M. Yang. (1995) The Making of the TVE Miracle—An Overview of
   Case Studies. In J. Wong, R. Ma & M. Yang (Eds.), *China's Rural Entre-
   preneurs—Ten Case Studies,* Singapore: Times Academic Press, 16–51.
Wong, K. Y. (Ed.). (1982) *Shenzhen Special Economic Zone—China's Experiment
   in Modernization.* Hong Kong: Hong Kong Geographical Association.
Wong, K. & D. Chu. (1985) The Investment Environment. In K. Wong & D. Chu
   (Eds.), *Modernization in China—the Case of the Shenzhen Special Eco-
   nomic Zone.* Hong Kong: Oxford University Press, 176–207.
World Bank. (1993) *China—Urban Land Management in an Emerging Market
   Economy.* Washington, D.C.: World Bank.
World Bank. (1992) *China—Implementation Options for Urban Housing Reform.*
   Washington, D.C.: World Bank.
World Bank. (1990) *China: Between Plan and Market.* Washington, D.C.: World
   Bank.
World Bank. (1988) *World Development Report 1988.* New York: Oxford Univer-
   sity Press.
Zhang, S. & A. Zhang. (1987) The Present Management Environment in China's
   Industrial Enterprises. In B. Reynolds (Ed.), *Reform in China—Challenges
   & Choices.* Armonk, N.Y.: M. E. Sharpe, 47–58.
Zhou, D. (1997a) On Rural Urbanization in China. In G. E. Guldin (Ed.), *Farewell
   to Peasant China—Rural Urbanization and Social Change in the Late Twen-
   tieth Century.* Armonk, N.Y.: M. E. Sharpe, 13–46.
Zhou, D. (1997b) Investigative Analysis of "Migrant Odd-Job Workers" in Guang-
   zhou. In G. E. Guldin (Ed.), *Farewell to Peasant China—Rural Urbaniza-
   tion and Social Change in the Late Twentieth Century.* Armonk, N.Y.: M. E.
   Sharpe, 227–247.
Zhu, J. (1998) Equilibrium in the Property Market and Its Impact on Urban
   Growth—a New Measurement in the Context of Growing Economies. In
   P. K. Sikdar, S. L. Dhingra & K. V. Krishna Rao (Eds.), *Computer in Urban
   Planning and Urban Management.* New Delhi: Narosa, 48–59.
Zhu, J. (1996) Denationalization of Urban Physical Development—the Experi-
   ment in the Shenzhen Special Economic Zone, China. *Cities,* 13, 187–194.
Zhu, J. (1994) Changing Land Policy and Its Impact on Local Growth: The Ex-
   perience of the Shenzhen Special Economic Zone, China, in the 1980s. *Ur-
   ban Studies,* 31(10), 1611–1623.
Zhu, J. (1993) Property Development Process and Its Public–Private Cooperation
   in the Shenzhen Special Economic Zone, China, 1980–1990. Unpublished
   Ph.D. diss., Centre for Planning, University of Strathclyde.
Zwass, A. (1987) *Market, Plan, & State—the Strengths and Weaknesses of the Two
   World Economic Systems.* Armonk, N.Y. & London: M. E. Sharpe.

IN CHINESE

Bei, Q. Z. (1990) *Jingji Tequ Caizhen Jingrong* (Special Economic Zones' Fiscal
   and Financial Policies). Beijing: *Haiyang Chubanshe* (Ocean Publishing).

Beijing Tongji Ju (Beijing Municipal Statistical Bureau). (1995) *Beijing Tongji Nianjian, 1994* (Statistical Yearbook of Beijing, 1994). Beijing: *Zhongguo Tongji Chubanshe* (China Statistical Publishing).

Caizheng Bu (Ministry of Finance). (1992) *Zhongguo Caizheng Tongji, 1950–1991* (China Finance Statistics, 1950–1991). Beijing: *Kexue Chubanshe* (Science Publishing).

Cao, H. T, & Z. H. Chu, et al. (Eds.). (1990) *Dangdai Zhongguo de Chengshi Jianshe* (Urban Construction of Contemporary China). Beijing: *Zhongguo Shehui Kexue Chubanshe* (China Social Science Publishing).

Chengshi Jingii Yanjiu (Urban Economy Study). (1993) No. 1.

Gong, S. H. (1995) *Weishenmo Shenzhen Shangpinfang Jiage Jugaobuxia* (Why Prices of Commodity Housing in Shenzhen Staying High). *Zhongwai Fang-dichan Daobao* (Chinese and Foreign Real Estate Times), No. 36, 24–26.

Gu, H. Z. (1997) *Zhongguo Zhishi Qingnian Shangshan Xiaxiang Shimo* (History of Chinese Urban Youths' Rustication). Beijing: *Zhongguo Jiancha Chu-banshe* (China Jiancha Publishing).

Guangzhou Tongji Ju (Guangzhou Statistical Bureau). (1995) *Guangzhou Tongji Nianjian, 1994* (Statistical Yearbook of Guangzhou, 1994). Beijing: *Zhong-guo Tongji Chubanshe* (China Statistical Publishing).

Gui, Q. F. (Ed.). (1988) *Hong Kong Fangdichan* (Hong Kong Real Estate). Shen-zhen: *Haitian Chubanshe* (Haitian Publishing).

Gui, Q. F. et al. (Eds.). (1997) *Shen Gang Fangdichan Nianjian, 1997* (Yearbook of Shenzhen & Hong Kong Real Estate, 1997). Beijing: *Renming Zhongguo Chubanshe* (People's China Publishing).

Guo, R. J. (1997) *Zhuazu Shiji, Shenhua Gaige, Jiakua Qiye Zhuzhi Jiegou Taozhen Bufa* (Speech in the Meeting of SOE Structural Adjustment). In SQZGLXB (Ed.), *Shenzhenshi Jianli Xiandai Qiye Zhitu de Shejian he Tan-shou* (Practice and Exploration to Establish a System of Modern Enter-prises in Shenzhen). Shenzhen: *Haitian Chubanshe* (Haitian Publishing), 68–73.

Guojia Tongji Ju (GTJ) (State Statistical Bureau, China). (1997) *Zhongguo Ren-kou Tongji Nianjian, 1996* (China Population Statistics Yearbook, 1996). Beijing: *Zhongguo Tongji Chubanshe* (China Statistical Publishing).

Guojia Tongji Ju (GTJ) (State Statistical Bureau, China). (1980–1997) *Zhongguo Tongji Nianjian, 1979–1996* (China Statistical Yearbook, 1979–1996). Bei-jing: *Zhongguo Tongji Chubanshe* (China Statistical Publishing).

Guojia Tongji Ju Chengshi Shehui Jingji Diaocha Zongdui (GTJCSJDZ) (Urban Social and Economic Survey Organization). (1996) *Zhongguo Chengshi To-ngji Nianjian '95* (Urban Statistical Yearbook of China '95). Beijing: *Zhong-guo Tongji Chubanshi* (China Statistical Publishing).

Guojia Tongji Ju Chengshi Shehui Jingji Diaocha Zhongdui (GTJCSJDZ) (Urban Social and Economic Survey Organization). (1990) *Chengshi Fazan Shish-inian* (The Forty Years of Urban Development). Beijing: GTJCSJDZ.

He, J. S. (1997) *Jingji Tequ Guoqi Gaige yu Fazan de Chenggong Tansuo* (Explo-ration to SSEZ SOE Reforms). *Tequ Jingji* (SEZs' Economy), No. 4, 34–36.

Huang, C. Y. & X. B. Mo (Eds.). (1995) *Jingji Tequ Chuangye Shi* (Development of Special Economic Zones). Beijing: Renming Chubanshe (People's Publishing).

Li, D. (1991) *Guanyu Fandichan Zenzhifei* (About Progressive Tax on Property Capital Appreciation). *Zhongwai Fangdichan Daobao* (Chinese & Foreign Real Estate Times), No. 3.

Li, M. B. & X. Hu. (1991) *Liudong Rekou dui Dachengshi Fachan de Yingxian ji Duche* (Impact of Floating Population on Development of Great Metropolises and Countermeasures). Beijing: *Jingji Ribao Chubanshe* (Economic Daily Publishing).

Li, Z. B. (1997) *Jiefan Sixiang, Dadan Shejian, Yongyu Tanshou, Zengchuang Guoyou Qiye Xinyoushi* (Speech in the Shenzhen SOEs Workshop). In SQZGLXB (Ed.), *Shenzhenshi Jianli Xiandai Qiye Zhitu de Shejian he Tanshou* (Practice and Exploration to Establish a System of Modern Enterprises in Shenzhen). Shenzhen: *Haitian Chubanshe* (Haitian Publishing), 14–30.

Liu, W. (1997) *Zhongguo Guoying Qiye Gaige Jingchen* (On the Process of China's SOE Reforms). *Tequ Jingji* (SEZs' Economy), No. 1, 13–15.

Liu, Z. G. (1988) *Shenzhen Jingji Fazan Tanmi* (Exploration of Shenzhen Economic Development). Shenzhen: *Haitian Chubanshe* (Haitian Publishing).

Liu, Z. R. (1996) *Zhongguo Chengshihua Wenti Xueshu Tantao Jiyao* (On Chinese Urbanization). *Chengshi Jingji Yanjiu* (Urban Economy Study), No. 12, 12–18.

Ma, J. S. et al. (Eds.). (1991) *Dangdai Zhongguo Xiangzhen Qiye* (Township-and-Village Enterprises in Modern China). Beijing: *Dangdai Zhongguo Chubanshe* (Modern China Publishing).

Shanghai Shi Banian Jiejue Juzhu Kunnanhu Zhufang de Janjiu Ketizhu (SSBJJKZJK) (Shanghai Housing Situations Research Team). (1983) *Shanghai Shi Banian Jiejue Juzhu Kunnanhu Zhufang de Janjiu (1983–1990)* (Report on Solving Housing Problems in Shanghai in Eight Years [1983–1990]). Unpublished report.

Shanghai Shi Tongji Ju (SSTJ) (Shanghai Statistical Bureau). (1990–1997) *Shanghai Shi Fangdichan Shichang* (Shanghai Real Estate Market). Beijing: *Zhongguo Tongji Chubanshe* (China Statistical Publishing).

Shanghai Shi Tongji Ju (SSTJ) (Shanghai Municipal Statistical Bureau). (1981–1995) *Shanghai Tongji Nianjian* (Shanghai Yearbook of Statistics). Shanghai: *Shanghai Renmin Chubanshe* (Shanghai People's Press).

Shen, Q. S. (1995) *Shenzhen Qiye Zhichan Daocha* (A Survey of Shenzhen Enterprises' Assets). *Tequ Jingji* (SEZs' Economy), No. 10, 46–47.

Shen, W. X., X. Wang & S. Ba. (1997) *Beihai Pizhu Tudi Zhong de Chouwen Jiemi* (The Scandal in Beihai's Land Leasing). *Gaige* (Reform), No. 2, 122–126.

Shenzhen Danganguan (Shenzhen Archives). (1991) *Shenzhenshi Shinian Dashiji* (Ten Years of Main Events in Shenzhen). Shenzhen: *Haitian Chubanshe* (Haitian Publishing).

Shenzhen Fangdichan Nianjian Bianjibu (SFNB) (Editorial Committee of Shenzhen Real Estate Yearbook). (1991–1997) *Shenzhen Fandichan Nianjian, 1990–1997* (Shenzhen Real Estate Yearbook). Beijing: *Renming Zhongguo Chubanshe* (People China's Publishing).

Shenzhen Jianshe Ju (Shenzhen Construction Bureau) (Ed.). (1991) *Tudi he Fang-dichan Shichang Guanli Zhengzhe* (Policies on the Management of Land and Property Markets). Shenzhen: *Shenzhen Jianshe Ju* (Shenzhen Construction Bureau).

Shenzhen Jianshe Ju (Shenzhen Construction Bureau). (1990) *Shenzhen Fangdichan Kaifa Fangzheng* (Guidelines to Shenzhen Property Development). Shenzhen: *Shenzhen Jianshe Ju* (Shenzhen Construction Bureau).

Shenzhen Jianshe Ju (Shenzhen Construction Bureau). (1989) *Shenzhen Chengshi Jianshe Shi* (The History of Shenzhen Urban Construction). Shenzhen: *Shenzhen Jianshe Ju* (Shenzhen Construction Bureau).

Shenzhen Tongji Ju (Shenzhen Statistical Bureau). (1989–1998) *Shenzhen Tongji Nianjian, 1988–1997* (Shenzhen Statistical Yearbook, 1988–1997). Beijing: *Zhongguo Tongji Chubanshe* (China Statistical Publishing).

Shenzhenshi Guihua Guotu Ju (SGGJ) (Shenzhen Planning and Land Bureau). (1997) *Shenzhenshi Guihau Guotu Guanli* (Shenzhen Planning and Land Management). Shenzhen: SGGJ.

Shenzhenshi Guihua Guotu Ju Nanshan Fenju (SGGJNF) (Nanshan Planning and Land Bureau, Shenzhen). (1997) *Shenzhenshi Nanshanqu Fangdichan Daocha* (A Survey on Real Estate of Nanshan, Shenzhen). Shenzhen: SGGJNF.

Shenzhenshi Qiye Zhitu Gaige Lingdao Xiaozu Bangongshi (SQZGLXB) (Shenzhen Enterprise Reforms Committee). (1997) *Shenzhenshi Jianli Xiandai Qiye Zhitu de Shejian he Tanshou* (Practice and Exploration to Establish a System of Modern Enterprises in Shenzhen). Shenzhen: *Haitian Chubanshe* (Haitian Publishing).

Shi, S. Z., Q. S. Gao, et al. (Eds.). (1989) *Shanghai Baike Quanshu* (Shanghai Encyclopedia). Shanghai: *Xuelin Chubanshe* (Xuelin Publishing).

Su, Y. & X. B. Zhao. (1997) *Zhongguo de Guoyou Qiye Gaige Jinchen* (The Process of Chinese State-Owned-Enterprise Reforms). *Tequ Jingji* (SEZs' Economy), No. 1, 13–15.

Wang, C. G. (1995) *Shehui Liudong he Shehui Chonggou* (Migrations and Social Restructuring). Hangzhou: *Zhejiang Renming Chubanshe* (Zhejiang People's Publishing).

Wang, S. (1991) *Shenzhen Zhenzai Jinru Xinjishu Shiql* (Shenzhen is Jumping at a New Technology Era). *Renming Ribao, Haiwaiban* (People's Daily, Overseas Edition), 10 September.

Wu, W. (1988) *Zhongguo de Zhufang Wenti ji Duice* (Chinese Housing Problems). *Chengshi Guihua* (City Planning Review), No. 1.

Wuxi Tongji Ju (Wuxi Statistical Bureau). (1995) *Wuxi Tongji Nianjian, 1994* (Statistical Yearbook of Wuxi, 1994). Beijing: *Zhongguo Tongji Chubanshe* (China Statistical Publishing).

Xia, Z. G. (1992) *Guanyu Woguo Chengshihua Jinchen Ji Fazhan Bianhua de Huigu* (Retrospect on Chinese Urbanization and Its Changes). *Chengshi Guihua Huikan* (Urban Planning Forum), No. 2, 5–14.

Xu, F. G. & L. Xu. (1997) *Shanghai Gaocheng Jianzhu Jianshi* (Brief History of High-Rise Buildings in Shanghai). *Chengshi Jingji Yanjiu* (Urban Economy Study), No. 3, 30–32.

Xu, S. Q. (1996) *Guangzhou Kaifashang Huyu "Jianfei"* (Guangzhou Developers

Appealing for "Slimming"). *Zhongwai Fangdichan Daobao* (Chinese and Foreign Real Estate Times), No. 21, 6–13.

Yuan, S. (1988) *Chengbao Guanli Zi* (Contracting Managerial Responsibility System). Beijing: *Zhongguo Jingji Chubanshe* (China's Jingji Publishing).

Zang, G. (1995) *Shenzhen Gaokeji Gongyequ* (Shenzhen High-Tech Industrial Zone). *Zhongwai Fangdichan Daobao* (Chinese and Foreign Real Estate Times), No. 12, 30–32.

Zhang, E. Z. (1998) *Shanghai Zhufang Jinrongye Xianzhuang ji Fashan Shilu* (Shanghai Housing Finance). *Shanghai Touzi* (Shanghai Investment), No. 2, 4–9.

Zhang, Z. C. (1993) *Shenzhen Fangdichan Shichang* (Shehzhen Real Estate Market). Shanghai: *Tongji Daxue Chubanshe* (Tongji University Press).

Zhao, M. & Z. J. Zhu. (1998) *Chengshihua yu Liudong Rekou* (Urbanization and "Floating Population"). *Chengshi Guihua Huikan* (Urban Planning Forum), No. 113, 8–12.

Zhen, J. G. (1995) *Shenzhen Fandichan de Xingshi ji Duiche* (Countermeasures for Situations in Shenzhen Real Estate). *Zhongwai Fangdichan Daobao* (Chinese and Foreign Real Estate Times), No. 16, 12–15.

Zhen, W. X., X. Wang & S. Ba. (1997) *Beihai Pizhu Tudi zhong de Shouwen Jiemi* (The Scandal of Land Leasing in Beihai). *Gaige* (Reforms), 2, 122–126.

Zheng, Z., L. Zong & X. D. Song. (1984) *Guanyu Shanghai Weixing Chengzhen Jianshe Fangshen Zhenche de Jianyi* (Comments on the Policy of Satellite Town Development in Shanghai). *Chengshi Guihua Huikan* (Urban Planning Forum), No. 3, 15–23.

Zhongguo Shehui Kexueyuan (Chinese Social Science Academy). (1992) *Woguo Chengshi de Tudi Shiyong Zhidu Jiqi Gaige* (China's Urban Land Management System and Its Reforms). *Zhongquo Shehui Kexue* (China's Social Science), No. 2. 63–81.

Zhongguo Shehui Kexueyuan Renkou Yianjushou (ZSKRY) (Population Research Institute, CASS). (1997) *Zhongguo Renkou Nianjian '97* (Almanac of China's Population '97). Beijing: *Zhongguo Jingji Guanli Chubanshe* (China Economic Management Publishing).

Zhongwai Fangdichan Daobao (Chinese and Foreign Real Estate Times). (1996) *Shichang Fenxi* (A Market Analysis), No. 18, 20–21.

Zhongwai Fangdichan Daobao (Chinese and Foreign Real Estate Times). (1996) No. 17, 14.

Zhu, J. (1986a) *Chengshi Juzhu Renkou Midu Fazhan yu Logistic Quxian de Jiashou* (Development of Urban Resident Density and Hypothesis of Logistic Curve). *Chengshi Guihua Huikan* (Urban Planning Forum), No. 6, 2–16.

Zhu, J. (1986b), *Chengshi Juzhu Renkou Fenbu yu Zaifenbu de Jichu Yianjiu* (A Basic Research on Urban Population Distribution and Re-Distribution). *Chengshi Guihua Huikan* (Urban Planning Forum), No. 5, 10–19.

Zhu, X. H. & Y. C. Yuan (1997) *Guoyou Qiye Queishun Yuanyin yu Duiche* (Causes for SOEs' Losses and Countermeasures). *Tequ Jingji* (SEZs' Economy), No. 2, 48–49.

Index

About the Author

JIEMING ZHU is a Lecturer at National University in Singapore. His research has focused on urban planning and development in the transitional economy and real estate analysis in high-density East Asian cities.

ISBN 0-275-96427-2

EAN

90000>

HARDCOVER BAR CODE